NEW YORK REVIEW BOOKS
CLASSICS

DIARY OF A FOREIGNER IN PARIS

CURZIO MALAPARTE (pseudonym of Kurt Erich Suckert, 1898–1957) was born in Prato, Italy, and served in World War I. An early supporter of the Italian Fascist movement and a prolific journalist, Malaparte soon established himself as an outspoken public figure. In 1931 he incurred Mussolini's displeasure by publishing a how-to manual entitled *Coup d'État: The Technique of Revolution*, which led to his arrest and a brief term in prison. During World War II Malaparte worked as a correspondent, for much of the time on the Eastern Front, and this experience provided the basis for his two most famous books, *Kaputt* (1944) and *The Skin* (1949). His political sympathies veered to the left after the war. He continued to write, publishing a portrait of Tuscany, *Maledetti toscani* (*Those Cursed Tuscans*, 1956), and one of Moscow in the early Soviet era, *The Kremlin Ball* (1957). In his later life, he worked in the theater and the cinema. He died in Rome.

STEPHEN TWILLEY is the managing editor of *Public Books*. His translations from the Italian include Francesco Pacifico's *The Story of My Purity* and Marina Mander's *The First True Lie*, and for NYRB Classics, Giuseppe Tomasi di Lampedusa's *The Professor and the Siren*.

EDMUND WHITE is the author of twenty-six books, including the novel *A Saint from Texas*, which will be published in the summer of 2020.

OTHER BOOKS BY CURZIO MALAPARTE
PUBLISHED BY NYRB CLASSICS

Kaputt
Translated by Cesare Foligno
Afterword by Dan Hofstadter

The Kremlin Ball
Translated and with a foreword by Jenny McPhee

The Skin
Translated by David Moore
Introduction by Rachel Kushner

DIARY OF A FOREIGNER IN PARIS

CURZIO MALAPARTE

Translated from the Italian and French by
STEPHEN TWILLEY

Introduction by
EDMUND WHITE

NEW YORK REVIEW BOOKS

New York

THIS IS A NEW YORK REVIEW BOOK
PUBLISHED BY THE NEW YORK REVIEW OF BOOKS
435 Hudson Street, New York, NY 10014
www.nyrb.com

Library of Congress Cataloging-in-Publication Data
Names: Malaparte, Curzio, 1898–1957, author. | Twilley, Stephen, translator.
Title: Diary of a foreigner in Paris / by Curzio Malaparte ; translated from the
    Italian and French by Stephen Twilley.
Other titles: Diario di uno straniero a Parigi. English
Description: [New York] : New York Review Books, [2020] | Series: New York
    Review books
Identifiers: LCCN 2019041956 (print) | ISBN 9781681374161 (paperback)
Subjects: LCSH: Paris (France)—Intellectual life—20th century. | Paris
    (France)—History—1944- —Anecdotes. | Malaparte, Curzio, 1898–1957—
    Diaries. | Journalists—Italy—Biography.
Classification: LCC DC715 .M3313 2020 (print) | DDC 944/.361082—dc23
LC record available at https://lccn.loc.gov/2019041956
LC ebook record available at https://lccn.loc.gov/2019041957

ISBN 978-1-68137-416-1

Printed in the United States of America on acid-free paper.
10 9 8 7 6 5 4 3 2 1

CONTENTS

INTRODUCTION

CURZIO Malaparte is a phrasemaker before anything else—sensuous phrases that stick in the imagination for a long time ("the sun's baked-honey brilliance"). Although he fancied himself a thinker (and was quite jealous of the renown of Gide, Sartre, and Camus), his pronouncements on "the French" ("France is the last homeland of intelligence") or on communism or existentialism or on women are often confused or repetitive or banal or wrong, whereas his recording of a sensation or a bizarre anecdote or his memory of a strange phrase is always indelible if not unerring.

In fact he is what the French call a "mythomane," a compulsive liar who embellishes the truth, not necessarily for gain but out of an irrepressible compulsion. Anyone who has read his World War II masterpieces *Kaputt* or *The Skin* can never forget the memorable but improbable scene when the starving Neapolitans serve to American officers a boiled young girl in mayonnaise attached to a fish tail, claiming she is a mermaid from the aquarium, or the scene when horses plunging out of a pond in northern Europe freeze in place and offer visitors a stationary merry-go-round. Or the court of the Nazi "king" of Poland who, when he's not sensitively playing the classical piano, leads his courtiers to the ghetto where the Germans shoot Jewish children for fun, pretending they're rats. And where Malaparte himself offers a weeping little girl who's starving a fat Havana cigar after she proudly refuses money. Or there's a moment when a Fascist officer opens a pot of freshly shucked oysters and admits it's really forty pounds of human eyes. I'm not saying these events didn't happen but Malaparte seems to have observed more than his share of grotesque oddities. Whether true or not, these scenes render perfectly the horrors of war.

In his Paris diary, Malaparte ends with a magnificent tableau of an aristocratic couple in Italy, the Pecci-Blunts, who are snubbed by all of their hundreds of invitees because Blunt is an ennobled American Jew and new severe racist laws have just come into effect. Unsuspected, hiding in the bushes, Malaparte and a female companion spy on the ostracized couple, who are calmly relishing the festivities—the fireworks, the live opera from La Scala, the delicate food and rare wines.... Living well is certainly the best revenge. This was a beautiful scene Malaparte had first written years before but was unable to publish during the Mussolini era.

After the war, Malaparte came to Paris (which he'd last visited fifteen years earlier); he was expecting a warmer reception than the one he received. He spoke and even wrote French. He was very social and dashing and had cultivated many friends during the long periods he'd lived there and kept up a French correspondence when he was in Italy. He was a famous womanizer. As is apparent from his diary, however, many Parisians shunned him and suspected him with some justification of being a Fascist "collaborator." In fact, he had been a working journalist for the then-Fascist newspaper the *Corriere della Serra* in the 1930s and had published an over-the-top article praising the Wehrmacht and had sent in many other "patriotic" reports from the front. He had also fought as a Fascist soldier in the elite Alpine forces. In Paris he emphasized that he had been exiled for five years to Lipari, an island off the northern coast of Sicily, for criticizing Hitler, and that he had been placed under house arrest in his luxurious villa in Capri and several times imprisoned for short stays in Regina Coeli in Rome, all, he claimed, for his assiduous antifascism.

In fact, in the last days of the regime he was imprisoned for having siphoned off public funds for his own use. He had been a member of the Fascist Party from the beginning and a reliable supporter of Mussolini. The real reason he was placed under house arrest was that he'd verbally attacked Italo Balbo, a transatlantic pilot who was a hero in Italy, even more popular than Mussolini himself. Malaparte had written (or at least signed) a worshipful hagiography of Balbo. When the pilot didn't seem duly grateful for the book, Malaparte began to slander him. Malaparte was a touchy, complex man; at the end of his life he was reputedly both a staunch Catholic and a member of the Communist Party.

He certainly was eccentric. The greatest love in his life was his dog Febo. When the animal went missing, Malaparte searched for him desperately throughout Turin and finally found him being experimented on by a vivisectionist. Malaparte noticed that none of the tortured dogs was barking; the vivisectionist explained that the first step in the laboratory was to cut their vocal cords. The grief-stricken Malaparte convinced the scientist to give Febo a lethal injection and put the poor dog out of his misery. Certainly Malaparte felt closer to animals (more innocent, less evil) than to human beings; several times in this book he sits down to bark loudly at night in the country and sets all the dogs in the neighborhood to barking antiphonally. This eccentricity is accepted in France but in Switzerland it is forbidden.

He has an infallible eye and describes "the pink, pale-green, and faded-blue varnishes of Venetian furniture," or an evening sky that is "dark and red like the inside of a nostril." Or he speaks of seeing the cathedral of Chartres under a "very young blue sky." Or the sky above Chamonix as having "the cruelty the night stars have in Persian poems." At dawn in Paris the swallows "cried softly, so as not to wake the sleepers." Or he says that when seventeenth-century European diplomats described the Orient they seemed to be speaking about "tiny, fragile, transparent pieces of porcelain." Sometimes he comes up with a phrase right out of Ezra Pound: "She must have been beautiful, when she was beautiful." He overhears a Frenchman speak of a German city "like the women in Italian primitivist paintings juggling the infant Jesus in one hand" while holding in the other "the model of a city or a church."

We're not sure what he means exactly and his descriptions don't seem verifiable, but they can instantly be visualized. His statements, his "ideas," are often more dubious if no less striking: we learn that

"Cartesianism is the substitute for the Reformation in France." Or that as an old man Bonnard makes "his youngest, most beautiful paintings." Malaparte declares himself extremely Christian but notes: "If Jesus Christ hadn't been resurrected, I wouldn't give a damn about Catholicism." He has unlikely bits of knowledge, for instance that the overcivilized courtiers of Versailles called the countryside "that place where birds are raw." He tells us that "the crueler a people is, the more intellectual it is." He's not the first great prose writer suspicious of culture, refinement, and deep thought. Maybe he was anti-intellectual because the French didn't take him seriously. Or perhaps his exposure to Italian and German fascist intellectuals had convinced him there was an inverse relationship between culture and cruelty.

He's full of opinions. He declares that the Place de la Concorde in Paris "is an idea, not a piazza; it's a way of thinking." He keeps worrying over Cartesianism as a dog might gnaw at a bone. One wonders if he ever studied Descartes, or if for him the name may just be shorthand for the rule of reason over instinct. Another preoccupation is the difference between two seventeenth-century playwrights, Racine versus Corneille. He despises women as much as he lusts after them; he tells us of a beautiful woman "full of ovaries up to her neck." He has a wonderful evocation of the great dressmaker, Schiaparelli: "Tall and slender, her forehead high, narrow, immense, the forehead of an Etruscan statue, the oblique eyes of an Etruscan statue, the mouth of an Etruscan statue. All the noise of the sea envelops her, and the smell of the sea follows her, and the blue and green light of the sea surrounds her, and I see again her naked foot on the sands of Forte dei Marmi, I hear again her blue and pale green voice perch atop the crest of the waves like a white gull." The sea imagery comes from their encounter at a ritzy Tuscan sea resort, Forte dei Marmi; who knows where the Etruscan allusions originate. (She was an Italian aristocrat from Rome and the most famous couturiere of her day and did have a flat, wide face and a prominent nose.)

There are lots of big names in these pages—Cocteau, the playwright Giraudoux (who'd just died), a cold, reserved Camus—but not enough friendly ones to make Malaparte feel that he'd returned to his true

homeland. Although he lived another decade and began many projects, he never completed any of them, not even this diary. (This book,
never revised, was published in 1966, nine years after his death.) In
these pages he admits that "the least thing...robs me of all confidence."
Which is hard to believe, considering how many times he'd pulled it
out of the fire. In France he was out of sync with the existentialists
and the Communists, the two leading cabals; in Italy he'd been
eclipsed by Alberto Moravia. In America he was denounced by a
knowledgeable woman who'd put together a careful dossier of all his
lies; she wrote: "Truth with him is always a molecule buried in an
enormous cocoon of lies...."

In an interview with the *Paris Review*, Moravia said, "Italians
prefer beauty to truth." That may be why Malaparte is perennially
popular in his own country despite his prevarications. He certainly
serves up a lot of beauty. As he himself puts it in his Paris diary, "I
think about Italy, where affection flows to a name, to friendship, to
beauty—never to intelligence." For such an anti-intellectual, Malaparte
is extraordinarily intelligent. He was never provincial—he knew
Eastern Europe, Russia, Finland, Spain, and of course France; he
could endear himself to anyone and called himself Mister Chameleon.
As his brilliant biographer, Maurizio Serra, writes: "The Chameleon
who knows how to play the aristocrat with aristocrats, the diplomat
with diplomats, the soldier with soldiers...."

Throughout this book he seems rattled or at least he's always taking umbrage. He makes French intellectuals responsible for Dachau.
When the French keep asking him why he didn't desert Mussolini's
forces, he chalks the question up to "coarseness." He tells us, "I prefer
real collaborators to fake resistants." He does tell French friends a
funny story. When he was twenty he was summoned to the Palazzo
Venezia, Mussolini's headquarters. After being kept waiting for hours
he crosses an empty room on tiptoe and stands before Mussolini's
desk without anyone acknowledging his presence.

At last Mussolini looks at him and is astonished he's so young. He
knows every detail of Malaparte's background. Then he says, "I'd
advise you, from here on out, not to concern yourself with me. I don't

like that you're a gossip and a malicious type." When Malaparte asks him how he has offended him, Mussolini replies, "Two days ago, at Caffè Aragno, you told several of your friends I always wear ugly ties." Malaparte apologizes and is dismissed. Halfway to the door he turns back and says, "You're wearing an ugly tie today as well," which only makes Mussolini laugh at the young man's cheekiness.

We're still laughing today at his outrageous remarks and discussing his singular character. What is indisputable is the beauty of his prose and the fascination of his personality.

—EDMUND WHITE

TRANSLATOR'S NOTE

BY MID-1947, Curzio Malaparte couldn't wait to get back to Paris. World War II was over, and he had ended up on the right side, serving as a liaison officer between the Italian army and the Allied forces that had driven the Germans up the peninsula and into surrender. But the aftermath of the conflict, which in its final two years had turned into a civil war in the country, still presented dangers for anyone associated with the Fascist regime.[1] Thanks, it appears, to his friendship with Palmiro Togliatti, the leader of the Italian Communist Party, he had avoided being officially purged, yet repeated arrests and continuing personal attacks from both the right and the left took their toll.[2] Having reacquired his passport that March, and fearing the potential consequences should a united Left prevail in the 1948 general election, Malaparte decided to leave while he still could.[3]

Back to Paris, because the Italian writer had previously spent several years in the city in the early 1930s, when the succès de scandale of his 1931 book *Technique du coup d'état* (not published in Italian until 1948) put him at the center of the French political and literary scene, ushering him into the grand salons of the age, introducing him to leading writers and intellectuals such as François Mauriac and Jean Giraudoux, and allowing him to establish or deepen friendships with the likes of Blaise Cendrars, Jean Cocteau, and Daniel Halévy.[4] Before that, across multiple visits between 1923 and 1925, as the most prominent Fascist intellectual in Paris, he had openly pursued collaborations with French right-wing publishers, while discreetly engaging in the more morally compromised task of monitoring the first gatherings of Italian exiles in France.[5] Before *that*, in 1919, he was assigned to the Italian delegation to the Paris Peace Conference, after having enlisted in the French Foreign Legion in 1915 and fought as part of the Italian Army sent to the Western Front in 1918;[6] and this experience of Paris at the age of twenty, and of the relationships established then, was unsurprisingly formative, and would become a future source of inspiration and nostalgia. So, after World War II, Paris seemed like a natural destination, a good place to write and build up his reputation again while things settled down politically in Italy.

In this period Malaparte was working on multiple projects at once, most prominently *The Skin* (1949), which would become his second enduringly famous book, after *Kaputt* (1944), but also the unfinished novel *The Kremlin Ball*, a book of poetry, two plays, a series of newspaper articles on the political situation in Italy, and this *Diary of a Foreigner in Paris*.

Malaparte's stated aim with the *Diary*, which was probably never conceived as a private document, was to offer a "portrait of a moment in the history of the French nation, of French civilization, that coincides with a particular moment in my life, in the story of my life." The second half of this statement is every bit as significant as the first. After all, the protagonist of virtually all his books is "Malaparte," in the first person, a slightly embellished and heightened version of the empirical author in his experiences near the center of European politics and culture in the first half of the twentieth century. Malaparte conceived of the *Diary*, he continues in a preface, as "a theatrical work brought to the boards of the page...centered on the character called 'I.'" And it is perhaps the theatrical present-moment-ness of most of the *Diary*, even as there are also tales of more distantly retrospective nature strewn throughout, that most sets it apart from his other works. Not incidentally, though he scarcely alludes to it in the text of the *Diary*, during this time Malaparte also worked on getting his two French-language plays—*Du côté de chez Proust* (1948) and *Das Kapital* (1949)—performed on the Paris stage, which he did, drawing crowds but also some fierce criticism.

Among the most important *unstated* aims of the book was to explain to the French how he had always been a friend, even during the last war, and to offer some tough-love advice on how to recover from occupation. He wants them to accept that there are different ways to resist tyranny, that the French weren't the only ones to do so in the last war, and that they are open to charges of hypocrisy as well: "When I was in the Regina Coeli prison, when I was on Lipari, how many Frenchmen climbed the grand staircase of Palazzo Venezia and went to pay homage to Mussolini!" And yet, he adds, "I don't hold a grudge against them; they were within their rights." At the same time, if Malaparte repeatedly expresses his faith in France, that it will recover its guiding spirit and sense of self-worth, it is perhaps in part because a strong, confident France would be more likely to relinquish its own grudge against him and move on; a France still traumatized by occupation and fueled by resentment, rather less so. But, of course, he first had to convince the French while he was there, before the book came out. It may be that one of the things Malaparte was doing in the more discursive portions of the *Diary* was rehearsing and rehashing the arguments he employed in the salons.

Happily, the book also abounds in anecdotes and repartee shared among actors, painters, and writers (most memorably among them Jean Cocteau, Véra Korène, and André Malraux), and with statesmen, diplomats, and minor aristocrats, about art, literature, and history. There are, too, some fantastic set-piece narratives, like the story of the Spanish prisoners captured on the Finnish front in World War II, the ball of Count Pecci-Blunt, and how Malaparte got hauled in to meet Mussolini after being overheard insulting the dictator's ties; diverting scenes of the author in the Alps, taking on pistes that are much too difficult for him and upsetting Swiss innkeepers by barking with the dogs at night; some relatively less fun passages comparing the dramatists Racine and Corneille and how they do or don't express the French character; and episodes showing Malaparte's sympathy with and esteem for the working class, as opposed to the petty bourgeois, among whom he numbers Sartre. Malaparte damns the doyen of French existentialism with faint praise, as a talented fellow whose philosophical ideas are less important or influential than his postures: "a new, artificial bohemianism, which proposes to replace principles with slovenliness, ideas with a sweater."

As a journalist, Malaparte traveled widely in both Western and Eastern Europe and met with leading artists and writers wherever he went. However, a major source of tension in the *Diary* is the changed relationship with this leading edge after the Second World War. As across much of the continent, the most prominent postwar cultural figures in France were generally those associated with resistance to fascism and Nazism; there was an earnestness and purist morality about this group, a focus on questions of freedom and authenticity that were light-years away from the lush aesthetic, ambiguous provocations, and cynical wit of Malaparte. Where the Italian does make a case for freedom in the *Diary*, he does so on literary rather than political grounds: "My freedom (and the freedom of each of us, of each individual) has nothing to do with the freedom of a people, of Europe. Whether or not Europe is free, the problem of individual freedom, and above all that of a writer's freedom, doesn't change." It is in this light that he claims the "most noble example of resistance" to be that of Luigi Pirandello, an admirer of Mussolini who was nonetheless "perfectly uncompromising" on the ground of art: in response to the dictator's attempts to tame him, he "obeyed orders that were not of a literary nature, and remained deaf to injunctions and flattery." Unsurprisingly, the French writer-resistants whom Malaparte encountered in this stay tended to find such a position unsatisfactory.

It is clear from biographies of Malaparte, as much as from the *Diary* itself, that on his return to Paris he was in fact rebuffed by the city's new literary lights, to which he responds by declaring his affinity with the men of the World War I generation, *his* generation. Nonetheless, he mostly has nice things to say about French writers, aside from Sartre, even if it's not always reciprocated. It is decidedly *not* with Camus, to judge by Malaparte's account of their first meeting:

I recall that, at a certain point, someone having asked me what kind of man was Bottai, the former Fascist minister, etc., Camus said sententiously that such men should be dragged before a court, and then shot. I didn't like this brisk manner of understanding justice, and I asked Camus what made him think Bottai should be shot. Camus, without looking at me, replied that all these men, assassins, etc., should be shot. I replied that not only was Bottai no assassin, he was in fact quite incapable of hurting a fly. But I understood very well that Camus wanted to imply that I too should be shot.

Malaparte is convinced that the likes of Camus, Sartre, and Malraux have false ideas about foreigners, including those who have immersed themselves in French culture and fought for France and its ideals, and he suffers from their lack of understanding and affection. The experience doubtless informs his advice to a young Polish writer, Artur Sandauer, whose career he promoted. Don't Westernize yourself, he urges; you have something particular to offer; use that and don't become the pale imitation of a Valéry, Aragon, Éluard. For his own part, Malaparte declared that such advice didn't apply to him, because he wrote in French as though it were his own language—which, as it turns out, wasn't entirely true; when native-speaker friends offered to correct his plays' language, he refused, insulted.

By early 1949, Paris had apparently had enough of Malaparte. He was increasingly shut out of the salons, his lifeblood, and even risked a duel with one of his fiercest critics, who had followed up a withering review of his play *Das Kapital* with calumnious personal attacks.[7] The last dated entry is from December 19, 1948. He may have realized then that this story wasn't to have a happy ending, and he wouldn't be publishing the diary. For several stretches in 1949, Malaparte was back in Italy, mostly in Forte dei Marmi, and he also spent some weeks in Switzerland. When he finally decided to definitively repatriate, in December, it was, he told friends, because his beloved dog was sick. By this time, though, the consolidation of power by the centrist

Christian Democrats in government and the clamorous success of *The Skin* meant that he could return to Italy safely and in triumph.

I came to Malaparte through working on a new English-language edition of *The Skin*, while I was an assistant editor at NYRB Classics. Before that, I mainly knew the author as the owner of a spectacular house atop a rocky promontory on Capri, thanks to Jean-Luc Godard's 1963 film *Contempt*. In the course of negotiations with the Malaparte estate to secure the rights to reprint the existing English translation of *The Skin*, by David Moore, I learned that one of the editors of the most recent Italian edition, published by Adelphi, had in an afterword noted a series of omissions and euphemizing mistranslations in the Moore version. I wrote the editor, Giorgio Pinotti, asking if he had made a list of the translation problems, but he politely declined my request to return to the project.

I eventually ended up comparing the translation to the original, line by line, noting the discrepancies, and translating any missing or mistranslated text. What was missing or changed tended to deal not with sex, exactly, since that doesn't really feature in Malaparte, but with sex-adjacent matters, like in the scene of American soldiers in Naples paying to ascertain whether an Italian girl was a genuine virgin, or the blond pubic wigs that Italian prostitutes would allegedly wear to cater to the perceived tastes of black soldiers. In both cases, the most explicit details had been left out. Some of the harsher stuff about Catholicism and capitalism had been cut too. After making the comparison between the latest Italian and American editions, I discovered by chance that the British edition of Moore's translation had made a different set of cuts. In general, with the exception of an entirely omitted chapter, the British edition cut *less*, and I was subsequently able to add back some of the passages I had marked as missing from the American edition. Occasionally, though, the Brits had cut more, especially with regard to the names of real aristocrats and military officers—probably owing to the stricter libel laws in England.

Because of such restorations, a friend joked that our edition of *The Skin* should have a special sticker on the front: "Additional smut translated by Stephen Twilley." Meanwhile I was asked to do a reader's report on an unfinished work by Malaparte about his 1929 stay in Moscow, *Il ballo al Kremlino*, which I did, recommending publication. A few years after I stopped working for NYRB Classics, the series' editor, Edwin Frank, asked me if I would be interested in translating another unfinished work by Malaparte, one that had recently been reprinted in France and covered the author's stay in Paris from June 1947 to December 1948.

Diario di uno straniero a Parigi was published nine years after the author's death, by the Florentine publisher Vallecchi, in 1966; the following year Denoël, in Paris, brought out *Journal d'un étranger à Paris*.[8] This *Diary of a Foreigner in Paris* was created on the basis of these two editions, both of which are presented as combining the parts written in one language with the parts translated from the other language—but the case is hardly so straightforward. For starters, of the typewritten pages marked "Journal" that the author's family delivered to the editor of the Vallecchi edition, apparently only a small minority are numbered, while many entries suddenly break off, their continuations to be sought among the undated material, or considered lost in the confused course of Malaparte's many moves.[9] What's more, while a bibliographic note in the Vallecchi edition refers to the "preponderant" Italian portion,[10] a glance through the Denoël edition, which italicizes material translated from the Italian, makes it look as if a clear majority of the text was originally composed in French. The two editions are also at variance at several dozen points, at scales extending from a word or two up to several paragraphs.[11] What happened? And what does this mean for the present edition?

There are clear errors in both the Vallecchi and the Denoël, but, with the exception of the spelling of proper names, which are more likely to be correct in the French edition,[12] considerably more care seems to have been taken with the Italian edition, including more coherent paragraphing and section breaks. The most serious errors are the multiple instances in the Denoël edition of text being run together in senseless ways, speech being misattributed, and missing material making nonsense out of certain transitions. A striking example of the last-mentioned error can be found in the entry for November 16, 1947, which begins: "I wake up anxious and tired again this morning. I try to work, but I can't write a single line. I'm depressed, as I am on so many days. Charles Du Bos, in his journal, expresses this sense of dismay and anguish quite well." The Denoël edition's omission of the corresponding first two sentences of the Vallecchi might invite speculation as to whether Malaparte himself was responsible for the difference. While there is little reason to suspect that he would wish to be relatively more candid about a period of self-doubt when speaking to an Italian audience, as opposed to a French one, perhaps the French version here represents a later draft, the result of a general misgiving, and that any version revised for publication in the author's lifetime, in any language, would not have included these sentences? Possibly, and yet because the French edition contains the orphaned reference to "this sense of dismay and anguish," it seems more likely that someone—Malaparte, or someone responsible for establishing the text of the French edition—just made a mistake.

Only in rare instances does editorial censorship seem to have potentially played a role. For example, Malaparte's reference, in the entry for February 14, 1948, to "second-rate intellectuals and artists, such as the playwright and Académie Goncourt member Salacrou," is limited, in the italicized text of the Denoël edition, to the equivalent of "second-rate intellectuals and artists." Could it be that the Denoël editor cut from the translation Malaparte's slight against the playwright Armand Salacrou (1899–1989), whose abundant official honors also included being a grand officer of the French Legion of Honor? It doesn't strike me as out of the question. In the same entry, where the Denoël edition's italicized text ends a paragraph with the observation that "a good number of the communist intellectuals are fresh converts, or fakes, or hypocrites, who have followed the interest of the moment, or the fashion," the Vallecchi edition proceeds to name names: that of "Aragon and Éluard, who passed from surrealism to communism, from communism to surrealism, and again from surrealism to communism during the war," and of Claude Roy (1915–1997), "who, prior to being elevated to the rank of communist poet, belonged to Action Française, and so was a monarchist and a reactionary, and during the war he was an important part of the collaborationist Radio-Vichy." Again, perhaps the Denoël editor judged it impolitic to faithfully reproduce such aspersions.[13]

At any rate, of the two editions, the Vallecchi seems more comprehensive, judging by the small number of elements that appear in the Denoël alone, as compared to the considerable number of elements that appear only in the former. There are also a handful of discrepancies in dates, days of the week, and entry order, including with respect to two of the book's big set pieces, the story of the ties and the ball of Count Pecci-Blunt. I have made my own call in each case about which version seems more plausible, generally explaining my reasoning in a note. I also managed to add dates to several entries, based on references to theater performances and to a political demonstration whose dates can be verified.

What the abundance of variants between the editions suggests, more significantly than the surprisingly slapdash production values of the Denoël, is that there must be at least two versions of more than half of the *Diary*. It would appear, then, that the work was neither written partly in French, partly in Italian, nor written completely twice, once in each language. Instead it seems that Malaparte would often start writing in one language, then switch over to the other, and maybe switch back; or write about the same occurrence once in French, once in Italian, with slight or occasionally significant differences.[14] While the Vallecchi edition shows signs of consulting alternate-language versions of many entries in order to provide a nearly comprehensive text, and very likely imposes some paragraphing, all while preserving Malaparte's spelling errors, the Denoël edition corrects spelling and indicates translated sections but apparently fails to take advantage of alternate-language versions of some entries and in all likelihood introduces new, sometimes significant errors.

This English-language edition, then, is a sort of hybrid, seeking to reconcile the existing and not particularly authoritative French and Italian editions, taking the best from each and supplementing and correcting material where possible. One thing this *Diary* clearly is not is a strictly philological document, which would in any case be ridiculous to presume without access to primary sources. I'm hoping my English-language translation is appreciated by scholars, to be sure. But the principal audience I have in mind is nonacademic, and I have striven to produce a text that can be enjoyed by all kinds of readers.

I am grateful to Lance Rhoades and Nicola Sayers for their comments at various stages of the project; to the Casa delle Traduzioni in Rome, where I completed a significant portion of my first draft of the *Diary* during a February 2016 residency; to Franco Baldasso, who shared his considerable knowledge of the author and invited me to present on my translation at Bard College in October 2018; to Douglas Johnson for clarifying copyedits; and for the patience of my wife, Heather Haddon, who graciously made room for Malaparte in our lives over many years.

—STEPHEN TWILLEY

DIARY OF A FOREIGNER IN PARIS

SKETCH OF A PREFACE

EVERY "diary" is a portrait, chronicle, tale, record, history. Notes taken day by day are not a diary but merely moments selected at random in the current of time, in the river of the passing day. A "diary" is a tale: the tale of a *tranche de vie* (the very definition of the novel, according to one celebrated school), of a period, a year, many years of our life. And as life follows the logic of a tale, it has a beginning, middle, and end (a life is a series of beginnings, middles, and ends, within the closed circle of the beginning, middle, and end of life, in the circle of life). It's not true that a "diary" begins by chance, progresses by chance, has no conclusion but the end of life. A diary, like every tale, calls for a beginning, a plot, and a denouement. The subject of *Diary of a Foreigner in Paris* is my return to Paris after a fourteen-year absence. It's my discovery of a new France, of a new French people. It's the portrait of a moment in the history of the French nation, of French civilization, that coincides with a particular moment in my life, in the story of my life. I don't claim to be breaking new ground in the "diary" genre. I'm simply suggesting that a diary is a tale, as a play is a tale. And now I arrive at my point: a "diary" is a theatrical work brought to the boards of the page. It's the point at which a tale comes closest to the theater. Everything there tends toward an ending, a conclusion, following the classical rules of unity, but centered on the character called "I." It's *Das Da*, Kafka's "present moment," brought to the stage-page. My "diary," at least, is this.

1947

JUNE 30, 1947. I finally return to Paris after fourteen years of exile in Italy.

Those fourteen years were the most unhappy and dangerous of my life. In 1933 I left Paris and returned to Italy, where I was arrested, shut up for long months in the Regina Coeli prison in Rome, then sentenced to five years' confinement on the island of Lipari.

During this unhappy period, among the large number of people abroad I counted as friends—in England, in America, in Switzerland—only my Parisian friends, at least some of them, did not forget me, were always beside me, defended me in the papers, the magazines, and the salons. How kind France is, when it is noble. How amiable and steadfast the French are, when they love someone. I will never be able to express to my Parisian friends the profound gratitude and affection I feel for them.

I finally return to Paris, to France, to this country where I have the right of citizenship. When we fly over Avignon, I recognize the Durance by its yellow bed, by its pebbles shining in the sun; I recognize the Rhône by the blue-green color of its waters. I say to Rossellini, who is with me:

"That's Avignon down there. In 1914 I was a soldier in the Palais des Papes. I had the madder-red pants, the broad sky-blue sash of the Foreign Legion, the short blue tunic with gold buttons, the little red kepi. I'd fled the Cicognini boarding school in Prato, my native city. I'd crossed the border at Ventimiglia at night, across the mountain, to enlist in the French Army, to defend invaded France. I was sixteen years old. Italy was still neutral. This city, Avignon—I love it as if it were my own. I love every one of its stones, every one of its trees, every one of its streets. I am not a foreigner in France."

Rossellini replies: "You are a foreigner. And there are certainly people in France who do not forgive you for being a foreigner. Even if you did fight for France when you were sixteen years old."

Then he closes his eyes again and goes back to sleep. I'm very fond of Rossellini. He's a filmmaker. He doesn't feel like a foreigner anywhere.

Cinema is the homeland of foreigners.

"Look down there. That black stream is the Rhône, those yellow ones are the Durance," I say to Rossellini, who is dozing in his seat.

The creator of *Rome, Open City* opens one eye, looks out the window, asks me how I am able to recognize the Rhône and the Durance. The Durance is one of my rivers, like the Bisenzio in Prato, like the Arno near Florence, like the Sesia, which springs from the foothills of Monte Rosa. They are the rivers of my childhood. "My veins," said Marsilio Ficino, the commentator of Plato, who commented on Plato in the Orti Oricellari, the gardens of Signor Oricellari, Count Rucellai, of Florence. I am Tuscan, but the Durance is one of "my veins."

I was sixteen years old in 1914 when I came to live in the Palais des Papes in Avignon. I had left behind the Collegio Cicognini, in Prato, site of my classical education; I'd crossed the border on foot, at Ventimiglia, and the French gendarmes had sent me to a tavern in Menton-Garavan, the Mère aux Bouchons, where some wounded French soldiers offered me food and drink. It was my first encounter with France. I was a pale, frail, and timid child, and France served as my mother. She embraced me as a mother embraces her son. Wearing my uniform of madder-red pants, the blue tunic with gold buttons, the red-and-blue cap, the sky-blue sash wrapped around my waist, I went walking in the evenings along the banks of the Rhône, or on the Île de la Barthelasse, near the Pont Saint-Bénezet, and sometimes I pushed on as far as the Durance.

"It's a very gentle river," I say to Rossellini.

France spreads out before my eyes: abundant, immense, all green.

It's the first time in fourteen years, since 1933, that I've slept without worry or anguish, that I've slept a sleep of the young and free. It's the first time in fourteen years that I'm sleeping in France. I love Italy, love my country, will always defend the Italians and take their side, even when I know them to be wrong. It's because I will never betray my country that I can tell the truth about my country.

Italy is a country of slaves. A country of men continuously exposed, day and night, to the worst violence of the police, the judiciary, and informers. Be it under Giolitti, Mussolini, or De Gasperi, the state despises the citizen, the justice system scorns him, the police threaten him. What does it matter if the Italian is, individually, a free man? He can think inwardly what he wants: in reality he is a slave, both of the state and of other Italians. If he doesn't have powerful friends in high places, he is at the mercy of the police, of the spite and jealousy of his neighbors, of the weakness and cowardice of the judiciary, of the subjection of the last mentioned to the executive and to the parties. I was arrested eleven times in twenty years; there is nowhere in Italy I can sleep easy.

I slept easy. The street noises entered gently into my sleep, like bees into the cells of their hive. All these noises, these nocturnal voices, this echo of footsteps, this murmur, this passage of tires on the cobblestones, brought into the hive of my sleep all the honey of the horse chestnut trees of Paris, all the honey of the Paris night. I woke at five, opened the window, and stood awhile gazing at the slate roofs, which were damp with dew and discolored here and there with patches of black, gray, and green. A cool breeze was blowing from the Bois de Boulogne. White clouds, very high in the pale blue sky, drifted slowly away toward the morning's pink crown. The swallows flying over the street cried softly, so as not to wake the sleepers. Cats, seated on roof edges with their front paws in the gutters, watched motionlessly as the sky slowly became heavier, denser, bluer. In these long instants I was young once more, I was twenty years old.

I stood at this window as I stood at a window of the Hôtel Lotti on Rue Castiglione, in June 1918, during a few days' leave. I would wake up in the morning and stand at the window to search the gray sky of Paris at dawn, after the bombardments. Big Bertha would begin at dawn.[1] A sound in the pink sky like the scratch of a diamond on glass—and I'd see the sky open, like a sheet of paper sliced in two, with the edges of the gash exposed, and a ray of deep blue appear, the same color as the live flesh at the bottom of a scalpel wound. My room was on the top floor, in the attic. I could see, emerging from the gray roofs, the statue of Napoleon on the column in the Place Vendôme, at the same height as the flowerpots in front of the mansard windows. I called him the "gardener," that gray man at the summit of his column amid the flowers of his aerial garden. Then the muffled noise of the explosion would bring the darker roofs of the Rive Gauche closer to me for a moment, and I seemed to see the reflection of the Seine trembling on the facades of the houses along the quays. A smell of toasted bread would rise from the streets, as well as that fresh smell of damp pavement, the delicate smell of the air of Paris at dawn, when the dust reawakens and vanishes.

It's this sensation of toasted bread, of dust, this slightly warm, feminine smell of Paris, that I rediscover this morning at the window after thirty years. How young the war was then! How pink then were the French faces against the blue horizon. How sad Paris was the morning of my departure. Sad to see me leave, this great pink maiden and blue horizon that was Paris in June 1918. Paris was twenty years old then, like me. It hasn't aged.

Windows are opened, interiors still warmish with sleep are disclosed to my curious gaze. Thousands of potted flowers open their petals at the sun's first ray. It hasn't aged, Paris. It is poorer. It offers up all its old furniture, its faded curtains, its old trinkets, like a flea market laid out on the rooftops. It's selling its old things to survive. The cats, the sparrows, the swallows, the white clouds, and the handsome young gentlemen who are the rays of the young sun pass through this flea market, looking, touching the objects, haggling. And a merry laughter runs from roof to roof, from attic to attic, from balcony to balcony: it's the murmur of the morning breeze. I have rediscovered the country of my childhood, the city of my youth, the Paris of my twenty-year-old self.

July 1. Yesterday, arriving at Le Bourget, I was greeted by Mme Jean Voilier and Guy Tosi, who had come to meet me. I couldn't hide my emotion, seeing Paris again after so many years.

That evening, when I left the hotel to go to Passy, I was unable to find a taxi. I set off on foot toward the Madeleine. On Rue Royale, at the corner of Faubourg Saint-Honoré, I saw a carriage coming, a landau, driven by a woman. I asked her to drive me to Passy. We chatted as we went.

The coachwoman's name is Mme Dorange. She tells me how, during the occupation, she and her horse and her open-top landau traveled 35,000 kilometers around France. She is kind, knows all of Paris, and speaks very courteously, turning around on her seat to look at me. She must have been beautiful, when she was beautiful. Upon my arrival in Passy, the friends who expected me for dinner marveled at my chariot. I believed that coachwomen were plentiful in Paris. Instead it seems I happened on the only coachwoman in the entire city. Later Louise de Vilmorin told me that Marie Laurencin had done a portrait of Mme Dorange and that from then on Mme Dorange resembled a portrait by Marie Laurencin.

This ride through the streets of Paris, the Place de la Concorde, the Champs-Élysées, on a fine summer evening (the air was warm, the swallows shrieked as they flew over the Place de la Concorde)— never had I dreamed of anything so enchanting in my sad Lipari evenings. It reminded me of the walk I took in 1915, in the company of a very young English official, whom I had asked if the Bois de Boulogne was far. "I'm headed there, I'll go with you," the official had replied. We walked all the way to the Pavillon d'Armenonville, where a handsome motorcar was waiting for the official. He was the Prince of Wales, future Duke of Windsor.

The leaves of the trees were luminous in the pink-and-green evening. It was the weary Paris of 1947, even dearer to my heart than the Paris of 1933.

July. Breakfast with Ambassador Quaroni at the Italian embassy.

Mme Quaroni, who is Russian, who has a sense of humor, who enjoys unearthing all manner of strange things at secondhand dealers and flea markets that have value in her eyes alone (the whole secret of happiness is to be found in such discoveries—as the Goncourts understood so well), returns from the flea market carrying I don't know what small object of extraordinary value in her eyes. We talk about Smolenski Boulevard, Moscow's flea market. From Moscow we head to Afghanistan, where Quaroni was Italian minister plenipotentiary during the war (he had been transferred there to put distance between him and Palazzo Chigi[2]), and Quaroni's conversation becomes that of an eighteenth-century traveler, marrying erudition with the spirit of discovery, an explorer's capacity for wonder with a diplomat's power of observation nourished by reading and experience.

He tells me about the horses and dogs of the King of Afghanistan, about the royal hunt, about the still-fresh memories that Alexander the Great left behind in those mysterious territories. He tells me about the extraordinary popularity of the Persian poet ——, whom every farmer can recite by heart. He loves Afghanistan, and when I tell him there is only one region in the world that excites my imagination, that I would like to visit and live in, and that it is Central Asia, the Altai plateau and the splendid isolation of the Persian and Afghan steppes of Turkmenistan, where the Himalayas are a blue pencil line on the horizon, he smiles, delighted.

I love diplomats, love their company and their conversation. These days there is no one but diplomats who might take the place in society of those learned Jesuits of the seventeenth century who returned from the Orient, Africa, and Central America with an entire treasure trove of knowledge, whose fragility and delicacy, when they spoke of a mountain or enormous river, of a desert, fort, or castle, gave their words the sense that they were speaking about tiny, fragile, transparent pieces of porcelain.

Quaroni speaks about the king's horses, the dogs, the mountains of Afghanistan, the Altai, the deserts, the horizonless steppes, like the Goncourts spoke about their Chinese porcelains. He smiles as he speaks, as is his custom, pausing from time to time to study the effect of his words on you. And since I know myself to be impassive when I listen to things that impassion me, I think about the effect that my impassiveness must have on him. And with his short-fingered, slightly pudgy but strong and agile hands, he touches the city of —— —its minarets, palaces, and castles, its walls of mud and red brick—which rises up white and red at the base of the yellow steppe; he turns it, flips it, spins it around, with the insouciance and grace of a Goncourt handling a Ming vase, knitting his eyebrows slightly, like the women in Italian primitivist paintings juggling the infant Jesus in one hand, the sphere of the world in the other, or the model of a city or a church.

Beside him Mme Quaroni listens in silence, supremely confident and serene: she knows that Quaroni won't let this city (this mountain, this river) slip from his hands onto his antique Bukhara carpets. She knows very well that this Himalaya of porcelain, which he handles with his short, somewhat hairy fingers, will not be allowed to shatter into pieces on the floor.

He describes how from the high Altai steppes, still scored by the tracks of Marco Polo's caravan, one spies the Himalayas in the distance, this blue pencil line in the white sky, an immense height like those mysterious signs that the mysterious Leonardo da Vinci sketched at the top of his pages, in the margins of his drawings, in that invisible exalted sky that he created around his heads of women and angels, around his designs for flying machines. He tells me it was on the Altai steppes that he understood for the first time just how high the sky is. From that blue line.

Then we talk about Moscow, the Communist nobility, Stalin.

Then we talk about France. He talks about it with an almost feminine elegance, choosing his words, caressing them with his refined, discreet smile. And here again are the Goncourts speaking of France, of Paris, of the French, in their porcelain-filled study. Once again he is the sage seventeenth-century Jesuit who returns to Europe, to this Europe, after having discovered in an unknown, mysterious, and distant fairy-tale land a city, a people, or a state, a splendid civilization threatened by the wind, which the desert sand threatens to swallow up and which, little by little, when the spring wind blows, sweeping away the sand, emerges from its tomb of dust, from its shroud of impalpable sand, and discloses its towers, belfries, roofs, and trees, the terraces of its mother-of-pearl palaces, the golden roof tiles, the green of its gardens, where the water fountains begin to sweetly sing again.

He speaks, smiling, and little by little I see this city rise at the base of the steppes of Europe; see this city, this people, this state, this nation, and its towers, statues, and domes, its people with the ironic gaze of disinterred statues, the gentle smile of peoples come back to life. He has faith in France, the affectionate faith that collectors have in their delicate porcelains, which it seems the mildest breeze could crack, and against which nothing has prevailed: not centuries, not wars, not revolutions, not floods, not fires, not barbarian invasions. He cites books and verses, speaks of paintings, of old Bonnard who makes—now that he is on the far edge of life, already brushed by death—his youngest, most beautiful paintings. He speaks of a certain old politician, of his wisdom; of the wisdom, despite everything, of the French people; of this French youth that is so generous, so courageous; of the supremely French way in which this youth has demonstrated its love of death, not a morbid but a smiling love, the ancient love of death that breathes in the verses of Ronsard, that shines through in the young French knights of Francis I. He cites the verses of a French poet of our own time: "King Francis did not die in Pavia."[3] No, it is possible to save one's honor and not die.

Then he asks if I'm happy with the way I've been received in Paris. I tell him that I am. Then he recounts how, one day, two months prior to my arrival in France (which is truly odd, given that I applied for a visa from the French embassy in Rome only two days before leaving, and obtained it in ten minutes), Bidault told him, as if in passing, "Did you know? Malaparte would like to come to Paris. But I haven't yet decided whether I'll give him a visa."

"And why not?" Quaroni says.

"Because during the war he wrote against France."

"But that's not true," I say. "During the entire war, I didn't write a single line about France!"

"I know," Quaroni replies, "and I told him as much. But I didn't want to make it a personal matter. I know, from personal experience, that during twenty years of Fascism you were under attack by the Fascist newspapers for your friendship toward France, and that during the war you did your duty as a free man, that you were part of the Resistance. I wanted to make it a matter of general regulations. I told Bidault that I currently had on my desk the passport of Pierre Cot, who hoped to travel to Italy. If he had denied your visa, I would have denied Pierre Cot's, and I was confident that Rome would have approved. Bidault was quite amazed by my reaction, I believe. But he said nothing. He probably considered you a collaborator."

"He's not the only one," I say, "and it's even quite amusing to see how much the French consider me a collaborator. At times I have the desire to respond forcefully, to ask what certain people's Resistance really consisted of. But what would be the point?"

"It's of no importance," Quaroni says, smiling. "What one thinks of people has so little importance these days. When they tire of considering you a collaborator, they'll change their mind about you. As you will no doubt have already been told, it's the price of glory."

"But," I ask, "what would they say about me had I actually been a collaborator?"

Quaroni replies, smiling, "They would salute you as a hero of the Resistance."

July. Yesterday, during lunch at the embassy, Ambassador Quaroni told me a wonderful anecdote about Pope Pius XII. Returning from

Moscow in 1947 to take up his new position at the embassy in Paris, Quaroni stopped in Rome and took advantage of his brief stay to pay a visit to the Holy Father, who is a personal friend. The Holy Father spoke to him about Russia. "There are only two universal powers in the world: the Church and Moscow. They clash, etc."

Then he asked Quaroni what he really thought of the Soviet regime. "Every time I enter the Vatican," Quaroni told him, "I encounter the same atmosphere as in the Kremlin."

July 8. This evening I dined at France Muller's, at 12 Rue Clément Marot.

On Capri the previous winter, André de Vilmorin had said to me: "France is delightful. She has the most beautiful eyes in the world." If he had said, "the most beautiful eyes in Paris," I wouldn't have believed him. The most beautiful eyes in the world is something slightly less than the most beautiful eyes in Paris.

There's something of this sort in the letters of Horace Walpole, if I'm not mistaken. I've known Henry Muller for sixteen years, I'm his friend and remain affectionately and sincerely faithful to him.

I'm going to meet François Mauriac, whom I haven't seen since 1933. At the time I saw him rather often, especially at Édouard Bourdet's, or at Grasset's. I've always had a great fondness for him. I am supremely attracted to men who have made Catholicism their personal realm, made Catholic morality their personal morality, made the manual of the perfect Christian their manual for the conduct of life. A Frenchman doesn't know what Catholicism is, what, alas, a Catholic country is. One must be born in Spain or Italy. There is, deep within me, a sort of overwhelming hate for Italian and Spanish Catholics. How many misfortunes we Italians and Spanish owe to Catholicism, to Catholic morality, to the clergy, to the Church, etc.! We will never be free as long as we are dominated by the Catholic morality of Italy and Spain.

Is a Frenchman Catholic? I have my doubts. There is a depth of individual and national freedom in French Catholicism that turns it into a kind of national religion, well suited to the intelligence and temperament of this people. It's a philosophical, intellectual Catholicism, with very distinct political nuances.

Naturally, it can be objected that Catholicism in Italy and Spain is suited to the intelligence and temperament of the Italians and the Spanish. And yet it's Catholicism that has made us what we are. We are drawn by the horse; the French sit astride it. In the presence of an Italian Catholic I sense the abyss of wickedness, of hypocrisy, of slavery to superstition, of contempt for human freedom, of cowardice, of love of the macabre, of hatred of life. In the presence of a French Catholic I sense the breath of a free spirit, of free reason, of free conscience. In France, the Church has a share of power. In Italy it is the absolute ruler. A French communist is not, as an Italian communist is, a Catholic communist. A man like Pascal would not be possible in Italy. Everything that is free in Italian Catholicism is not Italian. Francis of Assisi declares that his mother is French. Even in Boccaccio, one senses the presence of French blood and French manners in his humor, his objectivity, his freedom.

I find François Mauriac little changed, physically. One of the last times I met him was at Édouard Bourdet's. He had just undergone a throat operation; his voice was weak, listless. I find his voice no longer weak, but sharpened by physical suffering. I find him a bit more agitated, more self-confident, more overbearing.

I immediately sense something in his greeting that surprises me: a hint of animosity, of repulsion, of dislike. He doesn't like me, I tell myself. I quickly make an examination of conscience. In what way have I wronged him? What has happened between us in all these years? Nothing. The war did not happen between us. I have the right to find him again as I left him. Why, then, has he changed toward me? I have no idea. France Muller points him to the seat on her right. Mauriac indicates he will cede the place on her right to me and sits down on France's left. This small gesture pleases me, reassures me, reconciles me with him.

Around the table I see Ollivier, Mme François Mauriac, others I'm meeting for the first time. I feel suddenly ill at ease. Everyone looks at me as if I were not only a foreigner but an uninvited guest. The conversation gets underway with some words from Henry Muller recalling my years in Paris, my time in prison. François Mauriac interrupts him to say that many people in France suffered a great deal in prison as well, that it's rare to find a Frenchman who hasn't been in prison, etc. I say nothing.

Henry asks me for news about the Italian writers he's met. I don't have a chance to reply: Mauriac interrupts him to express his astonishment that Italian writers were able to put up with Mussolini for twenty-five years, without a sign of revolt. I reply that Italian writers wrote and published, that Italian literature is not a literature of slaves or a Fascist literature. Mauriac goes on without looking at me, talking about the plight of French youth, of European youth. I tell him that the plight of youth is the same, be it in France or in Italy, that the youth suffered a great deal. He cuts me short. I give up and say nothing more.

Ultimately, none of this concerns me personally. I'm a foreigner, I'll play the foreigner. I feel weighing on my head the reproach that can be made against my country's policies, for which I am not responsible. It's not my fault if Mussolini declared war against France, if he behaved badly toward France. I think that certain foreigners who came to Rome before the war to pay homage to Mussolini are rather more responsible than the Italians, who had no choice.

July 9. At Jole Robinson's, in the Eiffel Tower area.

Jole R. is an American, a self-declared free woman. She considers herself a martyr and a heroine just because she was a correspondent in Spain for I no longer remember which American newspaper. She refers to all Italians as "bastards," "Nazis," etc., and is not very intelligent.

There are fifteen or twenty people in her apartment, the Italian painters ——, the illustrator Garetto, of *Vogue, Harper's Bazaar,* etc., the French communist painter Fougeron, the picture dealer Caputo, a few vaguely republican Spaniards, one vaguely republican Spanish woman, an old American woman, etc. Jole had called me on behalf of my American publisher, Dutton, whom she had seen in New York before returning to Paris. Jole has been drinking, and looks at us Italians with hate and contempt. I'm already sorry I've come, but what to do?

Fougeron, who was in Rome last month, where he was welcomed by Guttuso and the other communist daubers as a great Parisian painter, affects an air of contempt for us all. And so I decide to stay. Fougeron starts to talk about painting, neocubism, abstractionism, progressive painting. This last phrase makes us laugh. "Art," says Fougeron, "must be in the service of truth." The Italians present smile. When Paul Éluard came to Italy, in 1946, and publicly said, "*La poésie au service de la vérité,*" the public began to laugh: they were the same words we had heard for more than twenty years from the mouth of Mussolini. Fougeron becomes annoyed, talks about communist art, fascist art, and other follies of that sort. "*Nous avons fait la revolution, en France,*" says Fougeron. At first we think he's talking about the Revolution of 1789, but apparently he means that of August 1944. Everyone starts to laugh, including the Italian communist painters present.

July 11. Dinner at Henry Muller's, on Rue François Premier.

What a joy it is to see little Muller again, after so many years! Of all my Paris friends, Muller was—along with Daniel Halévy, Pierre Bessand-Massenet, Henri Sabatier, Montherlant, Bedel, Guéhenno, and so many others whom I will doubtless have the chance to see— one of the most loyal, the most devoted, during the time of my stay on Lipari. His wife, France Boutelleau, is Gérard's sister. She is vibrant, cheerful, witty.

At dinner I'm seated across from François Mauriac, whom I last saw in 1933, at Édouard Bourdet's.[4] Time passes. Returning to Paris, I had planned not to show any awareness of the intervening years. But time passes. What surprises me, even upsets me a little, is the way François Mauriac looks at me. It's a look of reproach, from on high, as if since our last meeting many things had happened that might be held against me. I make a rapid examination of conscience. I have done nothing wrong, nothing I can reproach myself for, nothing against France and the French, nothing against honor, justice, freedom, nothing against François Mauriac. During all those years, I suffered like everyone else; I spent many years in prison, like so many others. For me, François Mauriac has remained the same. Why am I not the same for François Mauriac?

Ah, I am Italian. My country declared war on France, my country's soldiers occupied French territory. So it was. But when I was in the Regina Coeli prison, when I was on Lipari, how many Frenchmen climbed the grand staircase of Palazzo Venezia and went to pay homage to Mussolini! Politicians, writers, Frenchmen of every stripe. All the same, I don't hold a grudge against them; they were within their rights.

At the end of dinner I tell Mauriac how, on the occasion of our last meeting at Bourdet's (also present were André Maurois and his wife, François Porché and Mme Simone, Mme Bessand-Massenet, the Italian writer Alberto Moravia, and others), I heard him say something to Moravia that has stayed with me. Mauriac had just undergone a throat operation; his voice was hoarse, deep, and sorrowful. He was sitting on a sofa next to Moravia, with whom he was discussing the religious crisis in Europe. At a certain point Mauriac said...

"Let's hear what Mauriac said," says Mme Mauriac, coming up to me. Her tone is condescending and she looks at me in a strange way. I tell her what Mauriac said: "If Jesus Christ hadn't been resurrected, I wouldn't give a damn about Catholicism."

"Ah, that's what Mauriac said?" asks Mme Mauriac.

"Ah, so that's it," says Mauriac. "A fairly wretched statement. But did I really say those words?"

They're close to the door, on the verge of leaving. Mme Mauriac says, "I'm disappointed, I'm disappointed." And with these words she walks out, without saying goodbye to anyone.

Returned home, I open *La Rencontre avec Barrès*, by François Mauriac, published by La Table Ronde in 1945. On page 100 I read these lines: "But a young Catholic of my stripe, joints stiffened by what a contemporary has called 'the cramp of salvation,' violently insisted that Christianity be metaphysically true. If they had demonstrated to me that Jesus is not the Christ and that there is nothing divine in the Church of Rome, in that very moment I would have rejected with horror and disgust the straps and fittings that harnessed me, though it meant society crumble all around me."

It is, in other words, the same thing Mauriac said at Édouard Bourdet's in 1933 to Alberto Moravia. Why, then, does Mauriac today deny ever having uttered it? Why that "I'm disappointed, I'm disappointed" on the part of Mme Mauriac? Why this air of reproach, of an injury received, on the part of François Mauriac?

Time passes, to be sure. Oh, does time pass. No one is still Catholic in 1947 the way one was in 1933. Then one was Catholic in a freer, more personal way. Today it's more political. Caution enters even into one's faith. Today one is afraid of having said things that can be damaging. But no, no. The truth is that, in 1947 as in 1933, if Jesus Christ hadn't been resurrected, no one really would give a damn about Catholicism.

People cease to give a damn today for less, much less. Therein lies the entire difference.

July 11. Yesterday evening at Pierre Bessand-Massenet's, something said by Burckhardt, the author of *Richelieu* and Switzerland's minister in Paris, surprised me.

We talked about Böcklin in connection with my house in Forte dei Marmi, which was designed in 1898 by Hildebrand, the sculptor from Munich, and whose construction was overseen by Böcklin, who lived in Forte dei Marmi in those years. The close of the last century is very important for German culture, I say, given how it highlights the "modern" misunderstanding between European culture and German culture. This is when Europe, because it knows Nietzsche and Herder, remembers Heine, loves Wagner, etc., believes it knows German culture, which is actually rather little known in Europe.

Burckhardt was saying that the French know German culture better than any other people in Europe, a judgment that, I confess, amazed me. I offer as evidence[5] the excessive importance France attributes to German literature, which is rather inferior to its philosophy, its artistic culture, its historical culture, etc. In my opinion, the true German literature is its philosophy, its best writers being philosophers.

Cited against my opinion are Kleist, Chamisso, and naturally Schiller and Goethe. Someone refers to Valéry's admiration for Goethe.

I reply that, according to Benedetto Croce, in 1934 Valéry had yet to read Goethe. And I relate how one evening in 1943, when Croce was taking refuge on Capri, living in Alberto Albertini's Villa d'Unghia Marina, he said (in the presence of Tarchiani, since emigrated, and currently Italian ambassador in Washington; Mario Soldati, etc.), that, returning from Oxford, where he had traveled for a philosophy conference, he had met Paul Valéry in Paris, and, speaking of Goethe—whom naturally Croce placed at the summit of Parnassus—Valéry had told him that he was preparing a course on Goethe and that he was then reading Goethe, whom he had not yet read. There are German literature experts in France, of course, and I cite the magnificent book by Vermeil, professor at the Sorbonne, in my opinion the best book, along with *De l'Allemagne* by Madame de Staël, to have ever appeared in France on Germany. But I add that French writers do not know, or hardly know, German literature; they judge it without knowing it, and in consequence believe it more important than it really is.

"It seems to me," I say, "that the influence of German literature on French literature has been nil, or nearly so, and it could not have been otherwise, given that German writers and poets, from the time a German literature, strictly speaking, exists—that is, from the seventeenth century—if they're great, they're influenced by France and Italy, and if they aren't, they aren't great. It seems to me," I say, "that the influence of the German spirit has been greater than that of its literature, and that Germany has been more important for its national character, for the quality of its spirit, etc., than for its literature, strictly speaking."

Bessand-Massenet cites the surrealists, who made so much use of Novalis, etc.

"Is Novalis," I ask, "a great poet? No, certainly not. And Goethe? But Goethe did not have any influence on European culture. Let them cite me data about his supposed influence. One characteristic of German youth is its scarce affection for Goethe, whom they consider scarcely German. The German poets are Kant, Hegel, Schopenhauer, Nietzsche, etc., not its poets and writers. Ultimately," I say, "the greatness and originality of the Germans consists in the way they see the world, not in their artistic interpretation of it."

In their way of seeing God, in their relationship to man, in the relationship of man to nature, to God, life, death, etc., not in their way of representing all this in art. I say that the influence of German art on Europe dates from the Middle Ages, and that since then the German genius, in its artists, has been corrupted by its contact with Italian and French culture, and on this question I share the opinion of the Germans themselves, who have always deplored, and deplore to this day, the French and Italian influence on their culture, and the corruption and decadence that followed. From Germany we moved on to the current situation of French culture, which, in my opinion, is in crisis: no longer capable of defending the universal ideas that are the basis of French culture, it makes do with ideas and themes that are not universal values. It's on its way to becoming a literature—a culture, if you like—of manners and not of ideas. It no longer has a French philosophy, or a French vision of the world. It has too much good taste, and taste is of secondary importance in art, etc. For me, this is what constitutes the crisis of French culture. Naturally, I believe French culture will overcome this crisis, but I don't believe it will be able to get out of it with —— (names I won't repeat).

August 16, Royaumont. This morning at breakfast, the Polish writer and communist M. Sandauer spoke about Warsaw, about the Warsaw Uprising against the Germans, in 1944, which he participated in as a Polish soldier in the formations incorporated into the Soviet Army, from the bank of the Vistula to Warsaw's Praga district. From Praga one takes in at a glance the upper town, the Royal Castle, the churches of Stare Miasto, the Citadel and the open space behind it, all the way to the Nalewki ghetto district. I point out that it was Warsaw alone that revolted against the Germans at the approach of liberation. Its destruction is perhaps owed to the fact that no other European city rose up against the Germans with the arrival of the Allies.

"*Pardon*," Gadoffre says to me, "Paris revolted; there was the insurrection of Paris, etc., etc."[6]

"I have no doubt," I say, "since you say so."

"Dear Malaparte, I do hope you don't believe it was Rome alone that rose up against the Germans."

"But Rome didn't revolt against the Germans," I say, "not when the Germans were there, and not after they'd left! Warsaw is the only one that revolted. Warsaw alone."

"And Paris. You're forgetting Paris," says Gadoffre.

"I wasn't in Paris at the time of liberation, so I don't know what happened there. My status as a foreigner prevents me from speaking about things I'm not acquainted with."

September 1.[7] This evening I took a stroll in the Place de la Concorde. It is not, as Hemingway said to a friend, a *promenade à la campagne.*[8] The Place de la Concorde is as far from the countryside as Versailles was from the countryside—that place where the birds are raw. (Nothing more clearly demonstrates the French nobility's estrangement and detachment from country life than this definition.) Of all the public squares in France, the Place de la Concorde is the most French. It obeys the same intelligence, the same sense of tradition, the same sensibility that created Piazza del Popolo in Rome. (Here too we find the same presence of trees, both in the name—"Popolo" doesn't mean *people*, but *poplar*, in Latin—and on the flanks of the Pincio. And the French name of the architect, Valadier, even if he was Roman, even very Roman, and a papalist.) The Place de la Concorde is a piazza that obeys geometry, a Cartesian piazza. Cold, logical, rationalist, mathematical, miserly. It's the ghost of France, an X-ray of the French people. Entering it from the Champs-Élysées you have the Tuileries Garden as a backdrop; on the left, the Hôtel de Crillon, the Naval Ministry, the arcades of Rue de Rivoli. You have before your eyes one of the most representative landscapes of France. And entering it from Rue Royale you have before you the National Assembly, that colonnade of counterfeit Greece, a sort of Greece constructed for the use of the French bourgeoisie, and the trees of the Champs-Élysées, and the river air, the Seine's reflections in the blue and gray air, in that French air that is so French in the Place de la Concorde. But an art is required to stroll in the Place de la Concorde. And it seems to me, or I fear, that the French of today have lost it.

It used to be that only the French knew how to stroll in the Place de la Concorde. Today not even they do. It's a difficult art to practice. It's an art that resides not in the physical, but entirely in the moral, the intellectual realm. It is not possible to stroll in the Place de la Concorde—that is, to be acquainted with this art—without a clear vision of France, of what France is.

I saw Édouard Herriot cross the Place de la Concorde. He was a Radical,[9] but he was acquainted with this art, albeit in its decline, and only approximately. As he walked he showed he knew very well that the freedom of the Place de la Concorde is only apparent. In essence, in reality, it is a piazza enclosed within the high, invisible walls of tradition, logic, and dignity, of the good manners of the golden age of the French spirit. It is possible to be a Radical, a Socialist, a republican of the left or the right, and be more or less acquainted with the art of strolling across the Place de la Concorde. But I very much doubt that a Communist could be acquainted with it, or a Gaullist, or an Action Française.[10] It is a piazza that refuses every extremism. Nonetheless, it is not the piazza of the middle path—far from it. There is a very evident extremism in this piazza, the extremism that is identified with an achievement, with an extreme result.[11] It is a piazza at the extreme limit of a civilization. On the far side of that frontier is democracy, the Republic, bad taste, confusion.

It is a piazza that cannot be assimilated by the Republic. It is of an extremely refined and intransigent modernity. What is truly modern in France is only the France of Louis XV. All of French modernity evolves from, proceeds from Louis XV, and ignores Napoleon, the Restoration, Louis-Philippe, the Second Empire. Everything modern built in France proceeds from the elegant, refined, essential, pure, lean rationalism of Louis XV. The Place de la Concorde does not believe in progress as it was understood in the nineteenth century. It doesn't believe in human perfectibility. It believes in the perfect man—as he was realized and conceived at the time of Louis XV. Darwin, Marx, all the perfecters of man (including Hegel, Freud, etc.) are foreigners in this piazza. Perfection, in the modern social world, would be a Marx with the proportions, the rigor, the logic, the leanness, the harmony of this piazza. A rigorous, scientific Marxism, conceived according to the architectural measure and logic of this piazza. How different this is from the Marxism conceived in the Place de la Bastille, at La Villette, in the Place de la République! Everything that is truly French finds its measure here. Picasso, Rouault, Matisse, Manet, Renoir, and the abstractionists, and the new School of Paris, Gischia, Fougeron, Manessier, are recognizable as French by their adherence to this piazza. Certain impressionists above all, starting with Manet. The same with certain literature. Even Racine, Corneille, La Fontaine are not for here. At most André Chénier. Read Éluard, Aragon, Apollinaire, even Valéry and Gide, here, in this piazza, and you will immediately become aware of what separates them from the true, profound, authentic French spirit. More than any of the others, though, Éluard, Gide, and Valéry approach it; more than any of them, they resemble the Place de la Concorde. But how far away is Proust! Euripides is close to it, and Sophocles, and Virgil, and certain things by Anacreon, and Xenophon, and Plato. And consequently Christ. But the Greek Christ, Saint Paul's Christ, the Hellenistic Christ. Certainly not the Catholic Christ, or the Reformation's. A Christ of the Parthenon. Because the Place de la Concorde is the Acropolis of France. (And not the Louvre, or the Place Vendôme, or the Arc de Triomphe, or Versailles.)

I've always wondered why Renan ended up in Athens, why he

climbed all the way to the doors of the Erechtheion, in order to say his prayer on the Acropolis. What place in Athens is more Athenian than this Place de la Concorde? What place more pure, perfect, essential, logical than this? More intellectual in nature? It's here that one grasps the close kinship between Descartes and Plato, and Descartes's Christianity. It's upon entering this piazza that one realizes how false the sets and the costumes and the very diction of the Théâtre-Français, of Racine and Corneille at the Comédie-Française, really are. What better stage set, for Racine and Corneille, than this piazza? Hermione, Andromache, Britannicus, and Horace are all at home here. It's their palace, their temple, their true homeland. It's Ilium, Thebes, Corinth, Athens, Sparta, and Troezen, lovable Troezen, at the same time. The heroes of Corneille and Racine—have any heroes ever been more French?—breathe there the pure air of Ilisos, of Boeotia, of the Peloponnese, of the Troad, of the sea. The god of this piazza is Poseidon. Severe Poseidon, with his salty breath. Because the presence of water there is continuous and unavoidable. This presence is due not just to the river, but also to the white marble of the statues variously arranged across the immense piazza, to the green crowns of the trees, to the bright blue of the sky. What is white and green in the French landscape, as everyone knows, in French poetry and painting becomes gray and blue, which are the colors of the French landscape, of French nature, in the Île-de-France. In all of French poetry there is no trace of white and green, just gray and blue. And it was the Frenchman Poussin who made the landscape of Lazio—so green with trees, so white with clouds—French, or gray and blue.

Upon entering here, one has the impression of entering an aquatic land: the trees are submarine flora; the water flows among the plants and the statues, taking the place of the air; and the rare birds that cross the piazza (it's the piazza where birds are the rarest in the world—and I believe that's because birds fly, not swim) seem mysterious, like sea swallows. They quickly return to the surface, and look from on high at this pale blue lake populated by trees and statues. And this aquatic impression occurs early in the morning, and in the evening at sunset, more than at other hours of the day.

The Place de la Concorde is an idea, not a piazza; it's a way of thinking. And the transformation undergone by the French these past fourteen years is visible precisely in their evident disharmony with this piazza today; that is, in their different way of thinking, which is perhaps no longer so French as before. What the Frenchman is today, I don't know. There is little trace in him of what is shaping Europe today. What's repellent about him today above all is a fault that he already had in spades: provincialism. Before, there was no one but him in the world; he was everything. The French "do everything and know nothing, know nothing and do everything," as Alfieri said, exaggerating, in his *Antigallican*[12]; the rest of the world didn't count, and Paris was the navel of the world. This way of thinking was a defect, and a very serious one, in a world that was already on its way to becoming autonomous not only from France, but from Europe. And it was certainly a form of provincialism, of petty-bourgeois nationalism. Today it's the other way around. Today France is nothing and counts for nothing; France is finished, cut down to size; France is ruined and washed up; everyone, even the Hottentots, are worth more than the French, etc., etc.

And this is another form of provincialism, more repellent, perhaps, than yesterday's. When I listen to such arguments—in the Métro, in buses, in cafés, in drawing rooms; as a non-French person, as a foreigner, as what, in France, is the greatest handicap, an Italian—I have to force myself not to give in to the temptation to shout the fool down. I always do so in the end, no matter who it is, especially with young people, even if they're hard-up types, as is often the case. And when I feel overwhelmed by the cowardice of others, by this morbid mania for denigrating France that is particular to the French today, I come to take a stroll in the Place de la Concorde. Here is France. And I feel like I am in the belly of France, like Jonah in the belly of the whale.

Tuesday, September 2.[13] At the Théâtre-Français tonight to see *Andromaque*. I had never entered the House of Molière before in my life. The room is full. I like the audience.

Devotees of the classics, they all know Racine's text by heart. Large numbers of modestly dressed women, young students, office workers—the only audience truly worthy of this glorious house. Unlike the audiences in almost every other theater in Paris, in Europe, they don't smell. There's no trace in the theater of that odor, as Paul Morand says, of the "little lion," the odor of today's poorly washed, poorly looked-after Europe. Racine himself has not changed. The war, the suffering, the universal misery: all have increased his tenderness, his humanity, his truest and most profound intonations.

It's a curious contrast, this immobility of art face to face with the debasement of the crowds. The set design is mediocre, the staging pathetic. The actors are each performing in his or her own show. Orestes, M——, is dressed like an Assyrian, a Babylonian, maybe a Phoenician. At times he resembles a man dressed up as a nun. He shouts, screams, thrashes about, throws his arms up to the sky and can't manage to bring them down. His entire body struggles with these arms that are continually getting away from him. Andromache, Mme ——, weeps, despairs as if her son had been taken away by social services. She doesn't know what it is to be Hector's widow. Pyrrhus, M. Eyser, performs very well. He has the sense of the tragic, even as he too is badly dressed. Greece! Do they know ancient Greece at the Comédie-Française?

I was deeply moved by Véra Korène. She has Racine in her blood. Her performance is of a rare, stirring purity. She knows the value of words, of Racinian subtleties, of Racinian passion. She is by turns full of love, hate, vengeance, pity, regret. Her violence, so restrained, is terrifying. She's the only one onstage to never forget that Racine is no ancient Greek, that French tragedy of the Grand Siècle is a kind of chamber music in comparison with the tragedy of Aeschylus, Sophocles, Euripides; chamber music in comparison with symphonic music, with Beethoven. Corneille and Racine were performed in the Royal Theater, before an audience of noblemen, of grandes dames, of princes, in an atmosphere belonging to the age of Louis XIV, of his court and his time.

Racine's words, in his own time, did not travel far, but went deep.

Véra Korène has a very precise and very gentle sense of the gestures, of the accents, of the looks. There is no gesture in her that mars the smooth and shiny surface of the verses. Racine's verses, on her lips, are sparkling and sweet, fresh, succulent, and shiny like a piece of fruit, a fruit she savors with feminine gluttony. She never cries; her desperation has the particular dignity that sorrow and joy have in a woman's heart that is humiliated, or exalted, by the passions.

I like Hermione. She is age-old in the French manner. I wonder if the women of the court of Versailles, in Racine's time, had Hermione's nature. I have the impression that Racine's feeling for women was retrospective, as if they were women of Cardinal de Retz's time.[14] Women in Cardinal de Retz have the same complexity that Racine gives to Hermione, that perversity of the grande dame, which makes Hermione a lover, an assassin, a temptress, a woman completely free of deference to the gods, laws, or good manners. She was the grand-daughter of Leda and the Swan, the granddaughter of Jupiter, the daughter of Helen and Menelaus. Her mother seems a bit embarrassed by her daughter, but what progress! What irony! What cruelty in her pity! What cruel pity! What piteous cruelty! I like Hermione. In her, and in Véra Korène, I rediscover the romanticism of Tasso's heroines in their continual attempts to escape the limits of the human, the chivalric, the fairy tale; to penetrate that enchanted, truly feminine world where every gesture, every word, every look, already has the poignant, noble, and, I would say, almost depraved accent of death. Hermione exudes death and damnation from head to toe, and for-giveness and pity and resurrection and nostalgia and remorse and rancor toward life. Véra Korène is the only one on that stage who knows what Racine wants to say, what today's Racine means for a French audience; the only one who tactfully recalls that Racine's tragedies were performed in a theater rich with velvets and silks, soft, perfumed, a bit warm, gently illuminated by rosy candlelight, and by the smooth white luminosity of female faces, female hands; the only one, in a dusty and faded theater, who remembers the frivolity and dignity of the France of yesterday, compared with the France of today dressed in cotton prints and cardboard shoes; the only one, surrounded by the poor, embarrassed, insecure, and fearful Paris public of 1947, to bear the message of French tenderness, which is the only still valid message of France's greatness.

After *Andromaque*, Véra Korène performs Musset's *Caprice*. The distance between them is less great than it seems. The actors, Mme —— ... and Jean Weber, are excellent. For the first time I am struck by the Polish character of Alfred de Musset's plays. There's a grace to them that isn't simply French. Something there sounds familiar to my ear, and it's the Polish accent of Musset's stagecraft and repartee, his frivolity, lightness, and whimsy. I don't know why, but I have the impression that Véra Korène's costume, a great black cloak studded with small white beads, comes from the closet of Anna Karenina. There's something Russian about that cloak. It seems as if Véra Korène comes onstage from a Saint Petersburg street, as if a bit of snow sparkle remains on her shoulders, and it slowly melts in the warmth of Countess Mathilde de Chavigny's drawing room.[15]

Later, Véra Korène telephones and asks me, among other things, if I liked her cloak. I tell her about my Saint Petersburg impression. "That's strange," Véra says, "it's a cloak that was made for my grandmother in 1901, in Saint Petersburg." I don't tell her about the Polishness I sensed in Musset. About the Pushkiness. It's strange, these French impressions that come to me from my memories of Russia and Poland.

After the play, in Véra's dressing room. Lily Brady is there, along with the cultural attaché of the United States embassy and his wife, and Miss More, who is leaving on a plane for Boston tomorrow. And the enchanting voice of Véra Korène resounds through the room, filling it completely, and makes the air tenderly vibrate, like the sound box of a violin.

September 4. I had dinner this evening at Cécile Gaillard's, at 20 Rue Barbanègre, across from La Villette in the Pont-de-Flandre neighborhood, on the Canal Saint-Denis.

It's one of the most proletarian neighborhoods in Paris, and the mist of Flanders, the gauzy fog of that region of ponds and forests that extends north of Paris—the region of Chantilly, of Luzarches, of Ermenonville, of Senlis, of Compiègne, the region dear to Gérard de Nerval—of that foggy region, is already rising on the horizon, beyond the buildings of the Villette slaughterhouses, the factory smokestacks, the little shacks that extend, beyond the Canal Saint-Denis and the Canal de l'Ourcq, through Buttes-Chaumont, Pantin, and La Villette.

The war has left its traces of want and dereliction everywhere. The proletarian youth of these poor Parisian neighborhoods have dull eyes, gestures weighed down by malnutrition and the anxiety of those lean years. The Villette Métro, with its little yellow garlands, its glowing yellow glass stuck up there like the sign for a lazaretto, rolls along like a lazaretto train of cholera sufferers from Louis Blanc to Stalingrad, to Crimée, to Corentin Cariou. The crowds that squeeze into the cars are dirty, sad, and tired; the women have that air of neglect, of surrender, that betrays the sufferings they've endured, the fear, the desperation, the calm desperation of Paris, of Europe today. The girls have on just a bit of makeup, their dresses too short, cheap sandals, their hair damp with sweat; the boys wear sweaters and espadrilles, with their pointed chins, their slightly vacant eyes, their thin lips. Among the crowds are many men between forty and fifty, soldiers from the other war, the type of Frenchmen I like best. It's always the France of 1914 that obsesses me, this generation of soldiers, of victors, of *poilus* that is my own. Their faces are completely different from those of the men of younger generations, those born between the two wars.

How the French people have changed. The men of my generation have harder, and at the same time more poignant, faces, more manly features, more childlike eyes, and that trace of the timeworn, the weary, the decisive, the austere found in French faces in the periods in which France distinguished itself from Europe more profoundly than today, in which France was more France and less Europe, in which it was France. Almost all the men who were twenty or twenty-five years old in 1914 have mustaches, short, unkempt hair, low foreheads, clear eyes in dark faces, dull skin. They are the Frenchmen I saw for the first time in 1914, on the streets of France, in the forest of Argonne, in the trenches of Champagne, in the villages of Burgundy, of the Champagne Pouilleuse, in the factories and in the streets of the Gare de l'Est at dawn, as we left for the Champagne front in the spring of 1918, and Big Bertha fired on Paris, on the Rive Gauche. It's a harder race of men, who dress more simply, remaining faithful to the heavy-soled shoe, the tight-ankled velveteens, the peaked cap, the narrow tie over a shirt of coarse cloth.

Each mustache droops at either side of the mouth, a mouth stained by smudges of lipstick, by the Pernods and absinthes of old, by the ever-present Caporal stub at the corner of the lips. They speak from the throat, with an argot that is not the proletarian argot of today, the one spoken by the young heroes in René Fallet's *Banlieu sud-est* or in Barjavel. The language spoken by the men of my generation is the language of Cendrars and Apollinaire and Pierre Mac Orlan and Francis Carco.

One must come here, to La Villette, to Saint-Denis, to Pantin, to Buttes-Chaumont, to Villejuif, to the towns on the periphery, the towns of the ring road, of the fortifications, to rediscover, camped out beside each other—but not mixed, not confused, still foreigners to each other—the ancient race of Frenchmen, of Frenchmen of France, and that new race that is little by little taking shape in Europe, the European race. Little by little it invades the ancient nations, chasing away the ancient peoples, the old, the tired, the defeated, the citizens of a France, a Germany, and an Italy that no longer exist if not in the testimony of the men of my generation. Because a European race, with the characteristics common to every nation, really is taking shape in Europe; in democratic countries as in the countries that until yesterday were fascist, it's the same race: young, nervous, more attractive, both frailer and healthier at the same time. The same race that one finds in Moscow, Berlin, Rome, Paris, and London, and which I would call the "Marxist race," because it is less the product of cross-breeding than of better nutrition, sports, the spread of good hygiene, and the slow evolution of social ideas and feelings, because ideas and feelings influence the body to the same degree as sport, hygiene, and nutrition. A twenty-year-old in Moscow, Kiev, Berlin, Prague, or Italy has very distinct characteristics in common with the young people of every other country: feelings, appearance, and that attitude toward life that characterizes epochs and races, generations and peoples.

The Métro at La Villette is full of the same people who fill the trains in the outskirts of Berlin heading toward Spandau or Tempelhof, those in the outskirts of Moscow toward Krasnaya Presnya, of Rome toward Quadraro or Garbatella, of Milan toward Bovisa, of Odessa, of Kiev, of Warsaw in the Praga district or at the end of Marszałkowska, or of Lviv, or of Vienna. As a race they are more cynical, more detached, more distrustful, perhaps; and perhaps less courageous, less moral in the bourgeois sense, with a morality of their own that may repel those who fail to perceive the profound transformation the human species is undergoing in these years and in this century.

The "transformation of man" that Marx regarded as the foundation of Marxism, this concept that passed from Darwinism into what I would call the social field of ideas and feelings, is taking place in Europe and in the world at a faster and faster clip. A strange kind of moral evolution, which Darwin failed to foresee, and which takes place in the deep mental and psychological recesses of the species as well as in the body. A moral as well as a biological fact.

What is strange for me is that I don't feel like a stranger to this new race, though I belong to a pre-Marxist generation, and though I've remained faithful to my generation, to what there is there that is everlasting, unchanging, stable. Maybe I too have undergone the transformation that young people are undergoing today, maybe it's my Nordic roots, the proletarian upbringing I received in the working-class family where I was raised, the working-class environment in which I lived to the age of fifteen, my continuous efforts to understand, to mix with the people, to judge the life of the masses from close up, and that instinctive tendency to justify my cynicism, my freedom of spirit, outside my own cultural environment, by contact with a moral world that is not that of my own culture.

Cécile Gaillard is waiting for me outside the exit of the Corentin Cariou Métro station, just past the railway bridge. Cécile is a great gal, a friend of Juliette Bertrand's. She's a Cantalienne, and on her breast she wears what in her region is called an *esprit*, one of those little crosses with three gold pendants, encrusted with topazes, which a red enamel colors with a strange vermillion reflection. It's the little cross that the Protestants who took refuge in Cantal brought to the Auvergne region.

We return up Rue Rouvet, through the squalid houses caught between the Canal Saint-Denis and the railway. It's a smoky and foggy neighborhood, filled with the incessant lowing of oxen falling under the butcher's hammer in the slaughterhouses of La Villette.

Cécile lives at 20 Rue Barbanègre, on the corner between the Quai de l'Oise and the Quai de Flandre, at the end of Rue Rouvet, in a sad, gloomy house built into an acute angle. Cécile works for social services, earning 7,000 francs a month, which are starvation wages. All her time is taken up by a few hours of sleep, her visits to the factories, long shifts in the clinics, injection services for the poor, assistance to "at-risk" children and women who have recently given birth, and TB screenings in the workshops and hovels of the Flandres neighborhood. Her life is a life of poverty, of hardship, of continuous self-denial—but I've never seen a more cheerful, more courageous woman than Cécile. I've known her for twenty years, and for twenty years she hasn't changed. Always smiling, active, full of goodwill, overflowing with courage and with that simplicity in her courage that is the only admirable thing in women; in fact it's a sort of tenderness, the most beautiful form of feminine tenderness. No longer young, she too belongs to the old race, to the generation of 1914. Her courage is the firm, stubborn, patient sort of the France of those courageous, virtuous years (I'd like the word *virtuous* to be understood in the Latin sense, from *virtus*: courage, fortitude, a light rather than a dark force of the spirit, hope amid the struggle), of those last years of old France. All her life has been toil, sacrifice, renunciation, poverty, solitude. The solitude of women in proletarian neighborhoods is terrible. Cécile lives with her books, which she binds herself in her off-hours: she designs and colors the paper, coats it with wax to make it shiny and smooth, cuts, glues, sews, binds, all on her own.

She reads some Italian authors: Papini, Palazzeschi. Lots of French ones: Antoine de Saint-Exupéry, the classics, Gérard de Nerval. She knows Italy: Assisi, Siena, Florence, Naples. How long has it been since she was last in Italy? She returns from her travels with drawings of cities, villages, and trees, which she draws herself. She has an idea of the world that is her own, that is female, that is honest; I mean she has an idea of the world that is of her sex and of her class. What's hers is the feeling she places in books, countries, peoples, men, events.

She tells me about the occupation, about the Resistance, in the same way the workers do, the real workers of the proletarian neighborhoods: with simplicity, without even the most remote thought of making it a badge of honor, of gaining some privilege by it, of basing a rhetoric on it, a metaphysics of feelings and interests—without, in other words, what disgusts and repels in the grand European speculation about the Resistance, speculation in equally bad faith as that about collaboration, cowardice, treason. (Those who speculate on the Resistance are the only ones in France with a feeling of inferiority, the inferiority complex of defeat. They feel like losers and look for an explanation. Collaboration was born from the sense of feeling like a winner alongside the Germans. And I wonder why those in the Resistance, why I myself, don't feel like winners alongside the Anglo-Saxons and the Russians. What is so indigestible for us Europeans about the Russian and Anglo-Saxon victory? I think it is worth seriously reflecting on this singular contrast, between the optimistic psychology of collaborators and the pessimistic psychology of those in the Resistance.)

We stop for an aperitif at the tobacconist's on the corner of Rue Rouvet and Rue Barbanègre, and I notice that everyone is nice to her. A young woman asks if the shot she got should hurt. She hasn't been able to sleep. In response Cécile says that she will get used to it, and assumes what she calls her "*toubib*" manner:[16] her bearing imperceptibly changes, along with the tone of her voice and the sweep and weight of her gestures in the smoky air of the tobacconist's, air dimmed by the black reflections of the sepia-painted facade of the house on Rue Barbanègre.

We go out onto the quay, passing in front of the sad, wretched slums of the alley between the canal and Rue Rouvet. Disheveled women stand at the windows, breathing in the foggy air and the slow, heavy smell of the canal. Children sit and play on the doorsteps of the hovels. It's a strip of Naples, but a sad Naples, a Nordic Naples, with something Belgian or Flemish about it, and that gray sky where the trees beyond the canal plunge their stiff peaks, with their still, static leaves shining like tin, caught in the hazy sky like a syringe needle in a wad of cotton.

At this point of the canal there are the locks. It is here that the Canal de l'Ourcq joins the Canal Saint-Denis and forms a kind of large inner harbor, where the big barges that come from the north, from the channel ports, from the canals of Belgium, sit rocking at their moorings. The barges are loaded with coal, wood, barrels of tar, iron pipes, bricks, bags of cement, twisted metal. A woman sweeps the bridge of one barge, wearing tall rubber boots and with her head covered by a large red handkerchief. At the bow, a dog barks, staring at a fisherman who stands motionless in the twilight shadows, his line in hand, a hamper at his feet. The illuminated cliffs of Buttes-Chaumont throw a reflection of smoky fire against the low sky. Beyond the Canal de l'Ourcq rise the fire-blackened towers of the mills and silos of Pantin. Toward Saint-Denis the sky is a dense, opaque black. A train whistles in the distance.

Groups of young people romp past; they're headed toward the pool on Rue Rouvet.

It's a proletarian pool, wretched in appearance. The whir of a motor in the sky above Le Bourget sounds like the whir of a skein winder. The whir coils like the thread of a skein, just like the whir of a winder. At times, the lowing of the oxen in the slaughterhouse snaps the thread, which the invisible Parca reknots with her glowing fingers: Le Bourget searchlights scouring a sky that is dark and red like the inside of a nostril. There's something that is human, carnal, and physical, and at the same time metallic (the smell of scrap iron, of iron filings, and the heavy smell of cow dung and blood that wafts from the slaughterhouses across the canal). The water that falls into the locks creates a sense of freshness; it sounds like a mountain cascade. We enter the pool building.

I've brought my bathing suit. I change in a communal room for men. I sit down for a moment at the edge of the pool, which is weakly lit by some reddish lamps. A crowd of adolescents, girls and boys, run alongside the pool, dive into the water, romp, swim, and shout. Some working-class kids emerge from the changing rooms with newspaper pages stuck around their middle in place of a suit. They dive in, having placed a newspaper at the edge of the pool to cover themselves with when they return to dry land. The newspapers are *L'Humanité*, *Ce soir*, *Combat*, the papers of the left or the Resistance. There's also a front page from *Figaro*, a few copies of *France soir*. I dive in, but it's not possible to swim, so great is the press of people in the water. A young woman sits and soaps herself at the edge of the pool; she washes her hair with hurried and almost timid care. Everyone is laughing and speaking, but the din seems muted, almost as if they were laughing, speaking, and shouting in a whisper. The swimmers without bathing suits wrestle at the edge of the pool, calling loudly for their friends to give them a newspaper. The matter of the newspaper and the bathing suit is a pretext for scuffles, jokes, and games, for a whole delightful comedy of youth, free from obscene or vulgar innuendo.

I marvel at the particular dignity of these young working-class people, at their sense of measure, of reserve, which before the war seemed a privilege unique to the bourgeois and is something essentially French. Such dignity excludes every obscene thought. A young woman returns to her bathing suit a breast that had slipped out in the effort of swimming. She performs this gesture with the naturalness of a nymph. The scene I see around me is out of a Greuze painting, transposed into a proletarian environment, where lasciviousness is replaced by simplicity; malice by absolute disinterestedness in the gestures, words, and smiles; vice by modesty, by this particular working-class modesty, which is realistic in nature and can't easily be shocked. I get out of the water and go to the changing room to dry off. I find Cécile again, who shouts at me from the edge of the pool to hurry up, dinner is ready.

Cécile's apartment is small: one room and a kitchenette, a bathroom, a doll-sized entrance hall. The walls are clean; everything seems new. From the window I take in that Flemish landscape of canals, hovels, locks, trees rising up between the slaughterhouse buildings beyond the canals, the fog that rises to the horizon from the ponds and woods of the Valois countryside—and little by little the moon, a red moon mottled with yellow, already fraying at the edges, rises dreamily over the roofs and the canals. And as the moon ascends into the sky, the houses, the roofs, the factories, the water in the canals, the leaves on the trees, they all take on a dark color, which little by little becomes black, until the supreme moon shines over a landscape sculpted from the pitch and coal of the night. I look at my hands: they're black. I think about that expression among blacks: "the black moon."

Crowds, gangs of young people returning from the pool, pass beneath the window. On the floor below, a radio sings with the hateful accent particular to the voices of those who sing and speak *pour le peuple*, or, as the French say, *pour le populo* (as if the people were a bunch of louts, of persons without taste, of imbeciles).

The master of the locks describes how, during the days of the Liberation, a German wanted to explode a barge loaded with explosives right in the middle of the locks. The master successfully persuaded him not to do it, and the barge exploded in front of the mills, near Pantin. The German wanted to return to Berlin in a rowboat, by means of the canals. Everyone laughed.

We cross the Pont-de-Flandre and enter the bistro on the corner. The walls inside are frescoed with copies of paintings by Horace Vernet. Not the Vernet who does the horses, Charles, but Horace. The proprietor of the bistro is proud of his paintings. The bistro is full of those Frenchmen of 1914, with weary eyes, with the face of those who have suffered. I buy a round of drinks. We talk about the other war. Everyone suffered. Man suffered much more in that other war than in this one, except for the Jews.

"But not everyone has the honor of being Jewish, right? In the other war, everyone suffered; in this one, it was mostly the Jews who suffered. But that was a war of decent people, of men. We were soldiers, we respected each other. On the whole, that war does honor to every person who fought it. But this one. It's a big step down, I assure you. We've sunk very low, these days. There are no men anymore, that's it. There are nothing but scoundrels in every field."

They speak solemnly, shaking their heads. I think that these are all Frenchmen, that they put France above politics. They're courageous men, who have suffered; they're the remains of a people, of a France, that has almost already disappeared. I like these men, these Frenchmen: they're of the same race as me. I too am a man of 1914. But my heart aches at the memory of how I saw them return home after the war, after the victory, in 1919. Every time I meet these men, I can't help remembering this episode.

It was the first of May, 1919, a great gathering of protesters against the cost of living, against I don't know what, assembled in the Place de la Concorde. From all corners of this immense city arrived columns of men still in horizon-blue uniforms, thousands of disabled veterans supported by their comrades, enormous formations of ex-servicemen, to a man in the muddy, faded, rumpled uniforms of the trenches.

In the early hours of the afternoon, the Place de la Concorde was occupied by an immense army of former soldiers, by thousands and thousands of soldiers among the most valiant in the world. They were the soldiers who had won at Soissons, at Reims, on the Marne; held out at Verdun; sown the fields of France with dead. They were the best soldiers in the world, the most steadfast, the toughest, the most stubborn, the most courageous. They sang their songs of war, "La Madelon," *La Madelon pour nous n'est pas sévère*, and "La Madelon de la Victoire," *Après quatre ans de souffrances, Madelon, on les a eus!*, and refrains from the trenches. Here and there over that army, red flags waved. The disabled veterans, gathered beneath the Hôtel de Crillon, shook their crutches, shook their canes. It was an army of veterans up for the fight, invincible and victorious.

From the terrace of the Hôtel de Crillon, mingling with the small crowd of spectators from the foreign peace delegations, I contemplated that immense army with which I had suffered and fought. They were my comrades in arms. I was proud of them. All at once, from the Tuileries Garden, from Rue Boissy-d'Anglas, from Rue de Rivoli, from the Champs-Élysées, from the bridge, sprung large groups of police officers, armed with batons, who launched themselves against that invincible army of veterans. They bludgeoned them, beat them, scattered them, chased them with kicks up the backside. That immense, invincible army of veterans fled, was scattered; abandoned on the cobblestones of the vast square, wretched and forlorn, were caps, crutches, flags.

Leaning back against a column, I could scarcely restrain my tears. That was the day I dimly felt for the first time that my generation had lost the war.

September 5. This morning the Polish writer Artur Sandauer, author of a book of stories, *La Mort du libéral*, came from Royaumont to see me. He's in Paris to talk to Laudenbach, from La Table Ronde, who took my recommendation to publish Sandauer's book. Sandauer is happy.

We go out for lunch in a bistro on Avenue Marceau. He tells me about his life in Poland, his despair, his fears. After the Russians returned to Galicia (he's from a village in the area around Przemyśl, near Lviv), he enlisted in the Polish formations of the Soviet Army.

He tells me about the destruction of Warsaw, in August 1944. He was on the banks of the Vistula, in the Praga district, and there before him, for four months, the rebel city defended itself against the Germans, battling heroically. The massacre of 400,000 Poles, the flower of Polish youth, under the impassive eyes of the Russians, who did not lift a finger to aid the revolt, which had broken out at the behest of the Polish government in London. He tells me about Russian soldiers thronging the banks of the Vistula, their childlike cries of wonder and horror, that strange gaiety so typical of the Russians, which spreads so felicitously over the pages of *War and Peace*.

Then he talks about Polish literature.

He was commissioned by the Warsaw government to write a history of Polish literature, but the work weighed on him, and he would have abandoned it, if he had not already accepted the commission, and the money. How else could he live?

I tell him to write a "journal of a Polish soldier in the Soviet Army"; La Table Ronde would be happy to publish it.

He half-closes his eyes, thinks about this "journal." Then he talks about French literature. It's clear he would like to Westernize himself, to become a Western writer, a French writer.

I tell him, "If I were a Polish writer, I'd like to remain one hundred percent Polish. You'll never become a French writer."

"And you?"

"Don't look at me, I'm Italian. I lived in France for many years, and my culture is Latin, essentially Italian and French and English and German. I'm a Westerner in both the broadest and the most precise senses of the term. As a writer I'm as French as I am Italian. I can write in these two languages as if they were my own, equally. Not so for you. You are a Pole, and a Jewish Pole, from a region where the farming communities are already Ukrainian, where the East begins with forests of sunflowers, and the smell of honey in the air, and the buzzing of flies in the tall grass. You're from the far side of the Carpathians, beyond the extreme limit of the West, on the other side of the Eastern frontier. Yes, I know, you're in love with Paul Valéry, with Éluard, with Aragon; but above all with Valéry. And because of this you think you're a Westerner? I've read your *Mort du libéral*. It's the work of a writer from *over there*, with its irony, its cruelty, that brand of realism that belongs less to Polish writers, who are inclined to the verbose, the flowery, and the vacuous, than to some Jewish writers from the outer Eastern reaches of Europe. There's Gogol in you, and Chekov, and that magnificent Russian Jewish writer Babel, the author of *Konarmiya* (*Red Calvary*), the most beautiful book published in Russia since the Revolution. All of it is in you, in your way of writing, of seeing things, of narrating matters, of describing people. It belongs to your people: to that blood, that atmosphere, that weather. Don't commit the error of believing it's possible to become a writer like us. You would be a bastard, like so many others. You were born in that place, you have its genius; stay what you are, and you will make beautiful things. At the end of the day you're a writer, no? What do you care about the rest? Stay dressed as you are. Don't put on a mask or a costume, you would be ridiculous."

Sandauer listens to me, eyes half-closed behind his glasses. Then he looks at me, lifting his eyes, and says: "I've been in Paris for six months and haven't been able to write a page. I feel disoriented. You may be right. I'm a foreigner in France, in the West. I must remain a foreigner. You're right. So it would be an error to naturalize myself in French literature? But there are counterexamples: Turgenev. Here is a Westernized Russian. And a great writer."

I reply that Turgenev is not a great writer and that what is worthwhile in him is what is Russian, not what is French or Western. The same could be said of Tolstoy, or Dostoevsky. There are obvious traces in Dostoevsky, here and there, of his efforts to Westernize himself. Fortunately, they are failed attempts. "What do you think of Pushkin?"

Sandauer hesitates before replying. "Pushkin," he says, "is not a great poet. The Russians consider him very great, the greatest of their poets. They are clearly wrong. Pushkin is Parny, he's Byron. He's France, he's England. He's Western romanticism arrived at its highest degree of perfection, an extremely refined taste. I recently read Montherlant's *Carnets*. On September 7, 1935, he writes: 'Pushkin's *Stories*. Absolutely insignificant. The same as Gogol's *Dead Souls* or "The Portrait."'"

I don't agree about Gogol, but what he says about Pushkin is justified. Pushkin has what the same Montherlant of the *Carnets* calls a "gentlemanly style." Montherlant apologizes for it; Pushkin didn't apologize for it. It's the gentlemanly style that pleased the cultured society of his time; that is, the nobility, which made his reputation. *Eugene Onegin*, in particular, is Parny. Some of his pages

are worth saving: the story of his journey to Erzurum, during the
Russo-Turkish War; the description of the Hermaphrodite, and the
death of the young warrior prince, beside his young lover, this death
of a pederast in the wild and tender Armenian landscape, at the heart
of a battle, with the horses neighing and stamping far from the grass-
land, among the green and yellow trees (I see them as green and
yellow) of the forest in the bright morning (I see it as bright, like in
Poussin, a sky seen through the young leaves of the trees, a stream
that flows at right and makes the same sweet sound as the Thève in
Gérard de Nerval's *Sylvie*). Here it's no longer the "gentlemanly" style;
here Pushkin reveals himself for what he was, a great writer when he
forgot Western models, or recalled them only unconsciously. A taste
for the pastoral always lives on in him, even in his most sincere pages.
The other day at Royaumont, reading Diderot's critique of the painter
Boucher, I felt like I was reading a critique of a certain kind of literature, even a critique of the works of Pushkin. (And perhaps,
speaking of Boucher, Diderot was performing, unconsciously or not,
an act of literary criticism.)

"I don't want to be a second Pushkin," says Sandauer, laughing. "I
prefer to remain a Polish writer, a Jewish Pole, with all the power of
irony, cruelty, and realism that entails. I want to remain the poet of
the 'Eastern Far West,' as I call that part of Poland where I was born,
eastern Galicia, Carpathian Ukraine. In any case, in all of Polish
poetry, in all of Polish literature, it's the Eastern Far West, Ukraine,
this immense lost Polish empire, this boundless land beyond the
Dnieper, that gives it its grandeur, a pathetic grandeur." (It's the feeling Ulysses harbors in his faithful heart when, having returned to
Ithaca, he thinks of the sea, looks at the sea, his lost realm.)

Here Sandauer pulls a piece of paper from his pocket, reads me a
sentence from Valéry, taken from *Degas, Dessin, Danse*: "What is
interesting to me is not always what is important to me." "The West,"
he adds, "is much more interesting to me than it is important to me.
What is important to me is my unhappy country, the unhappy lands
where I was born, where all my family lies, in unknown graves, a
bullet in the back of the neck, their faces consumed by lime." I look

him in the face. His lips quiver. "All the same," he says, "if I could become a French writer…"

That afternoon, at six, at the Théâtre-Français, where Véra Korène waits to show me her dressing room, which I have been charged with decorating and furnishing.

Véra Korène is dressed in black; a large black hat with a wide brim hides her forehead, giving her an odd look that reminds me of the black butterflies one sees in the Alps, close to the glaciers. (The black butterflies on the Marmolada Glacier in the Dolomites. They would fly as evening came on, when the first shadows rose from the bottom of Fedaia Lake. They would flit over the dead atop the trenches of Mesola, caressing their faces with wings of black silk. I would think of the transparent black hands of the Volsci in the Etruscan tombs of Tarquinia, of Populonia, of Tuscania, where as a child I would hide, trembling with marvelous fear. I would watch the black butterflies of the Marmolada flit over the faces of the dead, caress their lips, their eyes, their hair, and I would say to myself, "The butterflies eat the corpses," and I no longer know who had told me this, perhaps poor Enzo Valentini, whose mother was a Bonaparte, from Perugia.) I like to see the intelligent and slightly anxious face of Véra Korène beneath the big wings of her black hat, and to think that she is one of those black butterflies that rise from the glaciers in the evening.

She motions me to follow, we step onto the stage, I hear a voice that says […] is in the fourth act of *Britannicus*. Tragic actors who perform dressed in their everyday clothes, without costumes, without makeup, with their neckties that clash just like their suede-soled shoes. It's the same as seeing swimmers in the water fully clothed, gloves on hands, top hats on heads. (Certain caricatures by Daumier, certain scenes of a Russian film seen in Leningrad in 1929, the passengers of a small ship sunk off the coast of Aboukir, in 1930.)

Mme Annie Ducaux strolls backstage with her large wolf dog, wearing a pretty, very simple gown, what was called in Musset's time an *indienne*.

Véra Korène's dressing room is the one that until her death belonged to Mme Segond-Weber, on the Talma floor. One can still make out on the door, under a coat of dirty paint, the names of Mounet-Sully, of —, of —. The room is big; its two windows look out over Rue de Richelieu, with views of the Louvre, Rue de Rivoli, the end of Avenue de l'Opéra. I take the measurements of the windows and of the section of wall between the windows, which must be covered with large old Murano glass mirrors, perhaps of a tender pale green, or a light sky blue, the faded blue of the Venice sky as evening comes on. I tell Véra Korène that I have already written to the Italian painter Orfeo Tamburi, asking him to come to Paris to make drawings of her dressing room's decoration.

We talk about styles, about the different nuances of eighteenth-century style in different countries, about calm, beauty, and delicacy, about the tenderness of Venetian furniture, about curtains, fittings, Venetian silk, about the pearl color that is the color of the lagoon, which is reflected in the pink, pale-green, and faded-blue varnishes of Venetian furniture and fabrics. The room's *cabinet de toilette* is as chosen by Mme Segond-Weber: an Empire style slightly contaminated by a certain bright shadow of 1902, 1903, by a suspicion of Viennese art nouveau, but "repressed" (precisely Freud's term) to the deepest depths of consciousness, to the ground floor, where the bust of Préville dominates with a grave and ironic air.

We exit, from backstage, onto the terrace overlooking the inner courtyard of the Palais-Royale. What harmony, what rhythm, what measured, demure delight! I understand now why Jean Cocteau chose to work in his apartment in the Hôtel Beaujolais, whose windows overlook this stupendous courtyard, this pure image of France! The children playing in the garden and the birds singing in the branches of the green trees—of a green that tends toward the clear blue of running water, the clear blue of streams; and I think of that subterranean river that crosses Paris, invisible beneath the cobblestones of the streets and the foundations of the houses, which I imagine to be not black like a Styx or a Lethe, but blue-green like an Île-de-France stream, like those pools reflecting the poplars in the Valois—make a sweet noise, similar to that "modulated tremor" Gérard de Nerval speaks of when he describes the voice of Sylvie.[17]

Véra Korène, in a gesture at once timid and sensual, gently indicates the fleeting rhythm of the windows, the columns, the amphora-shaped shafts that run along the upper balustrade, and seems to caress a child, the head of a dog, a crack in the crystalline air. I think of *Le Neveu de Rameau*, of his raspy voice, of the idlers poking their heads out of café windows to hear the motifs sung by that unhappy, music-besotted poet. Yes, what's missing is a false sound, a raspy voice that sings false, that would allow me to appreciate this admirable harmony, this music that modulates the tremor of the stones, of the moldings, of the trees, and the agile and pure dancer's movements of the dog accompanying Annie Ducaux, who strolls in the courtyard with a book in hand.

Later, descending the staircase, I encountered Mme Ducaux, followed by her wolf.

September 9. In the Concorde Métro station, a man falls. He's poorly dressed, in an American sweater, military pants, a khaki shirt. A short red beard covers his face.

He spins as he falls, hits his head against the wall, and gently collapses to the ground, his head upturned against the shiny majolica wall. He looks at me with his eyes rolled back. A dribble of red escapes his lips. He's stricken by a horrible tremor, which I can't watch. I kneel down beside him, take his head onto my knees, open his shirt collar. He takes my hand suddenly, sinks his teeth into my flesh. I say to the passing people who don't stop, who don't even turn their heads, "Messieurs, help me." No one stops. The crowd flows down the long corridor without even a glance.

It's the six p.m. crowd, the crowd of petty bourgeois, of salesclerks and typists, the horrible petty-bourgeois crowd of six in the evening in every city in Europe: dirty, tired, pretentiously dressed, bustling, selfish, spiteful, mean, cold, sovereign. The sovereign crowd of big European cities at six in the evening, when the stores close, when everyone rushes home, when the people are tired, meaner than ever, more selfish than ever. I hate this crowd, which jostles you, tramples you, flattens you. Never fall in the street, or on the sidewalk, at six in the evening. Don't require help from your neighbor in the street, at six p.m. No one will help you. Everyone will trample you, flatten you, turn to say to you, "What are you doing there, in the middle of the sidewalk! Falling in the middle of the sidewalk isn't allowed. Shame on you!" If you're a foreigner, the crowd will look at you with a nasty expression, will call you a "dirty foreigner." In every city in Europe at six in the evening. And it's not the war that has done this to the crowd in the big cities. It was the same long before the war, in every big city in Europe: in Berlin, Moscow, and Vienna, in Paris and London, in Turin and Genoa. The war has weighed people down, made them mean; but they were that way long before the war. The petty-bourgeois crowd, in Europe, is very dirty, very miserly, very cowardly, very mean.

I say, "Messieurs, help me." No one stops, no one turns. I see two sailors passing. I say, "You, sailors, help me." They stop, look at me, start to go.

I shout after them, "You're in the military. Do you know your duty? Do you think your only duty is fighting and winning or losing the war? Your duty is to help those in need of aid. C'mon, come here."

The two sailors approach, telling me, "Sorry, we're not trying to be mean, we're just late."

"Okay, okay," I reply.

To remove the man's teeth from my flesh, one of the sailors strikes him gently on the back of the neck with his knuckles.

"No, not like that," I tell him. "He doesn't feel anything, he has zero sensitivity. We need to distract his unconscious attention from my hand. Pull on his legs."

Suddenly the man unclenches his teeth, throws back his head. I see that his tongue is completely rolled up, choking him.

"Give me your cigarette," I say to one of the sailors.

With the lit end of the cigarette I burn the man's tongue, underneath. I know the method. It's the only way to make him unroll his tongue, to keep him from choking himself. The man sticks out his tongue; one of the men takes it between his fingers, in order to keep him from choking himself. The three of us stay kneeling over the sick man, watching him.

"He needs a doctor," I say.

I look at the man. He's a Jew, no question. An Israelite of the Exodus, perhaps. They've been crossing Paris for the past few days, in groups of ten or twenty, men, women, and children. Pale, dirty, tattered, feverish, they pass through the Paris crowds, shouldering sacks filled with all their riches, with their entire lives—memories, sorrows, curses, hopes, hates—and of those amazing rags that every Jew carries with him in exoduses—pieces of fabric, scraps of paper, old dirty laundry. They are their flags. But why is he alone? Perhaps he fell. He was walking behind a herd of other Jews, he fell, and no one saw him; here he is now, with his head on my knees, his tongue held between the iron fingers of a sailor.

A police officer comes up to us, asks, "What are you doing?"

He wants know if the sick man is my relative, what's my name, what's the man's name. I tell him my name. "As for this man, ask him his name yourself. I have no idea."

The officer wants to know why I'm concerning myself with the sick man, and "with what intentions." I answer back: "Are you a police officer or a doorman? Help me, if you don't want me to report you."

Immediately the officer starts to behave, says we haven't yet seen the last of people dying in the streets. Then he adds: "He needs to be moved."

At that moment a group of Jews arrive, sacks on their shoulders, dirty, pale, silent. One man detaches himself, takes the sick man's head on his knees, blows in his eyes. The man's tongue slips from the sailor's fingers, curls up in the back of his mouth. I take my cigarette and burn the underside of the tongue. The tongue relaxes and the Jew catches it. He looks at me and smiles. He's recognized from my gesture that I'm familiar with the disease.

It's the Jewish disease. The sacred disease of the Jews. How many Jews have I treated in this way, in Poland, in Ukraine, in Romania.

It's where I learned how to prevent a sick man from choking on his own tongue. The Jew looks at his companion. Other Jews grab the sick man under his arms, lead him in some small steps. The man closes his eyes; his face slowly regains its color. Then he opens his eyes, looks for me, smiles.

"Thank you," the other Jew, his companion, says to me.

"For what?" I reply.

The Jew looks at me and smiles. I hand him a packet of cigarettes.

"English?" he asks.

"No, American," I tell him.

"Ah, we don't smoke English cigarettes," he says, taking the packet.

I say to him, "The English too have suffered and still suffer. It's not their fault. We are all guilty."

The Jew looks at me and says, smiling, "Farewell, monsieur."

The crowd flows by without looking at us, without even turning. It's the same crowd that wants to build a new society, one in which men are kind, everyone loves each other, and is happy. To be loved by these people? To be happy with these people? I think that if that man had been stricken with the disease not in a corridor of the Concorde Métro station, but in a station in La Villette, or in the Saint-Denis area—in a working-class station, in short—the crowd would have stopped. Everyone would have rushed to help that poor man.

The workers are not good. Oh no, they are not! They are like the others, like the rest of us, like everyone. But they help each other. Their morality is more Christian than ours. They don't despise those who fall. They don't trample you, don't flatten you. Even the workers, one day, will be controlled by the petty bourgeois. Even worker societies are governed by the petty bourgeois. I feel close to the workers, in their fear of future tyrannies.

I know what awaits us.

Thursday, September 11. I dined yesterday evening at the home of Madeleine Le Verrier, 57 Avenue de Ségur, with Véra Korène, M. and Mme Marjolin, Maurice Schumann and his charming wife, Alice.

I like Maurice Schumann very much. He's an intelligent and very cultured man, very young and very much a free spirit. Madeleine's foot was bothering her and she was stretched out on the couch, her laughing eyes merrier than usual. It would be difficult to sketch Schumann's character, if France weren't full of men completely different from him. He's the opposite of today's political men. He's independent, plainspoken, unafraid to say what he thinks.

I've noted many times during my stay in France that the current political class is made up of men who are afraid of their opinions, when they have them, and even more when they don't have them. I know this fear, I recognize it, alas! It's a political class, the same all over Europe, that doesn't feel comfortable in power. They fear for their place, sense the insecurity of the moment, this universal insecurity that undermines all European public life. They're parvenus. I'm sorry for them, but you've got to call things by their name. They are, of course, parvenus in good faith.

I don't share the opinion of those who claim to find in the words, gestures, and attitudes of the new French politicians the mark of bad faith. No, these men are in good faith. Their fear would not make any sense, or be of any interest, if it were not in good faith. These men, like all men, don't believe in anything, but they're paid to make the people believe that they believe in something. In France, for example. But France is precisely what they believe in less than anything. They've created a rhetoric for themselves, to replace the prewar version, the rhetoric of the Resistance above all. If they didn't have this rhetoric, they would be nothing.

The very nature of this rhetoric that they have created and on which they ground themselves, however weakly, means that their power is not only provisional, but illegitimate—and even were it neither provisional nor illegitimate, they would make it seem so, since everything in them makes it seem so. And what's more, they themselves believe it is so.

It's easier to observe this fact in the French to the extent that it's common to all the new political classes of Europe: they believe themselves to be illegitimate, and therefore provisional, and live in fear of having to abandon their place and return to what they were, which is not much. The same fact can be observed just as readily in Italy as in France, more than in the countries occupied by the Russians, where the rhetoric on which the new political class rests is solid, justified, and enough to constitute the basis for a proper metaphysics and a proper mysticism. I mean that the new Polish political body, or the Romanian, or the Hungarian, is less illegitimate than the French or the Italian, because it rests on the interests of the proletarian class, on new ownership of the land and the means of production, and that to chase away the new political men from their places would require first chasing away the farmers from the lands given to them by the state, and the workers from the administration of the country. Less illegitimate, I said, but illegitimate nonetheless, because it arrives in power with the help of a foreign army, and profits from both positive Russian help and the negative work of the Germans in those countries.

But in France and Italy the new political class bases its rights on nothing but rhetoric. Such rhetoric is new in terms of slogans but old in terms of the interests it represents. And it is a provisional rhetoric, one that cannot remain effective, because it feeds on nothing but a feeling of aversion for the collaborators, a feeling that with the passage of time is destined to fade, to change from sectarian to conciliatory, due both to the force of circumstance and to the mental weariness generated by the spectacle of inevitable injustices and inevitable excesses that accompanies any sectarianism.

This makes the new political class feel unprepared, deprived of legitimate claims, and at the mercy of popular sentiment. It's clear that as the gradual reconstruction of the country proceeds, it generates ever-greater weakness in the new political class; that rousing the conscience of the country, its will to live, its awareness of its strength and its sense of order, generates a desire in the people for a deeper order, both in its institutions and in the men who represent them. Among the new political men, those who will be saved are the cultured ones, whatever their party may be; men with claims enduring beyond the provisional ones of the Resistance. We have certainly not spoken of this, Maurice Schumann and I, since, being a foreigner, I refrain for the sake of tact from speaking of things that concern the French alone. But this is what I'm thinking as Schumann speaks.

Maurice Schumann is a cultured man, in whom the fear of provisionality and sincerity appears strictly within the limits of the reserve and caution proper to political men. He is a cultured man; that is to say, a man who has a mental structure, a moral architecture, a conceptual framework, and thus a system of ideas. It's not from the Maquis alone that he comes to power, but also from the École normale supérieure. He's a *normalien* in the most serious and most French sense of the term. He speaks competently and in a measured way about literature and art. He's able to give a precise judgment on the various currents in French and European literature, a judgment that isn't small-mindedly nationalistic but European, international. He talks about Corneille, Racine, and Regnard, whose *Légataire universel* I saw at the Théâtre-Français last night. He talks about Racinian *tendresse* as a man who knows not only French theater of the Grand Siècle, but also the tragic theater of the Greeks, and the *tendresse* of Sophocles and Euripides. With Véra Korène he discusses the complex problems that Racine's own contemporaries saw in *Andromaque*, in *Phèdre*, about the various meanings they were already then giving to those tragedies.

Véra Korène talks about Corneille and Racine, and about their differing success in France. It's well known that Corneille had greater box office success than did Racine, already in his own time. And that's true still today. "Based on my discreet survey of all the French theaters, it seems that Corneille surpasses Racine in terms of success, and by a great deal, in this order: *Le Cid, Horace.* Then, some way back, comes Racine with *Phèdre, Andromaque, Britannicus,* and ——."

To me, a foreigner, it would appear that that is to be seen above all in the Corneillian character of situations and roles. French taste does not go in for strong things. It's only out of reaction that the public prefers Corneille, above all because the feelings of the French public, today as in the time of Louis XIV, are not Corneillian.

We love only what we don't have. Racine's pathetic quality, his tenderness, his sometimes morbid complexity, and his touch of the sweetest cruelty (the role of Hermione in *Andromaque*); that continual laying bare of the human soul, within the context of broad, slow gestures, the more feminine emotions (treachery, cowardice, cunning, abandonment, jealousy)—none of this is proper to the French people, which is arid, cold, reflective, and nonviolent in everything but political passions. Corneille is closer to the "reason" that is dominant in the French. I would dare say that Corneille is more "Cartesian" than Racine. Father Bremond, in his *Racine et Valéry*, has also discovered Descartes in the author of *Phèdre* and in that of *La Jeune Parque*.

To me, a foreigner, Corneille draws more on reason than on feelings. The French people are not Corneillian; that is to say, not heroic. But they better understand actions driven by reason (Corneille) than by feelings (Racine). The latter is an irrational poet, and thus the French, a rational people par excellence, do not understand him, or understand him rather less than they do Corneille, that Descartes with a face protected by a tragic mask, that masked man who, like Descartes, *larvatus prodit*.[18]

In short, it is precisely the absence of heroism in the French people, and at the same time their rationalism, that explains the greater success of Corneille: not so much because they recognize themselves in Corneillian heroes, but because they understand their acts, their actions; because such actions are made of the same stuff as the actions, base deeds among them, of the French.

Another difference is that Corneille is more *citoyen* than Racine, more political than Racine, because he has more of a sense of duty, a sense of civic-mindedness, a sense that common interest transcends private interest, and that the laws of honor, duty, and the *cité* ought to overwhelm private feelings. In other words, Corneille is more (republican) Roman, while Racine is more (admittedly decadent) Greek. Corneille is classical; Racine is romantic. Corneille's characters are ideas; Racine's are human beings, and their feelings. From a Corneillian character one can expect only a good, hard, logical action, while from a Racinian character one can expect any manner of accident, and any manner of dirty trick.

What I say here are not the ideas of Maurice Schumann or Véra Korène, but my own reflections listening to them both talk about Racine and Corneille.

At a certain point Véra Korène says: "I've drawn the role of Hermione entirely from one verse—*la haine en moi part de l'amour*—while in general those playing Hermione make her love come from her hate, and not the latter from the former."

Véra has an almost morbid sensibility for Racine, a surprising intuition. She "feels" Racine like the tuberculosis sufferer "feels" consumption, like one "feels" the snake in the grass. She is inhabited by Racine like the Pythia by Apollo. Although her power over herself is immense, almost excessive (it repels me to think that the tenderness of Hermione is under the power of the actress), there are moments onstage when Apollo overcomes her, when the tenderness, the irrationality of Racine enfolds her, subdues her, and releases the marvelous woman who is in the supremely intelligent and great actress.

At a certain point Véra talks about *La Rabouilleuse*, which she'll be performing in October. She talks about ——, the actor, and says that she can't bear the thought of having to perform with him, to be in the arms of, to love onstage, a man who disgusts her, whose hair she can't bear the smell of, whose skin she can't see up close. There's nothing in Fabre's *Rabouilleuse* that eclipses, for example, Hermione face-to-face with Orestes, whom she doesn't love, but to whom she pledges herself. Racine is stronger than the smell of Orestes's hair. But Balzac and Fabre are weaker than the smell of the actor ——'s hair. Then Schumann and the young François-Régis Bastide, author of *Lettres de Bavière*, who arrived after dinner, take to reciting some verses of Molière, and the conversation drifts to modern poetry, to Mallarmé, Valéry, Claudel, Giraudoux, Cocteau.

I describe how that afternoon I went with Laudenbach, the publisher of La Table Ronde, and Artur Sandauer, author of *Smierc liberala*, to Michel's, a hairdresser on Rue de Castellane. While Michel cuts my hair, we talk about Cocteau.

"Ah, you know Monsieur Cocteau?" the barber says to me. "He's one of my clients. A very respectable man, with a wonderful position. He's one of the most respected stockbrokers in Paris."

"Cocteau, a stockbroker?" I say. "But he's a poet."

"Ah, you mean Jean Cocteau!" the barber says. "I'm talking about M. Paul Cocteau, his brother. His brother Jean is my client as well. He often has me come to his house; he used to have me come to his house when he was living in the Hôtel Beaujolais. Yes, he's a chic fellow."

He marvels that Jean Cocteau is known abroad. "Well, well," he says, "I'm amazed."

Schumann says that it makes a strange impression, when you're on the 72 bus, to hear the conductor call out, "Paul Valéry!" It's the name of a bus stop on Rue Paul-Valéry, which used to be called Rue Villejust. I say that I go buy my eggs in a *crémerie* on Rue Jean-Giraudoux. And I observe that in Italy the name D'Annunzio is removed from streets, and poets like Ungaretti and critics like De Robertis are driven from universities, out of a spirit of sectarianism.

Saturday, September 13. If I'm not dead, it's because in Italy there was no Hôtel Majestic worth dying for.

It's very hot. I'm living on Rue Galilée.

On Rue Galilée, between Avenue d'Iéna and the Place des États-Unis, on the facade of the building at no. 17, on a marble plaque, I read this marvelous epitaph: "Here on August 25, 1944, Raymond Charles Bonenfant, husband and father, died for the liberation of the Hôtel Majestic. To his memory, from those he saved."[19] That is to say, the guests of the Hôtel Majestic.

I love and respect Charles Bonenfant. If, during the war of liberation, I had happened to die, I would not have wanted to die for Italy, for all of Italy. In Italy there are a lot—I mean a lot!—of swine, real bastards, for whom I would not have wanted and would by no means like to die.

I would not have liked to die for the liberation of Rome, either, or of Florence or Milan. Ah, no! Others, perhaps, but not me. I am of the same race as Raymond Charles Bonenfant. I would have liked to die for something very personal, very pleasant, very tidy, and not too grand. For example, for the liberation of the Hôtel Excelsior. At least I would have had someone who was grateful to me: not Italy, not the Italians, but the guests of the Hôtel Excelsior.

"It doesn't matter, because I'm writing *Paludes*."

Saturday, September 13. Boussinot tells me about his book *Maldemer*, saying he wrote it for the petty-bourgeois youth of France, and of all of Europe.

It's a new race coming up in Europe, invading nations and inundating everything. It's the race of young petty bourgeois who are disgusted with the bourgeoisie, who don't have the courage to think of themselves as proletarian, to mix with the workers, to break the ties that bind them to their class, the past, their comforts, and the possibility of a secure future (small jobs, small businesses, the minor liberal professions, inheriting the family business, some small family property, the family office with an existing client base, etc.); at the same time, they feel they lack the necessary culture, and the courage, to confront problems like a bourgeois.

The legitimate representative of this class, of this unconfident, cowardly, soft, discouraged race, is Sartre.

Boussinot has harsh words for Sartre. I wonder if it's worth wasting so many harsh words on Sartre, who is after all a good man, who does what he can, despite being a man of talent. Sartre's merit, if it is a merit, is to have found the formula befitting such a class of misfits. The formula of external proletarianization, with respect to dress, to letting oneself go, to neglecting cleanliness and decorum of the body, clothes, and manners. Manners that are neither bourgeois nor proletarian but those of a new, artificial bohemianism, which proposes to replace principles with slovenliness, ideas with a sweater.

Sartre's philosophical ideas do not interest me. What interests me are his postures, which logically spring from and depend on those ideas. It seems to me excessive to trouble Kierkegaard, Jaspers, and Heidegger, the concepts of angst and existence, to justify an entire generation of misfits who are not pederasts but pretend to be, who are not poor but pretend to be, who are not bohemian but pretend to be, who feel no angst but pretend to, who fear communism but pretend to have some sympathy for communism, who are against communism but proclaim not to want to be a priori anticommunist.

Sartre has a big influence not on French and European literature but on the customs of a certain class of young French people. French, not European. What in certain countries is communist slovenliness, communist fashion, in France is a petty-bourgeois fashion. In every country in Europe, the workers don't ape the bourgeois, including in France. But here the petty bourgeois ape the workers, and the toughs from the *banlieue*. It's enough to enter the Café de Flore to appreciate what is artificial or false about these postures.

Boussinot thinks that if Sartre were not ugly, if he were an attractive, healthy, vigorous man, his entire philosophy would change. The same old question of Cleopatra's nose, says Boussinot.[20]

I ask him what the "Resistance" experience means for these young people. Boussinot is of the opinion that for these young people the Resistance was not even an adventure. They aren't heroes out of a job, heroes nostalgic for action, for the struggle, for danger. They aren't human material available for a communist, or a dictatorial, adventure. They're not even Trotskyists. They aren't anything. They're a bunch of petty bourgeois who are ashamed of being bourgeois, without the courage to take the plunge and become proletarians, to accept the worker's fate in the factories and the neighborhoods of the *banlieue*.

If a communist adventure, or a fascist one, were to come about, these young people wouldn't be one thing or the other. They would remain undecided, amorphous, other than slowly lining up behind the winner, or waging resistance in slippers. It's surprising how this generation that so often and so insistently refers to the Resistance, to the school of courage and sacrifice that was the Resistance, lacks courage and a spirit of sacrifice.

Sartre proclaims his intimate difference from communism, but at the same time proclaims not to want to be anticommunist. He too is essentially bourgeois. He too is for the usual moderation, for the middle path, for French clarity. A Cartesian who has glimpsed the limits of Cartesianism, the insufficiency of reason, and is at the same time afraid of the uncontrollable dark forces that Cartesianism can neither master nor explain.

Sunday, September 14. Yesterday, as I spoke with Roger Boussinot, a triumphal march made its way down the Champs-Élysées: the music of the Republican Guard on horseback, the American Legion, the crowd, and the piercing sounds of the fanfare in the warm air, the notes of "Encore un carreau de cassé." I had to restrain myself from going out onto the balcony to see the parade. I belong to the race of old regimental horses; music gets me champing at the bit. And yet not even I still have the ardor of old. No one has the ardor of old. Even this Parisian crowd no longer has the ardor of old. Not only in France, but all over Europe, crowds no longer thrill to anything but sporting competitions, especially bicycle races.

I've often wondered about the source of the people's coolness toward military ceremonies, toward the lighting of the flame below the Arc de Triomphe. (I would see newsreel footage of the ceremonies in the Ciné-Actualités: small, chilly crowds, a few women and boys applauding and cheering, distracted and indifferent passersby, be it for the return of the remains of those who died in prison, or the visit from Marshal Montgomery, or the unveiling of a plaque dedicated to those who fell for the liberation of Paris.) What is the source of such evident coolness, especially with regard to all the ceremonies commemorating the last war? War-weariness? A desire to forget the sufferings, the humiliations? Or scant gratitude to those who died for us?

I think it is precisely a matter of a lack of gratitude to those who died for us. If I self-analyze, if I look inside myself, I'm convinced that it is precisely this lack of gratitude.

I find it intolerable to think that someone died for me. I can't bear the idea that a man, that human beings died for me. I didn't need anyone to die for my freedom. I don't believe that anyone died for me, for my freedom; that someone chose to die for me, for my freedom. I have always been a free man; I won and defended my freedom on my own, with my own strength, in spite of the indifference and hostility of everyone.

It's possible that it was necessary for someone to die for the liberation of France, of Italy, of Norway, of Europe, of Paris, of Rome, of a nation, of a city, of a people—but for my freedom it was absolutely not necessary, and if someone died for me, well, it was a mistake, an illusion, a useless act of generosity.

There are, of course, thousands upon thousands of young people who sacrificed themselves, or believed they sacrificed themselves, for the freedom of Europe, and to those dead go my respectful love, my affectionate memory. But there's no one who died for me. I find the idea intolerable. And if I were to discover that someone truly died for me, sacrificed himself for me, I would feel an intense sorrow, a sense of shame, of bitter remorse. Because my freedom (and the freedom of each of us, of each individual) has nothing to do with the freedom of a people, of Europe. Whether or not Europe is free, the problem of individual freedom, and above all that of a writer's freedom, doesn't change.

Men hate the freedom of individuals, especially the freedom of writers. Men hate writers. Especially those capable of defending their freedom with their own strength alone. I did not ask anyone to die for me, and if someone has died for me as well, I have no reason to be grateful to him. If someone believed in good faith to have died for me as well, that makes me smile about human illusions, about how easy it is for someone to deceive himself that he has died for something or for someone.

In general, men die for themselves. I have a certain experience with how men die, and why. Behind the death of a man in war or in a revolution, there is always a little "I," a little fear or a little vanity. One dies only for one's own faith, and for one's own cross. One dies only for oneself.

Love of country, revolutionary faith, altruism, all that is well and good, all that exists, albeit to an ever-decreasing extent. But there's also discipline, the military code, the spirit of emulation, self-regard, vanity, love of glory, and courage. Courage plays a big role in the death of a man who believes he's sacrificing himself for others. The desire to demonstrate to others, and to oneself, that one has courage, and at the same time the blind instinct of courage: that blind, instinctive, irresistible force that drives you forward to face death, which is courage.

But why analyze, why seek out the causes of a fact that repels me? I do not admit that someone died for me, I cannot bear it. No thanks. I have no need of corpses on my conscience, even if they are glorious corpses. I do not accept such weight, such responsibility, such complicity. I never asked anyone to die for me, and if someone has died for me, so much the worse for him. I know perfectly well that if that dead man had not fallen for me, but was still alive, he would hate me.

Is there perhaps someone who is grateful to me for what I've suffered for my freedom and that of others? For the books I've written in defense of my and others' freedom? For the imprisonment, for the confinement I've suffered for the common cause of freedom? For the dangers I've freely gone to meet? No. Those for whom I suffered are the same people who applauded those who persecuted me. And when those same people for whom I suffered were free, they too persecuted me.

The same thing is true for me and for others. People hate free men. And I hate and disdain those who hate and disdain me because I am free and they are not, and I say, "Thank you very much, but I do not accept," to those who claim to have died for me. It is in itself a measure of freedom that there is no tomb over which I must go to pour out tears of gratitude. Fortunately not. And if I admit that someone died for me, I do so only for Christ, only for him. And in his sacrifice, the only thing that bothers and saddens me is the idea that Christ did not die for me, but for everyone; not for me in particular, at any rate, but for me in general. And I'm saddened by the thought that his death was necessary for me as well, for my freedom. Because I am Christian, deeply Christian, and Christianity excuses me from praying on the tombs of those who claim to have died for me, for my freedom.

There is one part in the example of Christ that a good Christian is prohibited from imitating, and that is to die for others, to sacrifice oneself for humankind. I don't care for false Christs. And if there are some, because there are, I'd like to stipulate that they did not sacrifice themselves for me, but at most for everyone, especially for those incapable of defending their own freedom.

Sunday, September 14. This morning at Moulin de Saint-Roche, at the Serolles', with André and Antonia Lichtwitz.

It had been fourteen years since I last saw emerge on the distant horizon, at the far end of the yellow plain, the two spires of Chartres Cathedral. Rambouillet is one of the regions I cherish most in France. Perhaps for the memory of Barbara, of Glenway Wescott. A few kilometers outside Maintenon we take a left, pass Saint-Piat, head down the coast toward Jouy, cross the Eure, and soon after reach the Moulin de Saint-Roche.

The other day Michelin taught me the difference between *fleuve* and *rivière*. France has four *fleuves*, or four watercourses that flow into the sea: the Seine, the Loire, the Garonne, and the Rhône. All the others are *rivières*, or tributaries of the *fleuves*.

Among all the *rivières* of France, the Eure is one of the happiest, the clearest, the most serene. A watercourse, one would say, designed by Le Nôtre,[21] the great gardener who must have designed all the *rivières* and all the woods, the deep valleys and the coasts, in this happy landscape. Along each side of the Eure, no wider than twenty meters, with uniform banks no higher than half a meter above the slow, limpid water, rises a line of poplars and weeping willows. Now and then the Eure enters a forest of bright green leaves, shining in the September sun. The air is warm, windless. And yet a rustle of leaves runs through the air up there, and a magpie skims the top of the grass, hiding in the depths of the ferns. Swarms of long-legged flies glide over the current, scatter and reunite. The sky is high, it seems like the Ukraine sky, with thick clouds on the horizon, castles of white clouds over Rambouillet, Fontainebleau, Orléans, Chartres.

Despite being a region of farmers, and one of the richest regions in Europe; a land of golden earth, the cradle of wheat, under a flawless, unfurrowed, very young blue sky; despite being a region of plains (albeit one split by deep ravines and seamed by the Eure valley), Beauce has something mysterious, something secret about it. It's not a region of farmers like so many others (attached to the earth, stingy, smallminded, isolated, mean). There's something about Beauce I wouldn't know how to explain. There's Chartres Cathedral. It wasn't the kings of France, or the great feudal lords, but the small proprietors who, with their own money, built the most beautiful cathedral in France, one of the most beautiful cathedrals in Europe, the miracle of Chartres.

I was speaking one day in 1932 with Marcel Schwob, who devoted some very beautiful pages to Chartres. "Chartres," he said to me, "stands in a defenseless region, exposed to every assault, in the most vulnerable part of the Île-de-France. But the cathedral is both temple and fortress. It's like those ancient sanctuaries whose most revealing and famous example is Cumae, near Naples, which in a certain way represents the dwelling place, the house, the palace of God in the heart of the country. Chartres is the heart of France. Don't go searching for it hither and yon: the heart of France is here, at Chartres, in the middle of this region of farmers."

The ancients always placed their sanctuaries in regions rich in wheat, or olive trees, or vineyards. Delphi is in a region that is one of the richest in oil in all the world—the Itea olive tree forest is without a doubt the largest in the world. Cumae is rich in grains, as is the sanctuary at the mouth of the Sele, in Italy, and the shrine of Our Lady of Divine Love near Rome, and all the sanctuaries of antiquity: that of Diana in Ephesus, rich in grains and olive trees and vineyards; that of Jupiter with the dirty feet; of Neptune at Paestum; of Diana on Lipari.

I remember the veneration in which Daniel Halévy, who accompanied Charles Péguy in his peregrinations through France on foot, holds Chartres. And Péguy's pages on Chartres? Certain pages, which I read many, many years ago (1923) and have never reread, nor want to reread (I want the impression to remain uncertain in my memory), and of which I retain a distant, vague, and very beautiful recollection; certain pages, I say, where Péguy, having woken at dawn and taken to the road, suddenly sees appear, beyond the fields of grain, and the trees, and the clouds, and the light mist of the still-raw morning, the spires of Chartres Cathedral.

It's only a sudden flash of pale stone, swiftly snuffed out on the horizon; the sudden flight of a skylark through the wheat; the sudden gleam of a river, of a windowpane struck by the rising sun. What is it, what burns over there, what shines over there, what dazzles over there, at the far end of the horizon?

No, it's not a cloud that unburdens its breast, that refreshes the earth, a white cloud of the spring. It's not a river, a windowpane, or a haystack in flames. No, it's not the flash of a horse's eye, of a girl's smile, of a lark's wing. It's the face of God. It's the terrible face of God. It's the fixed, immobile, immutable flash, the sad and spiteful flash that is on the face of God. It's the face of God at its most absolutely naked. It's the face of God that man every so often meets where he least expects it. It's the face of God as the French used to see it, when the French were still full of blood and hadn't forgotten the history of France, and still knew that Chartres was without a doubt the seat of a very ancient druidic sanctuary, a land sacred to the Divinity; when they had that naked, severe image of God, and hadn't yet covered the face of God with the gentle, smiling, honeyed, feminine mask of their Christ, of the French Christ, of the blondish Christ with bluish eyes and a tidy beard (which at a certain point risked becoming a goatee like Napoleon III's), which is the French Christ.

France is the European country where Christ is discussed most subtly, and where Christ is represented in his most vapid, most feminine, most emasculated form. Christ for girls, starting with Louis XIII and going up through the Christ of Cocteau, of Maritain, up through the false Christ in porcelain of Maritain, through the terracotta Christ of Claudel. Up through the Christ no longer a shepherd but a shepherdess, the Christ done up with ribbons, the Christ as Trianon sheep. Up through the fashionable Christ of Schiaparelli that is really, despite everything, the Christ of Claudel. And I apologize.

The Christ of Chartres is a God that is still pure, a trembling of leaves and water and skylarks' wings at the far end of the horizon. And little by little as we make our way across the countryside from Maintenon to Jouy, the trees become greener, the road descends, and the Eure is there before us: clear and fresh and sweet water,[22] between the green of the poplars and the willows.

Moulin de Saint-Roche is a charming spot, built on an islet in the middle of the river, where the Eure, guided by the locks, widens and creates a small archipelago in the gentle current. The mill is painted a pale pink; the wheels of the old mill are covered with ivy; and the water never ceases to make a very sweet noise, a very pure song. It's the home of the Serolles, and Janine Serolle receives us with her warmest smile.

There too are the Alphands, and Couve de Murville, and Alphand's sister, Mme Charpentier, back from Moscow, where her husband was until last June an adviser at the French embassy there, and Mme Sturges, and Le Maresquier, whom I met in Rome many years ago, when he was living at the Villa Strohl Fern. Alphand, who directs the office of business and economic affairs with America at the Quai d'Orsay,[23] speaks to me about Italy, in that discerning and precise way of speaking about peoples that is particular to the French: without being carried away by the facility of the French language to soften every idea.

He asks me if I believe that an uprising, a revolt by the communist forces, is imminent in Italy. I start to laugh. I don't believe in such a heroic will.

Monday, September 15. In the introduction to his *Introduction aux existentialismes* (Denoël, 1947), Emmanuel Mounier writes: "The century's ultimate absurdity must have been the craze for existentialism:

the delivery over to idle daily gossip of a philosophy entirely geared at tearing us away from idle gossip."

Some French still haven't lost their old habit of believing that the whole world does nothing but chatter about and debate what they debate and chatter about.

Europeans are pretty well fed up with Sartre and "his" existentialism. Sartre is certainly a good man, a bourgeois man, a good *normalien*, a man of talent, but, especially outside France (and even in France), no one takes his philosophy seriously, and if Mounier believes that existentialism is the craze of the century, he is mistaken. Sartre is no longer fashionable not because existentialism is no longer fashionable, but because the literary personality that he represents is outdated with respect to the tastes, trends, concerns, and dramatic situation of Europe.

People in Europe are tired of seeing all their problems reduced to idle gossip in France. The *ars perpulchra* par excellence of the French, as Lulli had it, is to popularize; to make things pleasant, comprehensible, and mundane; to make theories, problems, and the ideas of other peoples fashionable and available to all. To reduce certain fish droppings to perfume. Just like Algarotti's *Newtonianism for Ladies*.

Sartre has written, in other words, *Existentialism for Ladies*. Well, Europe is tired of this way of doing things. It's not by returning to old systems that France will regain its preeminence in European culture.

I have already noted that not only did Sartre not invent anything, but not even the so-called Sartrism of young people is the work or invention of Sartre. The fashion for long hair, poorly shaved faces, and dirty fingernails, for espadrilles, sweaters, and slovenliness, is the way people dress all over Europe. It's a kind of social mimicry, the way the petty bourgeois have come up with, more or less everywhere in Europe, and starting already before the war, to blend in as much as possible with the proletariat. It's a result of fear (which dominates everything) and of poverty, of the scarcity of clothing items and their high price, and also of an unconscious need to resemble the basic element of modern society, the masses. Sartre fooled himself into thinking he had made a certain attitude fashionable, an attitude that already existed in Europe before him, and which existed in France before him as well.

The problems that trouble the French petty bourgeois, and young people in particular, are the same problems that trouble all of Europe—Sartre has nothing to do with it. The fauna that lives at the Café de Flore is called existentialist in Paris; everywhere else in Europe it doesn't have a name, is a fauna without a label. It's the new race that's coming up.

The French, due to their entirely characteristic insistence on cataloging phenomena, on classifying and giving them a name, a French stamp (and it is, in part, a praiseworthy insistence), have given the name *Sartrism* or *existentialism* to a phenomenon common throughout Europe, one that has nothing to do with existentialism. Young people in Moscow, Kiev, and Berlin, in Warsaw, Vienna, and Italy, everywhere, already dressed and behaved this way before Sartre existed. To believe, as Mounier does, that all over Europe people are debating and chattering about existentialism and Sartrism is ridiculous. Sartre's lectures in Germany and Italy made people laugh. In neither place was he taken seriously.

In Italy existentialism was being very seriously discussed well before Sartre took over the word after the Liberation and gave it a fashionable meaning. During the war, two years before the liberation of France, I personally devoted an entire issue of my literary magazine *Prospettive* (which was the center of Italian literary and cultural "resistance" during the war) to existentialism, with contributions from Moravia, from ——, from the greatest Jaspers and Heidegger enthusiasts in Italy. And since speaking about existentialism was forbidden, I called the special issue "The Last of the Beautiful Souls." The censors, who had neither the time nor the desire to read philosophical texts, and who were also fooled by the title, let the issue of *Prospettive* through. It was an enormous success, especially among young people, just like the issue devoted to surrealism (another forbidden subject), the one devoted to the defense of modern painting and Picasso (a subject and a name that were extremely forbidden), and the issue devoted to "workers' morality," titled "Workers' Blood."

In Europe existentialism was already being spoken about, and seriously, before Sartre turned it into a "French" craze—that is, before Sartre devoted his considerable talent to writing his *Existentialism for Ladies*, and, I must add, *for Young People Mentally Disposed to Homosexuality*.

But Sartre's position becomes more complicated from a sentimental point of view, so to speak. In the victorious countries (and I've already said what, in my view, victory means in France), it is outwardly believed, or maybe seriously believed, that only the French struggled for freedom, engaged in resistance, fought the Germans and the Fascists. For the French above all (but also for the Americans, for the English; as was not the case for the Norwegians, the Danes, the Dutch, the Belgians), anyone who belonged to the Axis peoples is a Nazi, a Fascist, a sellout to the Germans, a torturer of Jews, an enemy of European freedom. According to the French and the other victors, there is no one among the Axis peoples who resisted.

Let's leave aside the partisans, the armed resistance that began in Italy after September 8, 1943, and limit ourselves to "resistance" in the fields of literature, thought, and art.

The name of Benedetto Croce would be sufficient reply in terms of philosophical and historical thought. But what about literary and artistic resistance? Our resistance to Fascism began neither with the war nor with the armistice and the Allied landing in Italy. As far back as 1925, the "literary" resistance in Italy rebelled above all against those self-professed Fascist writers who accused other writers of not being engaged. The question of committed literature is an old one in Italy. It certainly wasn't born with the Liberation. For twenty-five years, Italian writers refused to commit themselves, with a resistance that was stubborn, continuous, intelligent, cunning, conniving at times, and always gratuitous; that is, not dictated by political concerns, the concerns of parties; a resistance that in certain instances assumed dramatic forms.

It can sincerely be said that Italian literature, during the twenty-five years of Mussolini's dictatorship, did not engage. More or less, with greater or lesser courage, Italian writers "resisted" not only violence, which was rare, but flattery, corruption, and fear.

The most noble example of resistance was not, as one might believe, Benedetto Croce, but Luigi Pirandello. One could cite truly stunning examples of Pirandello's stubborn, dogged, honest, severe resistance to Fascist pressure. It would be enough to cite his death and his last will and testament (of which Mussolini forbid the publication and the execution) to place the extremely noble behavior of Pirandello toward the Fascist regime and toward the "literary policies" of Fascism in its true light.

Pirandello was a Fascist, enrolled in the Fascist Party; he had great regard for Mussolini, and he never concealed it. But on the ground of art he was perfectly uncompromising and never gave in—not to fear, not to flattery. Mussolini tried everything to tame him. Pirandello obeyed orders that were not of a literary nature, and remained deaf to injunctions and flattery. Mussolini nominated him to the Italian Academy; Pirandello accepted the nomination, to which he had a right, as official recognition for his literary work. On the ground of the nation, Pirandello was with Mussolini; on the ground of literature, he was not. Fascism looked with disfavor at Pirandello's art (founded, roughly speaking, on doubt), since it could not admit that doubt existed in Italian life, in the society and therefore in the art of the Fascist period. The extremist Fascist newspapers attacked Pirandello; the public, too, poisoned by propaganda, remained cold to his theater, even when Pirandello's immense success in Paris provoked doubts about the truth of the Fascist propaganda against him.

Benedetto Croce and Pirandello were unmovable on their respective grounds, the former that of historical and philosophical culture, the latter of art. And the "political" position of each was similar in many cases. If Croce, like Pirandello, remained intransigent on his respective ground, and never for a minute ceased to glorify the liberal idea and to criticize, albeit with the necessary caution, antiliberal regimes, but still, on the ground of political practice, in apparent contradiction, voted two separate times in the Senate, at the conclusion of memorable discussions, for Mussolini, for his government, and for his politics, Pirandello was equally, in political practice, induced to compromises, which after all responded to his deep and sincere convictions, but in the literary field he did not bend: he was against commitment and did not change the foundation of his vision of life; doubt remained his secret, and public, God.

If the example of Croce's intransigence in the historical and philosophical field greatly influenced the behavior of some of his pupils, it can't be said that he greatly influenced young people, who were all Fascists and deeply antiliberal (as can be seen today).

September 17. I had dinner with Roland Laudenbach and Emmanuel Berl at Tallevant's, on Rue Saint-Georges.

For the first time in my life I ate fried frogs. I ate them with my eyes closed. I am a foreigner in France; I couldn't say no when Emmanuel Berl said, "I'm French, in terms of nationalism as well as gluttony; I will eat frogs." They were exquisite. Frog tastes like chicken. A tiny chicken. From that sentence all of Berl follows.

I met Emmanuel Berl many, many years ago, in 1932, at Édouard Bourdet's, in the happy times of *Marianne.* I used to read *Marianne* on Lipari, when I managed to procure a copy thanks to the kindness and complicity of poor Paternò (who died in 1939).

Berl has remained a Frenchman of the Third Republic. A golden age, seen from 1947. Even though I prefer the Fourth Republic, with all its defects and its disorder, its sectarianism and its petty-minded democratic rhetoric, the men of the Third Republic retain for me an extraordinary fascination.[24]

I love Herriot, Blum, Halévy, and all the rest. They were—I say they *were*, because even though they're still alive, they don't count like before—men of an intellectual class rather higher than today's. They represented a world, a France, that had yet to lose its sense of superiority over the other peoples of Europe. They represented a culture, a tradition, and mores that are now out of fashion, outdated, in their death throes. They had a "French" vision of the world. For them, to be French meant a total commitment of the mind, the heart, the spirit, manners, character. Their culture, while French, was European. Misguided nonentities politically, they were intellectually powerful.

France derived prestige from them. They had French ideas.

September 18. Dinner tonight at Maxim's, with General Béthouart, high commissioner for France in Austria, Ninon de Montgoméry, his wife, Antonia and André Lichtwitz, Mme Aydée, and her husband.

In the gilded frame of Maxim's, everything takes on an easygoing, debonair aspect, with an elegance that retains a good deal of the Toulouse-Lautrec poster or the devil-may-care attitude of the Prince of Wales, Edward VII, during his Parisian escapades. And yet there's more *alte Wien* in this very famous late-night restaurant than Parisian *entente cordiale*. The paintings on the wall, in the "modern style" typical also of Parisian Métro entrances, recall the younger Boldini, Toulouse-Lautrec, certain paintings from Munich, from the terrible Munich of Wilhelm II.

During the meal the orchestra softly plays pieces of old Viennese operettas, waltzes by Strauss and by Lehár, Schubert lieder, and it's all very much the Vienna of Franz Joseph, of Archduke Franz Ferdinand, of the Mayerling tragedy, that rises again in this room overloaded with moldings, gilded frames, and mirrors full of dusty light, with lights too dazzling, too bright, which light up the room and darken the eyes.

Owing to the shadow this too violent light produces in the eyes, the bare shoulders of the women have a pale, somewhat lifeless luster, the same as slightly older skin. The bare-shouldered women are not French but South American, American, Portuguese. The French no longer like to bare their shoulders. Their evening gowns—and I don't know if it's the fashion or modesty, a strange kind of modesty, strange for a beautiful young woman—jealously hide their shoulders. They have a strange modesty, not that of older women, but of adolescents. The war, those brutal and shameless years, has left a trace of virginity, this strange modesty, in them. They are composed, reserved, cold, almost severe. Unfamiliar.

The other day at Moulin de Saint-Roche, at the Serolles', a woman no longer young spoke in a sweet voice of "our Fourth Republic, so poor in beautiful women." The words surprised me, since they confirmed my own impression.

I don't trust impressions. One always has the suspicion that everything in the past, *jadis*, was better, more beautiful, younger. Something, certainly, a veil, has descended over the beauty of French women. They no longer laugh the way they once did.

Such modesty is the sign that the women, too, lost the war—a war that everyone, winners and losers, lost. This modesty, which in the men generally manifests itself as despondency, pessimism, or poor manners, as boorish acts that no one questions and of which they themselves are perhaps not even aware (take S. de R., a grand French name, who, seeing me again after fourteen years, asks me, "What, you come from Italy? There's still an Italy?"), in the women—more sensitive, more intelligent, more active than the men, in France as well—manifests itself in this reluctance to display, even in the most appropriate ways, their nudity.

I am very grateful to the women in this country that is almost my own (it's the country where I encountered death for the first time, at the age of sixteen: you never forget those first rendezvous) for offering me a face of France that is not that of futile, frivolous, superficial life, for showing me their soul only through the veil of modesty.

One truly needs modesty in Europe today, to stroll among so many ruins. The men chatter, laugh, and argue; the women listen in silence, at times smiling weakly, distractedly.

How far we are from Proust's woman! (Odette). It's Mme de Guermantes who has rediscovered all her value, modesty, and grace in these French women, in these severe and rather cold and distracted Parisiennes.

It has often been noted that the grace of French women, of the Parisienne above all (with *Parisienne* I refer not to the midinette, or to the mannequin, or to that modern variety, the typist, whose origin dates from the age of Musset, of Abel Hermant, etc., but to the socialite, the elegant woman; there are no Parisiennes but those who descend from a tradition of elegance, of esprit, etc.), rests on the traditions of the grand manners of the eighteenth century, which revive in her something of those admirable attitudes of which Bossuet spoke in one of his magnificent funeral orations ("supported by skeletons, whose attitudes are admirable," an oration for the death of Queen Christina, if I'm not mistaken)[25] that distinguished the socialite of the Grand Siècle and of the eighteenth century.

September 22. Dinner tonight with Villefosse, Charles Orengo (who brings me the first uncut copy of *Une femme comme moi*[26]), and Camus.

One day, when someone asked old Huret (Huret is Utrillo's father-in-law), who had met Picasso in 1900 when the Spanish painter came to Paris, what he thought of the man and his art, he replied: "He's the Musée de l'Homme, as seen by a horse."

When someone asked Picasso what he thought of the work of Matisse, he replied: "Matisse? He's aged a lot, but he's beginning to make some progress."

[*Late September*[27]] Saw Péguy's *Joan of Arc* at the Théâtre Hébertot. No, Péguy is dead. He died a long time ago. *All* of Péguy is dead. The only living part of him left is this typically French "remorse" (not nostalgia, but remorse), which is of an innocence, a purity, that the French Middle Ages consigned to legend, to poetry, and that no longer lives in the French genius, ever since the time of Charles VIII, of France's Italian adventure, of the French Renaissance. Charles Péguy didn't understand that French mysticism did not continue as a tradition in France, be it popular or intellectual. Péguy forgot the existence of Pascal. This union between Joan of Arc and France is something too pure to be translated into modern language.

September. Dinner with some men from the French Resistance. Around the table, in a room on the second floor of a restaurant in the Place de l'Odéon, some of the best-known men of the Maquis.

I am still astonished—almost sickened, I would say—by the remarks these brave Frenchmen made about France, its situation and its misfortunes.

The most striking characteristic of the state of mind of the French after the Liberation is, in my view (a foreigner, judging without passion, coolly, is in a rather better position to grasp the movements of the French soul in its misfortune than the French themselves), their tendency to exaggerate their woes, to attribute the cause of their present woe to moral causes that diminish and debase them. It's the sort of schadenfreude I've already remarked on as a novelty in the French of today.

They consider themselves a people in decline—when they don't consider themselves entirely finished. They cry over their woes as if they were the only wretches in the world, the only ones responsible for their own misfortunes. They talk about the German occupation from 1940 to 1944 as an irreparable calamity. They moan over their defeat in 1940 as if they were the only ones in Europe to have lost a battle.

I listened to them and kept quiet. It's not the first time I've heard their laments. All of French politics today is nothing but wretched exploitation, for political ends, of the presumed French disgrace, of French misfortunes. Is this a case of wounded pride? It's something deeper and sadder. Wounded pride is certainly there, in this immensely proud people, but couldn't there also be the sign of a lack of imagination, of a defect of the soul, that is the fatal consequence of three centuries of rationalism, of Cartesianism, which has burned the great vital and imaginative force of the French people down to the roots?

I would have liked to say to them: "Don't cry so over your misfortunes. Between 1914 and 1918, eleven departments of France were invaded and occupied by Germany—and they didn't die of it. The occupation you so heroically contributed to freeing yourselves from was no more than a transitory incident in the history of the French people."

How many times have the Flemish, the Italians, or the Germans been invaded and occupied in the course of their history? They always rose up again. They drew new strength from the calamities of foreign occupation, that indomitable strength in peoples that is faith in oneself, the will to live, the will to survive. Look at the Italians: What will to work, what faith in life and in their own strength! Could you be less than equal to the Italians?

It's true that you don't have the same, centuries-old habituation to calamities. Still, it's not your first test. Is it enough, then, that a calamity strike you, for you to lose faith in yourselves?

What disgrace are you even talking about? About 1940? What army of cowards and idlers are you talking about? It's not true that the French soldiers didn't fight in 1940. You had incompetent leaders, but your soldiers were brave.

Read German books about the war: you'll learn that the French soldier fought well. In an inefficient way, without unity of action, without intelligence, perhaps; without faith, without hope, perhaps; but he fought well.

Compare the losses suffered by the French Army in 1940 with those of the German Army. They equal out. If you hadn't fought, you wouldn't have left so many dead on the battlefields of Belgium, of the Somme, or on the dunes of Dunkirk. Do you forget that the glory of Dunkirk is in large part French glory? You're confusing the battle of May–June 1940 with the defeat that followed.

You were beaten in 1940, agreed. The defeat is the consequence of that lost battle. You would have the French soldiers retreat in an orderly manner in such tragic circumstances? They retreated as every army retreats, even the most courageous, after having lost a pitched battle. The English are brave. The Spanish are brave. The Russians are brave. The Germans are brave. When they lose a battle, they retreat in disorder, no more and no less than the French soldiers in 1940. I saw the English retreat from the Chemin des Dames in 1918, as far as Château-Thierry. I saw the Russians retreat in 1941 as far as the Volga. In both cases there was the most horrible disorder. And nevertheless, they were brave soldiers who fought well. Have you never heard of the Berezina?[28]

Read this book by a German, Ernst Jünger: *Entre routes et jardins*.[29] It's the story of the Battle of France in 1940. There are pages there that are a credit to the French soldier's courage, spirit of sacrifice, and sense of honor. Why doesn't your minister of propaganda put together an anthology of German books about the war?

You've given appropriate weight to the heroism of those in the French Resistance, to the courage of the partisans. Why have you forgotten the French soldier of 1940? Because he lost a battle? And if the Maquis had lost, would he be any less heroic? There's an injustice here to be put right.

Allow me, a foreigner, to tell you: Don't cry so over your misfortunes. You are better, much better, than it morbidly pleases you to believe.

France is a great nation. It remains a great nation. France produces less cast iron than America, Russia, or England does. It's not cast iron that makes a nation great. It's *autre chose*. And you know it well. If a nation produces nothing but cast iron, it's not a great nation. Well, the French produce this *autre chose* in rather larger quantities than England, Russia, or America. Every time France—even when it was the most powerful industrial, economic, and financial nation in the world—failed to produce this *autre chose*, it was beaten. Under Louis XIV, under Francis I, under Napoleon III, even under Napoleon I.

This state of mind threatens to distort the entire sense of your most recent history.

You persist in believing, and in making others believe, that your Resistance, your magnificent Maquis, made up for the disgrace of 1940. But there was nothing to make up for on the moral level! There is no moral connection between the Maquis and the French soldier of 1940!

The Maquis did not make up for any disgrace. It fought the Germans, the same enemies, in another kind of battle. It *continued* the war of 1940. It didn't have any disgrace to make up for. All the Maquis did was to complete, to continue, the courage of the soldier of 1940. That's it. I'll say something else: The Maquis is the French Army of 1940 led by other leaders. It's the leaders who were different from those in 1940, not the fighters. The French Maquis did not make up for the disgrace of 1940—it simply fought against those who believed, between 1940 and 1944, that the French soldiers didn't fight, that 1940 was not a battle courageously lost but a disgrace. The Maquis only prove I'm right.

Why, then, do you insist on believing and on making others believe that 1940 was a disgrace for the French soldier? Do you believe that in so doing the glory of the Maquis is thereby increased? Do you not understand that the only—I say the only—justification for what you call "collaboration," and which I honestly call "desperation," consists in the conviction on the part of those wretched French men and women that 1940 had been a disgrace, that in 1940 France behaved cowardly, that France was finished? The "desperate" were wrong, because France wasn't finished. And the proof is you, is the Maquis, is every good French resistant.

You are pleased to believe and to make others believe that the Maquis picked up the flag that the soldiers of 1940 let fall into the mud. Stop this stupid rhetoric. The French flag did not fall into the mud in 1940. The French soldier did not let his flag fall into the mud. The flag of the Maquis is the same as the soldier's of 1940. If you don't understand that the Maquis only continued 1940, continued the struggle, you dangerously distort the sense of your recent history; you allow people to believe this absurd, inconceivable thing, which is criminal to allow people to believe: that there were, in the history of France, French soldiers who did not fight.

No. In the entire history of France, no more in Pavia than in Sedan, no more in Rossbach than in Charleroi, no more in Belgium in 1940 than on the Maginot Line, there were no French soldiers who did not fight. We foreigners are the ones who know, who can tell you:

No, it's not true. There were French soldiers who were beaten, never French soldiers who didn't fight.

And if I happen to say to you, "If you allow this lie to be believed, you are a bad Frenchman," and you respond to me, "I was in the Resistance," I repeat, "You are a bad Frenchman." And if by chance you say to me, "You're a foreigner, you don't have the right to treat me like this, you don't know France, and you don't have the right to make a judgment about France, because you don't know it," I will respond to you, "When peoples suffer, when they're miserable, they lose heart, they humble themselves before their own eyes. Only foreigners can judge them coolly, dispassionately."

And coolly I say to you: "Do not humble yourselves. France is a great nation. It's a foreigner who tells you so. Your present woes notwithstanding, you are a great people. It's a friend who tells you so. It's a foreigner. Listen to what a foreigner tells you. And be ashamed to humble yourself like this. Don't allow me to be obliged to be ashamed for you."[30]

[*October 11?*[31]] I went to see Kafka's *Trial*, which André Gide adapted for the theater.

What to say about Gide? What to say about Barrault? This: that Barrault displays, in *The Trial*, much more intelligence than Gide. Which is no easy thing.

Throughout the performance I heard the audience deploring the nasty trick played on Kafka. I don't dare say that Gide has taken advantage of the fact that Kafka is not very well known in France. If Kafka were as well known to the French public as he is to the Italian public, for example, André Gide would have shown more caution. Because *The Trial*, as it was adapted for the stage, and as it was performed (and it could not have been performed differently), is precisely the opposite of the novel *The Trial*.

In the novel, Kafka's charm consists above all in the relationship between the dream and what Kafka calls *Das Da*, the "here and now." *Das Da* is not reality in the sense of being the opposite of the dream, because it is not possible to affirm, or deny, that reality is the opposite of the dream. *Das Da* is the sense of the present moment, of reality as time, as the "now," as the "moment." *Das Da* is the sense of the event; the sense of history, in other words. In Kafka's novel, the trial is an action brought against man as a living, existing being, against his entire life, his entire existence, against the very reasons for his existence, against, in a word, the history of man, of humanity, against history tout court. This type of half-consciousness in man, in Kafka's characters, in *The Trial*, in *The Castle*, in *The Metamorphosis* (man wakes up as a worm), is the irresponsibility of man as a living being, historical subject, protagonist of both his own story and the story of the world, of humanity.

On account of this irresponsibility, man enters the court of law, so to speak; becomes responsible; undergoes his trial. Who brings the action? Men? Certainly not. The state? (Some have wanted to see the Marxist or communist state in this trial of the bourgeoisie.) It's God. By what right does God mind our business, the business of men? Enter the silent protest of the accused during the trial that is life: "God exists. But we know so little about him, it's as if God didn't exist."

We're acquainted with Kafka's thinking on the relationship between men and God. We know of God's existence. But does God know of our existence?

One commentator on Kafka cited to this effect the words of a Dostoevsky character: "If God didn't exist, how could I be a general?" And so begins the trial of man, in his relationship with *Das Da*, with the present, with the "here and now," with history. The reign of the dream is over, now begins the reign of *Das Da*, of the present, of events, of history. Man enters history. He comes from this forbidden realm that is the dream, and I get the suspicion that God does not have access to the dream realm, that he waits for man to leave the dream, to enter the realm of *Das Da*.

"God exists, but this is the only thing we know about him. We are even unable to say whether God in his turn is aware of our existence. God exists, but since it is impossible to enter into communication with him, it's as if he didn't exist. So might we summarize the contribution of Kafka's novels to our belief in God" (*Kafka, ou Le mystère juif,* by André Németh, translated from the Hungarian by Victor Hintz, published by Jean Vigneau, Paris, 1947) (pages 14–15).[32]

[*Mid-October?*[33]] Ernst Bloch has said: "In his self-styled analyses of existence, Heidegger reflects a state of mind belonging to social classes in decline. Angst, elevated by Heidegger to an existential category, is illustrated with the situation (derived from the present world) of the petty bourgeois who feels threatened in his position and future prospects. Worry (*sorge* = concern), another Heideggerian category, corresponds to the state of certain *hauts bourgeois,* who, just as Heidegger defines the human condition in general, do not find themselves in the right position. It's the reason why, for him, existence is the worrisome thing par excellence. And the absurd is the bourgeoisie's unease raised to a metaphysical absolute. Death finally renders man indifferent to the stage in which society finds itself at that moment, and which, nevertheless, could also be capitalism's. The counterrevolution avails itself of the idea of death, putting it forward as the sole 'end' attributable to life, as in the past it made use of the consolations of a better beyond. Heidegger's man is representative of the decadent bourgeoisie, or the bourgeoisie stubbornly persisting in its accepted nullity" ([quoted in] ibid., p. 19).

[*October 27.*[34]] Lunch at André Lichtwitz's. I always feel at ease at André's. Jean-Pierre Aumont is happy about the success of his play *The Emperor of China* the day before yesterday.

He talks about English theater, which he knows very well, about London actors and actresses. He will return to London shortly and is very curiously anxious to know if people will like his work as much without him in it (he plays the lead role). An American lady, who has come to Paris to look for new works for Broadway, shows a good deal of interest in Jean-Pierre Aumont. Seated next to me is Duhamel, who has translated and adapted American plays. The conversation concerns theater; I don't say a single word. I'm afraid they'll ask me about my play. André is on the verge of bringing it up but I signal to him. Fortunately, he understands.

I observe Jean-Pierre Aumont: he's fascinating. In this Frenchman the new European race that invaded Europe ten years earlier sits alongside the old French race, that of the painters. Because there is a race of painters, as there is a race of poets, of sculptors.

Jean-Pierre Aumont belongs to the race represented by Clouet; his facial features, the line of his forehead and his lips, the sweep of his hair, are classical, with none of the intellectual contamination of the eighteenth century. The French of the age of the last Valois up through Louis XIII belong to a particular race; all the grace of the Renaissance (Florence, Fontainebleau, Chambord, the Louvre, Urbino, Ferrara) is gathered up in their features and their facial expressions; it is the flower of the "*latin sangue gentile*," of the noble Latin blood, as Petrarch says.[35]

Jean-Pierre Aumont speaks English with an accent both gentle and virile, and with a smile. He talks about French theater, about the risks to European theater posed by the invasion of American theater. I don't believe in the vitality of American art, theater included, which lacks grace. Grace is something European. The homeland of grace is Europe. Like good wine, which can't survive the ocean crossing, grace cannot emigrate to the United States. One day, Europe, when it has lost its political, military, and industrial strength, will be the realm of grace, like Pericles's Greece, toward the end of the Peloponnesian War. One forgets that the Parthenon is the work of a Greece already in decline, a decline in its material power. I think that in Paris, in France, one fails to appreciate the true value of what constitutes the real strength of our civilization: grace. More than beauty, grace endures in the customs of a people. In Southern Italy there is a people who were once famous for their beauty, since turned ugly, small, and ill formed. They have lost their beauty; their grace endures. Grace is our true beauty.

The French do not like for foreigners to have an opinion of them that is not their own. In their defense, they say: "You don't know France." Some time ago I read an article about Italy in a French magazine. In it the writer marvels that Cocteau is very well known in Italy, more than certain others whom the French consider to be greater than Cocteau. The fact is that Cocteau is grace, that France is grace, and that what one loves in the French spirit is not strength, or reason, but grace.

Europe is weary of the Cartesian spirit and admires above all the grace of the French. It was in the periods in which France was the most powerful that its grace flourished. There was nothing more singular, more astonishing, than the army of Charles VIII marching across Italy to Naples.

Talk to a Frenchman about grace and he will reply: "We have other qualities." Naturally. But to those other qualities, Europe prefers French grace. And by grace I mean something entirely moral, the awareness of one's own intellectual superiority, one's own strength, one's own power, one's own freedom, one's own wealth. Grace is the equilibrium of all one's strengths, all one's qualities. There are peoples who are stronger, or richer: Germany, Russia, Charles V's Spain, Pitt's England. But this equilibrium, this grace, is French alone. This is the light France spreads all over Europe. Order, clarity, reason, manners, good taste: this is grace.

[*October 29.*[36]] Big commotion last night at the Salle Wagram. The Communists had organized a demonstration in front of the hall, where the peoples oppressed by the USSR were holding a demonstration. The policing was impressive. Battalions of mobile guards barred all passage. The Communists came up against the barricade; the police began to disperse the crowd with heavy baton blows. At midnight everything was over. Word comes of hundreds of injured among the Communists. I had gone to dinner in Meudon at Tavernier's. A lovely evening in his little house, which is shaken continually by the passing of trains bound for Brittany. We spoke about literature. I returned on the train that goes to Montparnasse. It was very cold out. This morning, Boussinot, who doesn't hide his Communist sympathies from me, comes to visit. He's indignant about the violence used by the police to disperse the Communist demonstration. I tell him I'm a foreigner, that these things do not interest me, except as a spectator, and that I wasn't present at the spectacle.

"You're wrong," he says, and adds that he fears if these things keep happening, the Communist militants will eventually tire of being beaten with batons, to no purpose. He tells me a rather strange story. Some groups of demonstrators gather before a barricade. They talk to the officers, trying to persuade them to let them pass. A woman shouts: "I was in a concentration camp in Germany, I have the right to pass, the right to express my own opinions"; and she shows her deportee's badge. An officer says to her: "You were in a camp? And you didn't get enough?" And he strikes her a tremendous baton blow to the head. Boussinot is indignant. How naive these young Communists are!

October. Lunch at André Lichtwitz's. André is very struck by my mania for barking in the night. He claims that it's my liver. With us were a Hindu from Madagascar, a young colonial official just arrived from Indochina, Jean-Pierre Aumont, Duhamel and his wife, and Mme Vallery-Radot. Everyone looks at me with considerable astonishment, except for Jean-Pierre Aumont.

I changed the subject. I don't want them to take me for an eccentric. I find that there's nothing more natural, when you love dogs, than to bark with them.

November 11. I got up early to go see the parade. I'm no longer a child, but I still like the soldiers, the flags, the trumpets. The spahis with their fiery horses remain in my eyes for a long time; the naval fusiliers; the infantrymen in their white gaiters, the rifles held good and tight against their shoulders.

Condemn me if you will, but I am a man, and I love war. I'm not such a hypocrite as to say, "I don't love war." I love it, like every well-born, healthy, courageous, strong man loves war, like every man who is not content with men, or with their misdeeds.

The crowd massing on the Champs-Élysées is moved. The French people love their soldiers. The parade this morning is for them, something that touches them to the bottom of their hearts. France is reborn. France is not dead. The eyes of the people around me are moist with tears. I too am moved. And yet I am only a foreigner; this display should leave me cold. It's not my country; these aren't my soldiers. But I too was a French soldier, I too paraded down the Champs-Élysées one distant day in 1919, before this crowd.

A woman beside me says to me, "It's a lovely sight, isn't it, monsieur? Finally! We are glad to be French, are we not? I lost a son in 1940. He is avenged!"

"Yes," I respond, "We are glad. It's a lovely sight."

She rests her arm on mine and says to me, "Isn't it?"

How precarious and humiliating the life of a foreigner is! If she knew that I was Italian, she would insult me.

November 13. Dined this evening with Jean Cocteau at the restaurant Taillevent, on Rue Saint-Georges.

Roland Laudenbach, from La Table Ronde, and I waited on Rue de Beaujolais, at the Palais-Royal, for Jean Cocteau to return home from Bevin, where he's shooting *L'Aigle à deux têtes*. With us is the very young and charming Anna Maria Solaria, who is quite excited.

Cocteau gets out of the car, goes inside to change his shoes. He comes down minutes later in moccasins. "I put them on in your honor," he says to me. "They're Italian moccasins." I tell him they're from Franceschini, on Via Condotti in Rome. "You recognize them?" he says, a bit surprised, a bit flattered. Franceschini is the great shoemaker who caters to kings and princes in exile.

We set off on foot toward Rue Saint-Georges. Cocteau is dressed in gray, a sweater partially covering a blue striped tie. He wears a coat of Arab, or monastic, cut, with a little hood that hangs down his back. It's the first time I've met him. He immediately seduces me with his simplicity. His manners are simple, his voice subdued. Not a false gesture, not a false note.

This eternal youth has grown old. His cheeks are lean, the skin of his face is slightly wrinkled, his hair is gray. This surprising man has a surprised air. I understand his allure, an allure that gave rise to a legend. He has the surprised air of old monks when they emerge from the convent to collect alms. He tells us—discreetly, with absolute simplicity—about his new film, about Venice, about Paris.

Since my return to Paris I've often heard of Jean Cocteau. People gave me the book by Claude Mauriac to read, the book by Maurice Sachs.

It's strange how the French fail to understand, or no longer understand, what is French and what is not. They make a big deal about certain men and things, for example about Sartre and existentialism, and demand that foreigners see a French side to them that they do not have. Sartre is unquestionably a very interesting man, a man of considerable intelligence; but he could also be a French Swiss from Geneva. A Giraudoux or a Cocteau responds to a very precise and enduring need of the French spirit: the need for imagination, for the baroque, for the rococo, without which France would be an uninhabitable Cartesian country. Giraudoux and Cocteau correct what is too Cartesian in the French spirit. They bring to literature not emotion, that other great corrective to the Cartesian spirit, but imagination, grace, and that passionless madness of the eighteenth century. Madness that is cold, pale (if it can have a color), lean, blue and white, dry and polished smooth like a cuttlefish bone; that is the secret spirit animating the entire mechanism of French civilization. A civilization that is at this point the most fragile in the world, because it is nothing but a memory, regret, long habit. It is no longer love but the memory of love, etc., no longer hate but, etc.

I observe the sad and stunned mask of Jean Cocteau. In his *Difficulté d'être* he speaks gently, with affectionate detachment, about his face, about the crease or wrinkle in the middle of his face. I don't see any wrinkles in his pale and gray mask, but something silvery, gossamer, quivering, as if he had just passed through a forest and emerged with impalpable spiderwebs on his face.

We arrive at Taillevent. Among the handful of customers I recognize Mme Soèze and M. Vallon. The light is warm and pink. Jean Cocteau, seated opposite me, tells me about the Marchioness Luisa Casati; he gives the final touches to the portrait he made of her in *Difficulté d'être*. In the mouth of Cocteau, the tremendous bad taste of the Marchioness Casati, of her era, of her generation, takes on the accents of grace and affection.

I think about everything that provides the set, the choir for this actress without a theater, without a script: Fallières, Poincaré, the Paris of Proust, the war of 1914, a France that no longer exists, that begins to no longer exist even in the pages of Proust. Because Proust wrote on blotting paper, the writing has spread little by little, penetrating the paper; at this point it's no more than a pale stain of india ink, a sort of palimpsest on which the impressions, portraits, and memories overlap and blend into a shadowy embroidery of branches, like a forest in the fog.

Cocteau writes on thin, shiny paper, similar to glass. He tells me about the Marchioness Casati's boa constrictors and her pitiful tubercular tigers, about her eccentricities, her extravagances, her generosity, her present poverty, in which so many splendors blend with the images reflected in a broken mirror. He tells me about Venice, this city of nouveaux riches, where the palazzos built by Venetian merchants surpass and stifle one another. I tell him I've never been to Venice; he offers to take me the following year, in September, to reveal to me the attractions of this incomparable city. We talk about Italy and the smiling simplicity of its people.

"The French," he says, "are the Italians in a bad mood; the Italians are the French in a good mood."

He doesn't tell stories; he draws the portraits of things, men, landscapes, events.

November 16. I wake up anxious and tired again this morning. I try to work, but I can't write a single line. I'm depressed, as I am on so many days. Charles Du Bos, in his journal, expresses this sense of dismay and anguish quite well. On such days I have no one I can turn to in Paris. I have friends, but what can I say to them? I went into a church. Churches are rather poorly attended in Paris. I love the common people in churches. No common people in the churches in this city, just a few gossipmongers, very rarely a few old folks, and a kind of awful petty bourgeois, the petty bourgeois of the church, of the faith, which horrifies me. The church, too, every church, has its particular classes: the proletariat, who are believers out of poverty, out of desperation; the petty bourgeoisie, believers in their local priests, in the petty literature of their parishes; and the *grande bourgeoisie*, the upper class, those who read Mauriac. There are very few proletariats of the faith in the churches of Paris. In every Italian church the common people are very well represented. The visit to the foot of the cross: that's what you won't see in a single church in a single neighborhood in Paris, not even in Ménilmontant, in Pantin. I'm watched warily, with the suspicious eyes particular to the petty bourgeois, in politics as in church.

November 18. For a foreigner, the only acceptable condition, in France, is to be a foreigner. It's a difficult art, the only one that allows a foreigner to feel at home in some way.

[*Late November.*][37] Dinner at the Countess de V.'s. A lovely evening. We talk about Petrassi's ballet, which has just started a run at the Champs-Élysées. We marvel that the press coverage did not even mention the composer's name. They give the name of the stage designer, who is the Hungarian Nikosz; of the dancers; but not Petrassi's. The composer Petrassi is in Paris; I saw him this morning. I didn't talk to him about the Parisian press's strange omission in his regard. It's more than an omission. It's disdain. Petrassi looks very satisfied. He leaves for Rome tomorrow. He goes to gather the laurels of success, of Parisian glory, in Rome. How sad it is sometimes to be a foreigner, in this Paris that adores foreigners!

December 19. Last night I had the same dream I've had every so often for years. My mother enters my room at night and says to me in a hoarse voice, "Stop working, you're tired. Go to sleep." I look at her. She's pale, and smiles. Then she gets up and withdraws, leaving her white hand behind on my desk. I get up and take the heavy, dead hand, open the window, and throw it out. Below is the garden of my house in Forte dei Marmi. I hear the sound of the sea. A bird sings. I always repeat the same words: "March 21, 1948." It was in Forte dei Marmi, in December 1935, that I had this dream for the first time.

I need to leave Paris. Lichtwitz suggests I go with him to Chamonix. I will go to Chamonix. I'm afraid of this dream. It brings me bad luck.[38]

December. Count Augustin de Foxa, made famous by my *Kaputt*, has given an interview to the Madrid newspaper *A.B.C.* In his statements, doubtless in revenge for several passages in *Kaputt* he doesn't like, he claimed that anything that is witty in the book comes from him. Very well. I've always said, in *Kaputt*, when it is de Foxa who is speaking, it is de Foxa who is speaking. I didn't invent anything, not even the witty remarks I heard from his mouth. *Kaputt* is a historical novel, whose characters are not from the age of Louis XIII but from our own. The characters are historical but contemporary. De Foxa is one of the wittiest men I have ever met. When they are witty, the Spanish are the wittiest men in the world. Reading the statements he made to *A.B.C.*, I wondered why I didn't put the story of the Spanish prisoners in *Kaputt*. And since de Foxa didn't tell it, I will, so that the story isn't lost or forgotten. All the more so since, if de Foxa were to tell it, he'd ruin it. As good a speaker as he is, he's just as bad a writer. No offense to de Foxa, but I tell his stories better than he does.

In February 1942 I was at the Kannas front between Lake Ladoga and Leningrad, part of the retinue of General Edqvist, who commanded a Finnish division at that delicate point of the front. One day, General Edqvist sends for me.

"We've taken eighteen Spanish prisoners," he tells me.

"Spanish? Are you at war with Spain, then?"

"I know nothing about that," he says. "The fact is that last night we took eighteen Russian prisoners, who declared themselves Spaniards and speak Spanish."

"Very strange."

"They need to be interrogated. You speak Spanish, no doubt."

"No, I don't speak Spanish."

"You're Italian, anyway, so you're more Spanish than I am. Go on, interrogate them, and afterward we'll see."

I go, find the prisoners being held in a shed, and ask them if they are Russians or Spaniards. I speak slowly in Italian, they respond slowly in Spanish, and we understand each other perfectly.

"We are Soviet soldiers. But we are Spaniards."

And one of them explains to me that they are orphans of the Spanish Civil War, that their parents died in the bombing, in the reprisals, etc., and that one fine day they were put on a Soviet ship, in Barcelona, and sent to Russia, where they were fed, clothed, and educated, where they learned a trade and became Red Army soldiers.

"But we are Spaniards."

Yes, I remember reading in the papers at the time of the Spanish Civil War (I was on Lipari in those years) that the Russians had shipped several thousand children of Red Spaniards to the USSR, to save them from the bombings and the famine.

"Are you enrolled in the Communist Party?"

"Of course."

"Well, don't say so. You told me, for now that's enough. Don't repeat it to anyone. Understood?"

"No, we don't understand."

"That doesn't matter. If I think about it, I don't understand anything either. It's just that, right, I believe it's better you don't tell anyone you're Spaniards, Red Army soldiers enrolled in the Communist Party."

"No, we can't accept this compromise. We were raised to tell the truth. There's nothing wrong with being Communist. We won't hide that we're Communists."

"All right, do as you like. Know, though, that the Finns are an honest and humane people, that there are Communists among the Finnish soldiers as well, but that they're fighting for their country, which Russia attacked in 1939. It's not about being Communist or not, is what I mean to say, but you understand me, I think."

"No, we don't understand. We understand that you're spreading propaganda, that's all."

"No, that's not all. Know that I will do everything possible to keep you out of trouble. Do you understand me?"

"Yes."

"All right then, goodbye. I'll come to see you tomorrow."

I went to General Edqvist and recounted my conversation with the Spaniards.

"What is to be done?" General Edqvist asked me. "You understand that their situation is a delicate one. They're Spanish Communist volunteers in the Red Army. Obviously, they were children when they were sent to the USSR. They're not responsible for the way they were brought up. I want to save them. The best thing is for you to telegraph your friend de Foxa, the Spanish minister. Ask him to come, in my name. I'll deliver the prisoners to him, and he'll do what he likes."

I telegraphed de Foxa in the following terms: "Eighteen Spanish prisoners taken. Come quick to collect them." Two days later, de Foxa arrived on a sled, in foul weather, with the temperature 42 degrees below zero. He was freezing and dead tired. As soon as he saw me, he shouted, "What are you interfering for? Why did you telegraph? What can I do with eighteen Red Spanish prisoners? I can't put them up at my house. Now I have to deal with them. What are you interfering for?"

"But you're the minister of Spain!"

"Yes, but of Francoist Spain. They're Reds. Now I have to deal with them. It's my duty. But I'd like to know what you're interfering for."

He was furious. But de Foxa has a good heart, and I knew he would do what he could to help those poor wretches.

He went to see the prisoners. I went with him.

"I am the minister of Franco's Spain," said de Foxa. "I'm Spanish, you're Spanish, I've come to help you. What can I do for you?"

"For us? Nothing," they replied. "We don't want anything to do with representatives of Franco."

"You're throwing a tantrum? I traveled two days and two nights to come here, and you reject me? I'll do everything possible to help you. The Spain of Franco knows how to forgive. I will help you."

"Franco is our enemy. He killed our parents. We ask you to leave us in peace."

De Foxa went to see General Edqvist.

"They're stubborn. But I will do my duty, despite them. I will telegraph Madrid to ask for instructions, and we will do what Madrid orders us to."

The next day de Foxa set off again in his sled for Helsinki. He was seated in his sled, and he said to me: "Mind your own business, you understand? If they're in this mess, it's your fault. Got it?"

"*Adiós.*"

"*Adiós.*"

A few days later, one of the prisoners fell sick. "Pneumonia," the doctor said. "Very dangerous."

General Edqvist said to me, "De Foxa must be informed."

So I telegraphed de Foxa: "One prisoner sick, very serious. Come quick with medicine, chocolate, cigarettes."

Two days later de Foxa arrived in his sled. He was furious.

"What are you interfering for?" he shouted as soon as he saw me. "Is it my fault if the wretch has fallen sick? What can I do? I'm on my own in Helsinki, you know. I don't have attachés, aids, anything. I have to do everything on my own, and you have me running all over Finland in this foul weather. What are you interfering for?"

"Listen, he's sick, he's going to die. You really do need to be there. You represent Spain."

"Okay, okay, let's go see him."

He brought with him an immense quantity of medicine, food, cigarettes, and warm clothes. He had done things on a proper grand scale, my good Augustin.

The sick man recognized him, even smiled at him. His comrades were silent and hostile. They observed de Foxa with hateful contempt.

De Foxa stayed for two days, then returned to Helsinki. Before climbing into his sled, he said to me, "Why do you interfere in things that don't concern you? When will you learn to leave me in peace? You're not Spanish, in any case. Leave me be, understand?"

"*Adiós*, Augustin."

"*Adiós*, Malaparte."

Three days later the sick man died. The general said to me, "I could have him buried quite simply, but I think it would be better to inform de Foxa. This man is Spanish. What do you think?"

"Yes, I think de Foxa must be informed. It's a matter of courtesy."

And I telegraphed de Foxa: "Sick man dead. Come quick, he must be buried."

Two days later de Foxa arrived. He was furious.

"Would you stop hassling me?" he shouted as soon as he saw me. "What are you interfering for? Are you trying to drive me crazy? Of course, if you tell me the guy is dead, that he must be buried, and that I have to be here, of course, it's impossible for me not to come. But if you hadn't informed me, eh? I'm not going to resuscitate him, just with my presence!"

"No, but you are Spain. He can't be buried like a dog in these woods, far from his country, far from Spain. If you're here at least, it's different, do you understand? It's as if all of Spain were here."

"Of course, I understand," de Foxa said. "That's why I came. But why do you get mixed up in these matters anyway? You're not Spanish, *válgame Dios*!"

"He must be buried with respect, Augustin. This is why I informed you."

"Yes, I know. All right, let's not talk about it anymore. Where is the dead man?"

We went to see the poor dead child in the little shed where his comrades had laid him out and watched over him. The Spanish prisoners observed de Foxa with a sullen, almost menacing air.

"We shall bury him," said de Foxa, "according to the Catholic rite. Spaniards are Catholics. I want him to be buried like a true, a good Spaniard."

"We won't allow it," said one of the prisoners. "Our comrade was an atheist, like the rest of us. His views must be respected. We won't allow him to be buried according to the Catholic rite."

"I represent Spain here, and this dead man is Spanish, a Spanish citizen. I will bury him according to the Catholic rite, understand?"

"No, we don't understand."

"I am the minister of Spain, and I will do my duty. I don't care if you don't understand." And de Foxa walked away.

"My dear Augustin," I said to him, "General Edqvist is a gentleman. He won't like your flouting the views of a dead man. The Finns are free men, they won't understand your gesture. A compromise must be sought."

"Yes, but I am the minister of Spain. I can't bury a Spaniard without the Catholic rite. Oh, why didn't you bury him without me! You see, you see what you've done, with your mania for interfering in things that don't concern you?"

"All right, all right, don't worry. We'll make the best of things."

We went to the general.

"Clearly," said General Edqvist, "if the dead man was an atheist, as his comrades claim, and as I believe, given that he was a Communist, he can't be buried according to the Catholic rite. I understand, you're the minister of Spain, and you can't..."

I recommended that we summon the Italian Catholic priest of Helsinki, the only Catholic priest in Helsinki (in Helsinki there was also the Catholic bishop, a Dutchman, but we couldn't summon the bishop). Thus the Catholic priest was telegraphed. Two days later the priest arrived. He understood the situation, and arranged things for the best. He was a priest from upper Lombardy, a mountain man, very simple, very shrewd, very pure.

The funeral took place the following day. The coffin was carried by four of his comrades. A flag of Francoist Spain was placed at the bottom of the grave, dug out using dynamite in the frozen ground. A unit of Finnish soldiers was ranged along one side of the grave, in the small Finnish war cemetery, in a small clearing in the woods. The snow sparkled gently in the day's dim light. The coffin was followed by Minister de Foxa, General Edqvist, me, and the Red prisoners, and by several Finnish soldiers. The priest stood fifty steps from the grave, stole and prayer book in hand. His lips moved silently, saying the prayer for the dead—but at a remove, in order not to go against the views of the dead man. When the coffin was lowered into the grave the Finnish soldiers, all Protestants, discharged their rifles in the air. General Edqvist, the Finnish officers and soldiers, and I each brought a hand to our cap in salute. Minister de Foxa held his arm out in the Fascist salute. And the comrades of the dead man each raised a clenched fist.

De Foxa left again the next day. Before getting into his sled he took me aside and said, "I thank you for everything you've done. You've been very kind. Pardon me if I bawled you out a little, but you understand . . . You're always interfering in things that don't concern you!"

A few days passed. The Red prisoners continued to await the response from Madrid. General Edqvist was a bit nervous.

"You understand," he said, "that I can't keep these prisoners here forever. Something must be decided. Either Spain reclaims them, or I'll have to send them to a camp. Their situation is a delicate one. It's better to keep them here. But I can't keep them forever."

"Be patient a bit longer, surely the response will come."

The response came: "Only those prisoners who declare themselves Spaniards, accept the Franco regime, and express the desire to return to Spain will be recognized as Spanish citizens."

"Go explain the situation to them," General Edqvist said to me.

I went to the prisoners and explained the situation.

"We will not recognize the Franco regime. We don't want to return to Spain," the prisoners responded.

"I respect your faithfulness to your views, but I must stress that your position is very delicate. If you admit to fighting against the Finns in your capacity as Red Spaniards, you will be shot. The laws of war are the laws of war. Do what you can so that I can help you. I beg you to reflect on this. At bottom, you are Spaniards. All the Red Spaniards left in Spain have accepted the Franco regime, have they not? The Reds lost this contest; their allegiance doesn't prevent them from recognizing that Franco won. Do as the Reds who live in Spain have done. Accept your defeat."

"There are no more Reds in Spain. They were shot."

"Who told you this story?"

"We read about it in the Soviet newspapers. We will never recognize the Franco regime. We'd rather be shot by the Finns than by Franco."

"Listen! I don't give a damn about you, about Red Spain, about Franco's Spain, about Russia, but I can't abandon you, I won't abandon you. I'll do what's possible to help you. If you don't want to recognize Franco's regime, to express the desire to return to Spain, then, well, I'll sign the declaration for you. I'll be lying, but I'll save your life. Understood?"

"No! We'll protest, we'll declare that you fraudulently signed for us. We beg you to leave us in peace. And mind your own business. Are you Spanish? No. So what are you interfering for?"

"I'm not Spanish, but I'm a man, I'm a Christian, and I won't abandon you. I repeat: Allow me to help you. Return to Spain, and there you'll do what all the others do, what all the Reds who have honorably accepted their defeat have done. You're young, I won't let you die."

"Leave us in peace, won't you?"

I unhappily left them. General Edqvist said to me, "Minister de Foxá must be informed. Telegraph him to come here to settle this business himself."

I telegraphed de Foxá: "Prisoners refuse. Come quick to persuade them."

Two days later de Foxá arrived. The north wind blew violently, de Foxá was covered with icicles. As soon as he saw me:

"You again?" he shouted. "How is it possible you're still interfering in this? How do you expect me to persuade them, if they don't want to be? You don't know Spaniards, they're as stubborn as a Toledo mule! Why did you telegraph me? What do you want me to do now?"

"Go talk to them," I said, "maybe..."

"Yes, yes, I know...that's why I came. But really now..."

I accompanied him to see the prisoners. The prisoners were intransigent. De Foxa entreated them, begged them, threatened them. To no avail.

"They will shoot us. All right. And then?" they said.

"Then I will bury you according to the Catholic rite!" shouted de Foxa, foaming at the mouth, with tears in his eyes. Because my dear Augustin is good, and he suffers from that magnificent and terrible stubbornness.

"You won't do it," the prisoners said. "*Usted es un hombre honesto!*"

Because they too were moved, even so. De Foxa left again, exhausted. Before leaving he asked General Edqvist to hold the prisoners a little longer, and not to decide anything without informing him.

He was sitting in his sled, and he said to me, "See, Malaparte, it's your fault I'm in this state." He had tears in his eyes, his voice trembled. "I can't think about the fate of those poor boys. I admire them, I'm proud of them, they're true Spaniards, proud and courageous. But you understand...We must do everything we can to save them. I'm counting on you!"

"I'll do everything I can. I promise you that they won't die."

"*Adiós*, Augustin!"

"*Adiós*, Malaparte!"

I went to see the prisoners every day, attempting to persuade them, but in vain.

"Thank you," they said to me, "but we're Communists. We'll never agree to recognize Franco."

One day General Edqvist summoned me. "Go see what's happening with the prisoners. They've nearly done in one of their comrades. And we can't figure out why!"

I went to the prisoners. One of them of was covered with blood and sitting on the ground in a corner of the room, protected by a Finnish soldier armed with a Suomi-konepistooli, the famous Finnish submachine gun.

"What have you done to this man?"

"He's a traitor," they respond. "A *traidor*."

"Is this true?" I ask the wounded man.

"Yes, I am a *traidor*. I want to return to Spain, I can't take it anymore! I don't want to die! I want to return to Spain! I'm Spanish. I want to return to Spain."

"He's a traitor! A *traidor*!" said his comrades, looking on with gazes full of hate. I had "*el traidor*" confined to a separate shed and telegraphed de Foxa: "'El traidor' wants to return to Spain. Come quick."

Two days later de Foxa arrived. Snow was falling. He was blinded by the snow, his face stung by the shards of ice thrown up by the horses' hooves on the frozen path. As soon as he saw me:

"What are you interfering for? Why in the world are you minding other people's business? You're still out to drive me mad with your stories? Where is this traitor?"

"Over there, Augustin."

"All right, let's go see him."

"*El traidor*" received us in silence. He was around twenty years old, blond and fair eyed, very pale. He was blond like blond Spaniards are, with fair eyes like fair-eyed Spaniards have. He began to cry. He said, "I am a traitor. *Yo soy un traidor.* But I can't take it anymore. I don't want to die. I want to return to Spain." He cried, watching us with eyes full of fear, of hope, of entreaty.

De Foxa was moved.

"Don't cry," he said. "We'll send you to Spain. You'll be well received. You'll be pardoned. It's not your fault if the Russians made you a Communist, you were a child. Don't cry."

"I'm a traitor!" said the prisoner.

"We are all traitors," de Foxa said suddenly in a low voice. The next day de Foxa had him sign a declaration, then left.

Before he left he went to General Edqvist.

"You are a gentleman," he said to him. "Give me your word that you'll save these poor wretches' lives. They're good kids. They would rather die than disavow their faith."

"Yes, they're good kids," said General Edqvist. "I'm a soldier, I admire courage and loyalty even in my enemies. I give you my word. Besides, I've already reached an agreement with Marshal Mannerheim, they will be treated as prisoners of war. You can leave with an easy heart, I'll answer for their lives."

De Foxa shook General Edqvist's hand in silence, choked with emotion. As he took his seat in the sled, he smiled.

"At last!" he said to me, "you'll stop bothering me with all these hassles! I'm going to telegraph Madrid, and as soon as I have a response, we'll see. Thank you, Malaparte."

"*Adiós*, Augustin."

"*Adiós*."

A few days later the response from Madrid arrived. The prisoner was escorted to Helsinki, where a Spanish officer and a noncommissioned officer awaited him. "*El traidor*" left in a plane for Berlin, and from there to Spain. It was clear that the Spanish authorities wanted to play up the affair. The prisoner was showered with attention and left happy.

Two months later I returned to Helsinki. It was spring. The trees of the esplanade were covered with new leaves of tender green; birds sang in the branches. Even the sea, at the far end of the esplanade, was green; it too seemed covered in new leaves. I went to collect de Foxa in his Brunnsparken villa.[39] Together we walked along the sea, en route to the Kemp.[40] The island of Suomenlinna was white with the wings of seagulls.

"And the prisoner, '*el traidor*'? Have you had any news?"

"Again!" cried de Foxa. "What are you interfering for?"

"I too did something to save that man's life."

"I almost lost my position, thanks to him! And it's your fault!"

He told me how "*el traidor*" had been very well received in Madrid. They promenaded him through the city's cafés, its theaters, its bullrings, its stadiums, its movie houses. They would promenade him, and the people would say, "Do you see that handsome young man? He was a Communist, he was taken prisoner on the Russian front, he was fighting alongside the Russians. He wanted to return, he recognized Franco in Spain. He's an honorable young man, a good Spaniard." But "*el traidor*" would say, "This, a café? You've got to see the cafés in Moscow." And he would laugh. He would say, "This, a theater? A movie house? You've got to see the theaters and the movie houses in Moscow." And he would laugh. They brought him to a stadium. He said aloud, "This, a stadium? You've got to see the stadium in Kiev."[41] And he laughed. Everyone would turn around and he would say aloud, "This, a stadium? The stadium in Kiev, now that's a stadium!" And he would laugh.

"You understand," de Foxá said to me. "You understand? It's your fault. It's your fault too. In Madrid, at the ministry, they were furious with me. All this because of you. This will teach you to interfere in things that aren't your business."

"But in the end, this young man ... What did they do to him?"

"What do you think they did to him? They didn't do anything to him," Augustin said with a strange voice. "What are you interfering for?"

I understood. They had buried him according to the Catholic rite.

1948

JANUARY 1948, Chamonix. The moon on Mont Blanc. The mountain standing out in white against thick black paper, like certain sketches by Leonardo. The icicles glow in the cold glare. The Aiguilles lightly prick the blue sky, a dark blue sky that would seem black if it were not tempered by the golden splendor of the stars, stars of a cruel, impassive purity, the cruelty the night stars have in Persian poems, when the upholstery of flowers, birds, and deer that covers the sky opens up, and the night sky appears, pure and cruel.

I think different peoples must certainly have different senses of nature: their sensitivity to nature perhaps depends, in part, on the way they deify it.

The Hellenes and the Latins humanized nature: to describe a river or a forest, the sea or the sky, they simply described gods with human features. How did the ancient peoples of the Gallic race, the ancient inhabitants of Gaul, deify nature? From the little we know about their religion and their art, it appears they did not give it human features. Their sense of nature did not deform nature. They had a very naive sense of nature and its beauty. I think they were the only people in Europe to have a sense of nature.

Take Virgil. There has been a long-running argument over whether Virgil descended from the Etruscans, or from the Gauls who inhabited the Po Valley. The Etruscans lived in cities and devoted themselves to commerce, industry, and art. The surrounding countryside, especially outside Tuscany—the provinces of the Etruscan empire, in other words—were inhabited by native populations: Latins in Latium,

Ligurians in the Po Valley, Umbrians in Umbria, etc. The countryside surrounding Mantua, an Etruscan city, was in Virgil's time inhabited by the Gallic population that had arrived there in the —— century. Even in the city, the Etruscan aristocracy had mixed with the Gallic aristocracy, with whom they lived in peaceful coexistence. The family of Virgil was a family of rich farmers, small landowners who were probably Gauls, since the Gauls had divided the lands among the warriors. It is very unlikely that Virgil was from an Etruscan family: in the first place because the Etruscans did not directly cultivate the land, being more of an aristocracy than a farming people; secondly, everything leads us to believe it improbable that a small Etruscan landowner would have been able to hold onto his land after a savage and pitiless conquest like that of the Gauls.

Everything in Virgil's poetry reveals that he was Gallic. His sense of nature, his gentleness, and that sort of poetry *en plein air*, which, like painting *en plein air*, is decidedly French and doubtless has its origin in the sense of nature that is so characteristic of the Gauls. I would describe his poetry, then, as "plein-air poetry." Virgil is an impressionist. He looks at fields, woods, rivers, work in the fields, farmers, and shepherds with the eye of a Manet, of a Courbet. He is first among the ancient poets to perceive the magic of the moon, with a feeling for nature that is neither sadness, nor the sensuality of Sappho, nor that of Alcaeus. The moon that rises over the distant mountains, that lights up the plain and the forests, pouring out its luminous, clear, sidereal silence on the sleep of men, is not the moon of Aeolian poetry, a moon that is never seen; that is clearly discerned in Sappho's room and on the terraces from which Alcaeus contemplates the sea; that is observed on the temples and columns of ancient Hellas.

The moon of Virgil is the moon of the woods and the rivers, the moon of animals roaming the night in the tall grass of the plain. It is a chaste, demure moon. It is nature. It is not, as in certain Greek poems, an element of the human soul, of the human body, of its sadness or its sensuality. All Virgil is immersed in this clear light that is the light of the moon, even his most sun-drenched landscapes (certain passages of the *Georgics* and the *Aeneid* seem to us illuminated by a tepid, pale, and transparent light; the light, I would say, of a nocturnal sun, of a noontide moon).

With Virgil, nature enters ancient poetry for the first time—nature in a modern sense, not as seen by Rousseau (the philosophical nature of Rousseau, imbued with elements of German poetry, of the German sense of nature), but as seen by the French impressionists. Of ancient Gallic poetry, which one supposes with reason to have existed and been lost, nothing survives but the poetry of Virgil; and it is a poetry of nature.

From these savage and innocent ancient Gauls, whose emblem was the skylark (and the skylark is the flower of the fields, the bird of morning, nature still damp with dew), not one poem, painting, or sculpture has come down to us. As a people they did not burden the landscape with works of architecture; of their wooden houses perched on hilltops, or in valley bottoms, or at the edges of forests, naught remains. This people lived in nature with their horses. A people of warriors and farmers. Their nobility was a rural nobility, of *country gentlemen*, devoted to hunting, fishing, war, and agriculture.

Crans, January 31. And yet I had been warned that the Swiss were a peculiar people.

Yesterday evening, having just arrived in the little inn Pas de l'Ours, which is hidden away in the pine forest overlooking Crans, I called out to the dogs in the vicinity. I went out on the terrace and began to bark. And the dogs immediately responded, from near and far, through the night dimly illuminated by a slim crescent moon. I always do the same thing when I arrive in a new place. I become acquainted with the dogs in the vicinity. I don't do any harm. But this morning I received a visit from the Crans police, who asked me to stop barking at night.

"You are not a dog, monsieur."

"I like barking with the dogs, at night. I'm not doing any harm."

"Such things are not done in Switzerland, monsieur. The regulations prohibit it."

"Thank you. I won't do it anymore. But I won't stay in Switzerland, I'll return to France. There you can bark at night all you want."

"I'm sorry, monsieur. Foreigners very much enjoy themselves in Switzerland. It's just that they don't bark at night. I believe you are the first."

"I shall return to France, where foreigners can bark as much as they like."

"I do not doubt it, monsieur. France is a country of loose morals."

"To bark at night is not to have loose morals."

"It begins with barking, monsieur, and finishes with biting. The Swiss don't like being bitten."

I won't stay in Switzerland. I'll leave tomorrow. I don't like countries where you can't even bark at night. I like free countries.

January. Earlier this evening, returning to Chamonix from Col de Voza, I found Yvonne Printemps and Pierre Fresnay at the Carlton. They're staying in Thonon, and the mayor of Thonon is with them. Yvonne Printemps is young, attractive, cheerful. I like the rosy pallor of her face, so attuned during conversation to the solemn, deep, miraculously modulated sound of Pierre Fresnay's voice. Another two French people whom I seem to have known for twenty years, whom I seem to have always known.

As I listened to Yvonne, I reflected that France, notwithstanding the amiable if somewhat meager propriety of French manners, is the only country in Europe where a man is received as a friend not because he is pleasant, or handsome, or rich, or of high birth, but because he is intelligent. In France, there is still a great respect for intelligence. I think about Italy, where affection flows to a name, to friendship, to beauty—never to intelligence. Where intelligence is immediately fought. The Italians behave toward intelligence as the Jews do toward intelligence in non-Jews: with spiteful, craven hostility.

I feel at home in France. Safe, calm. Benjamin Constant, in his journal, expresses the same feeling.

Yvonne talks to me about Fresnay, Coppet, Voltaire, Madame de

Staël. The serene, gentle green expanse of Lake Geneva, laid out against the snow-white specter of Mont Blanc at the distant end of the horizon, and the gardens of Ferney return to my memory like a familiar landscape. Yvonne tells me about her pilgrimage to Ferney. Her slow wandering through the deserted rooms, through the park, and all of a sudden the thin little old man who skipped from room to room.

Yvonne asked the man where the owner was.

"That's me," he replied, at once querulous and affable.

He shows her the trees planted by Voltaire. The Ferney estate was once much more extensive; the contingencies of inheritance and sales greatly diminished it. All the French land on the shore of Lake Geneva is charged with the sweetness, together with the anxiety, that stirred the hearts of those grand shades and their small retinues of friends and visitors. The times in which writers and free spirits used to install themselves on the Swiss border, ready in case of danger to take refuge in the free territory of Geneva, are not so far from us. Voltaire, in his own park, could cross the frontier to safety.

What state are we reduced to today, we poor writers! We are afraid, living among sectarian hate, constantly in danger. Yes, France is still a free country, the freest country in Europe, ever since even postwar England began to be infiltrated by the poison of social sectarianism and sectarian intellectuals. I am grateful to France for its freedom. Nothing, for a writer—not love, not riches, not glory—is as valuable as this feeling of security. France is the last homeland of intelligence.

Yvonne and Fresnay set off by car for Lake Geneva and Thonon. Yvonne would like to return to Chamonix, to spend a few days resting there before beginning her tour of Switzerland and Belgium. I recommend Argentière.

January 8. It's snowing. This evening we went to a hole-in-the-wall place to eat fondue, with Marie-Pierre B., Patricia ——, and Gérard Simond. The place is full of novice skiers, raw, athletic young mountain men. Marie-Pierre tells us some of her delightful little stories, in that gentle, mellifluous voice of hers. Not yet seventeen years old,

Marie-Pierre is part of the Racing Club de Paris ski team. She leaves tomorrow for a race in Switzerland; on the fourteenth she'll be in Sestriere. She narrates rapidly, with a smile.

Tale of the Crab. A crab falls in love with a sardine. "No, I won't have you for a husband," the sardine says to him. "I could never love a husband who walks sideways." The crab is desperate. He tries and tries again, but he can't manage to walk straight. "No, I won't have you for a husband," responds the sardine to every fresh proposal. One day the sardine is at the window, and she sees the crab come toward her across the piazza, walking straight. "Will you have me for a husband now?" the crab asks the sardine. "Yes, now I will," replies the sardine, and they are married the same day. The next morning the crab begins to walk sideways again. "You foul, treacherous fraud," cries the sardine in tears, "you've tricked me! Why have you started walking sideways again?" And she weeps. "My dear," the crab replies, "I can't get drunk every day."

Tale of the Warbler. A very snobbish warbler bumps into her old friend the sparrow. "I got married," the sparrow tells her. "Ah, how wonderful!" says the warbler, "and you're happy?" "Very happy," he replies. "My wife is a treasure. Come to our place for lunch tomorrow, so you'll get to meet her. But please, be punctual. My wife is very orderly, and if you come late she'll be angry." "I shall be at your place tomorrow at one o'clock on the dot," the warbler replies. The next day the sparrow and his wife tidy up the nest. Lunch is ready. At one o'clock, nothing. A quarter past one: the warbler doesn't come. Half past one. No warbler. The sparrow's wife begins to get irritated, takes it out on the sparrow, and at a quarter to two decides to serve lunch. They're in the middle of their meal when the warbler shows up. "Oh, forgive me for being late," the warbler says, "but I couldn't resist. It was such a beautiful day out that I walked."

January 9. At the summit of Mont Blanc, Gérard Simond tells me, there are thousands and thousands of dead bees. They lie on the snow, and the warm wind, the föhn, gently stirs them. All about the summit black butterflies fly. The Col des Hirondelles is so called because in spring there are always hundreds and hundreds of dead swallows found there. In spring the Vallée Blanche, Géant, and Mer de Glace glaciers, as well as the Combe Maudite glacier, are black with glacier fleas. They are minuscule and cover the snow in their thousands, turning it black. Gérard Simond, an international ice hockey champion, is a passionate hunter of *coqs de bruyères*, or wood grouse. His pointer, Tex, is famous throughout the Arve Valley. Gérard tells me about the lives of *coqs de bruyères*, marmots, ermines, snow rabbits, chamois. In the winter, the *coqs de bruyères* dig tunnels in the snow and go from one myrtle bush to another, eating the berries that have fallen from the branches and scattered over the ground. They live like this all winter.

Gérard tells me about the chamois cemetery. Like elephants, chamois have their own secret cemeteries. In the Alps, no one ever finds a chamois dead of old age or illness. No one knows where they go to die.

This morning, from the summit of Le Brévent, a magnificent sun—almost too dense, too golden yellow, nearly the color of honey—gilded the immense, magnificent succession.

February 4, Chamonix. I returned to Chamonix yesterday evening after a six-hour journey. Finally, France! Last night I barked as much as I wanted, without anyone bothering me. I am the only guest at La Sapinière, and no one protested. Ah, France! Finally, a free country.

February 14. Yesterday evening at Roger Nimier's, I met Maria Casarès and Orson Welles.

I like Nimier very much. He is a young Frenchman, of an extraordinary and entirely new quality. His writings in *La Table Ronde* are cut by his intelligence as if by a razor. He has an acute gaze and lays out problems in the swift, precise, decisive manner of the French eighteenth century. Yet once the problem has been laid out, his entirely modern intelligence intervenes, cruelly and cynically. The problem dries out, becomes clear, blatant, like an insect pinned to the page.

With his acute, penetrating gaze, as if borne atop the two antennae of an insect, he touches the wings, the legs, the eyes, the ruffled hair on the head of the insect, cicada, butterfly, grasshopper, cricket.

Roger Nimier is certainly the most intelligent and the freest of the young French intellectuals, and also the liveliest. He possesses a quality that is lacking in much of the current generation in France. He has no respect for what I would call the tradition of pompous idiocy. I believe that, deep down, he has already gone beyond the rhetoric of resistance and collaboration.

Of course, he too runs the same risk as much of the bourgeois youth of France: fascism. It's undeniable that much of the youth is fascist. But in a French way, which is not the same as the Italian way, or the German. In less political words, to be fascist means to accept the formulas of national greatness at odds with the situation of modern man with respect to national greatness, just so. To realize that "glorious" Europe is over is already a sign of freedom, and of modernity. Man matters only as a human being, not as a Frenchman, Italian, German, or Englishman. Nimier laughs at everything. He has a way of laughing that reminds me of how the believer laughs at the atheist....

... Nor is it worth observing that in France, too, a good number of the communist intellectuals are fresh converts, or fakes, or hypocrites, who have followed the interest of the moment, or the fashion. Indeed, alongside the names of Aragon and Éluard, who passed from surrealism to communism, from communism to surrealism, and again from surrealism to communism during the war, there is the name, for example, of Claude Roy, who, prior to being elevated to the rank of communist poet, belonged to Action Française, and so was a monarchist and a reactionary, and during the war he was an important part of the collaborationist Radio-Vichy. The crisis, in the form of uncertainty, hesitation, and apathy, begins to seep into fellow travelers, generally recruited from among the aesthetes, such as the actor and mime Jean-Louis Barrault, the inverts (the number of inverts turned communists is enormous, in France as well), and second-rate intellectuals and artists, such as the playwright and Académie Goncourt member Salacrou.

What surprises me most about Soviet literature is the ingenuousness with which its writers show us man. Not humanity, not human life, but man, the individual, individual life. They are almost embarrassed whenever they find themselves needing to describe man's inner journey. Something has remained of the old obsessive introspection of authors like Dostoevsky or Tolstoy. But reduced to a schematic formula. The Western reader has the impression that the heroes of the Soviet novel proceed by fits and starts, just like the heroes of the American novel.

March 1. I go up to the top of Le Brévent. In the cable car the conductor asks me: "You're the Italian writer who's staying at Le Vieux Chalet, right?"

"Yes," I reply.

"How does it work in Italy?"

"Not too bad. More or less like here. There are strikes and riots, life is expensive, and chaos reigns. But it will pass. The Italian people have common sense. Just like the French people."

"Not that. I'd like to know how the cable cars work in Italy."

March 2, Chamonix. The source of French people's troubles is that they didn't use to take Europe seriously, and took France too seriously. Today their wretchedness derives from the fact that they take Europe too seriously, and don't take France seriously enough. It takes a foreigner to come and tell them: "You are a great people; you are still a great people. Aren't you ashamed to behave like you were a Balkan country after an invasion by the Turks?"

March 3, Chamonix. At the summit of Le Brévent I meet Gaston Bergery, skis over his shoulder, fair eyes narrowed against the sun's baked-honey brilliance.

As he puts his skis on he talks to me about Russia, which he knows quite well; about his stay in Moscow as French ambassador (I'm a foreigner, for me there is only one France, with due respect to those clever devils unwilling to acknowledge disinterest in these things); about the European situation; about the mood of the Americans.

He describes having lunch recently with some members of the United States embassy in Paris. These Americans were not charitable toward Roosevelt's memory. It seems the Americans are beginning to realize what an awful drama occurred at Yalta. The remarks these diplomats make about Roosevelt are such that Bergery says at a certain point, "Please, you're making me uncomfortable."

What occurred at Yalta is truly incredible. That sick man, his eyes already filled with night, his cheeks hollow, his hands trembling, is at the center of this awful drama that represents the delivery of Europe into the hands of the Russians, without any reason, without negotiation, without discussion—simply, it seems, because Roosevelt was sick, or mad.

I always enjoy considering how easy it is for a great man of state to be mad. The drama of Yalta is in the madness of Roosevelt, in his sudden weakness in front of Stalin, in his inconceivable optimistic faith in Communist Russia. It's at Yalta that Roosevelt not only sold Europe to Russia, but also betrayed America, put it in the situation it finds itself in today. I tell Bergery that I'm thinking of writing a play, *The Yalta Conference*.

But will anyone have the courage to put it on? Roosevelt, at Yalta, is a Shakespearean character: a king who, forgetting all the sacrifices made to save Europe, forgets everything, gives Europe away to the Russians, commits America, betrays Europe.

There is a photograph of Roosevelt at Yalta, seated between Churchill and Stalin in marshal's uniform. Roosevelt is wearing a black cloak; his gaunt white head stands out against the black. It's very strange and interesting, this about-face of American public opinion with regard to Roosevelt.

March 4. Dinner at the Rotary Club. The guests of honor were Arnold Lunn, creator of the greatest downhill ski race, the Kandahar, which will be run tomorrow and the following two days on the glaciers and Brévent pistes (with the slalom at Argentière); de Gignoux, secretary of the French Skiing Federation; and the French skiing champion James Couttet, the 1947 world champion;[1] and Oreiller, the 1948 world champion.

During the toasts, Arnold Lunn delivers some foul-tempered words. He's an Englishman of the same breed, I would say, as Norman Douglas, author of *South Wind*, one of the finest books in modern English literature. He speaks about skiing, about his idea for Kandahar. He's a sixtysomething Englishman with a red face and mocking eyes.

Then I stand up and speak about the race of Marxists that has invaded Europe. But I fear my idea is not understood. When you speak about Europe, the French always think you're speaking about France. They react as if you were speaking only about them. Nevertheless, this race of Marxists exists; nothing about it is comparable to the old race of Europeans. We are in a period of our history in which, under the influence of ideas, the new technology, the new economy, etc., etc., and of a new philosophy of life, the race of peoples is changing. It's like the time of the Gothic invasion. The Roman Empire is finished. The new races sprout from the trunk of the old races. They may be the same races, but how changed they are! Who would recognize, in the Po Valley farmer, the farmer of the age of Augustus? Even his language has changed. Nevertheless, he is still of the same stock.

Toasts are made to James Couttet, to Oreiller. I like the fine features of these Savoyard mountain men, their pure, calm eyes, their slow and profound gaze.

Yesterday, at the post office, I met two skiers from the Italian team, who are participating in the Kandahar. My heart leapt for joy at hearing the language of my country. They were two strong young mountain men from the north, one fair, the other dark, both timid, and kind in that Italian way that comes mostly from timidity. But how different they are from Couttet, from Oreiller, from these French mountain men from Val d'Isère, Megève, or Chamonix. Harder, with something brutal in their chin, their lips, their voice. What joy, even so, to see Italians again in the streets of Chamonix, in France, and to see them welcomed as friends, with a simple, touching warmth. The French are a gracious people. That's it: the French and the Italians suffer from the same embarrassment that at times makes them blush. But I would like the Italians, my Italians, to understand in coming to France that Italy has for some time been a cruel and unhappy country.

Breakfast this morning on Le Brévent with Bergery, the doctor Picaud, Gérard Simond. Picaud is a man of very great and very subtle intelligence. A modern Frenchman, clear and down-to-earth. We talk about Dr. Faltin, a Finn, whom he knows; about the hatred toward doctors in France. He talks about his mountains. He tells me that the valleys around Mont Blanc were invaded by Jews in the twelfth century. *Megève* means "bad Jew."

After the Rotary dinner the young architect Chevalier, son of General Chevalier, accompanies me out. He's a good Catholic, but has some sympathy for the race of Marxists. He's full of optimism.

March 4. Dr. Picaud says to me: "One looks at Mont Blanc as one would look at a dead man, a corpse. Only a doctor, accustomed to seeing dead men, can understand Mont Blanc, or the mountains. It's a corpse."

March 4. My American publisher, Dutton, telegraphs me from New York asking for the English-language rights to "your wonderful *The Skin*," of which he's read the chapters published in *Carrefour*.

This word *wonderful* in the mouth of a publisher restores my faith in my work. When I work, I'm at the mercy of everything. The least thing discourages me, robs me of all confidence. I tremble if some piece of news I read in the paper bothers me. For the whole day I'm no longer capable of working. A letter, a word, a line in a newspaper is enough. This sensitivity with regard to the outside world is nevertheless my whole strength.

How far I am from resembling the figure they make of me in France! They know nothing about me, and yet they say and write the most unbelievable things. At times I wonder if my success depends on the false idea that the public has of me. Do they have the same false ideas about Montherlant, about Cocteau, about Giono? I wonder. And what idea do they have of me, precisely? They take me for a collaborator, a friend to the Germans, a Nazi. What an idea! I can only laugh about this, and the Italians would laugh as well if they knew. I am neither a hero nor a martyr; I don't do politics. All my avatars are literary avatars. I was put in prison for literary, not political, reasons. They want to make me into a political figure, and clearly this doesn't square with me, and people don't understand anything anymore.

They don't want to understand that I am toward the antifascists what I was toward the fascists; that the reasons I despised the Nazis are the same reasons I despise the Russian Communists; that I have the highest contempt for politicians, of whatever party; that I'm interested only in ideas, in literature, in art. That I am a free man, a man above everything that stirs this poor mass of men.

As the first Italian writer to find success in France after the war, I am saddled with all the complaints they have against Italy, against Mussolini, against the Italian people, etc. There is nevertheless a clear wish to hear me say what I am. I won't say it. It's not worth the trouble. Let them think of me what they like; they won't think of me what they ought to. Essentially, this proves that for the French I am much more than a foreign writer. They would love it if I were French. They love what in me resembles some French defect or quality. There is love in this mania for painting me as different from what I am. They say to me: "These are the inevitable disadvantages of glory. It has always happened this way."

I think instead there is some secret worry in all this. The French are in search of new men. They would like for these new men to be French. They believe they are more down than they are. A curious error! Were not the French of the end of the reign of Louis XIV perhaps wrong when that wave of pessimism washed over France? I think that one of the deep, subconscious causes of the Revolution of 1789 was the French people's fear of falling short of what it was.

I find nevertheless that France is on its way to recovery. It will recover, despite everything. There is a kind of fear, dread, and pessimism in all *encyclopédistes*.

March 7, Chamonix. Sir Arnold Lunn, president of the Ski Club of Great Britain, asks me why I love Chamonix so much.

"I love Mont Blanc."

"Of course, but, really, you're not a great skier, you're not a great climber. So what do you do with Mont Blanc? Maybe you're writing a novel about Mont Blanc?"

"I wouldn't dream of it."

"And so?" says Sir Arnold Lunn.

"Mont Blanc," I tell him, "is my Ingres's violin."[2]

March 9. Skied Le Brévent. Without help. I don't know how to turn, or stop, or snowplow, or slalom.

I hear people say: "You're crazy, you're not capable of skiing a Le Brévent piste. The snow is nasty and wet. You'll hurtle down the famous 'wall' and break a leg, in the best of cases."

I take off all the same, with Gérard Simond, who, after the first fifty meters, well before arriving at the "breach," advises me to turn back. Indignant, I refuse. The snow is truly awful.

I pass through the "breach" and look down. I feel nauseated. Muckembrun, who was informed of my decision at Planpraz, and who has come up in the cable car, reaches me, wants to help me. His help refused, he yells. I yell back. He takes me by the arm; I wriggle free, furious. I shout at him to leave me in peace.

"You'll break your leg," he yells in his high-pitched voice.

I continue. It's very hard going for someone who doesn't know how to ski. From the top of the wall a group of students from the school in Les Praz watch me, stupefied. I take on the wall. I don't look down, because I didn't come here to feel nauseated, and the sight doesn't interest me. What interests me is doing the "wall." I fall, slide down under the eyes of the astonished students.

I stop because Muck has grabbed the end of one of my poles. I'm furious, I abuse him. Poor Muck. He goes away, followed by his dog Totou. Gérard is lower down, watching me. I do the wall.

A woman passes close to me. "Do I know this woman?" I ask myself. I've seen her somewhere. But where? I continue the descent. A woman passes close to me. "What the devil," I say to myself, "where have I seen this woman?" I'm now about a hundred meters from the famous grates, when a woman passes close to me. "But I know her," I say to myself. I address her, asking if we know each other. "Maybe in Paris."

"No, it's the fourth time I've descended Le Brévent, while you labor."

It's Countess de Voguë.

At last I arrive at Planpraz. Everyone is furious with me. But I've skied Le Brévent. In two hours and forty-five minutes. For the Kandahar, the record is two minutes and twelve seconds. Yes, but they were skiers. And finally, why not?

Monday, March 15, Paris. I search Italian literature in vain for a writer who can be compared to Gide. I don't find any. Maybe a Greek or two: there was surely a Gide in ancient Greece; but his name, his works, have disappeared.

This aridity and this rigor are above all Greek. His Protestant spirit is, too. And this anxiety, and this love of youth. And this curiosity, and this fear of man. It seems to me that nothing can better express the extent, depth, and scope of the disarray of intellectual France than Gide.

The Nobel Prize pays tribute to . . . what? His literary glory? His influence over the youth of Europe? His conduct during the war? The beneficent lucidity of his spirit faced with the cruelty of the times, of men, of war? I doubt it.

The cruelty of Gide is the same cruelty as that found in the actions of men, of Germans. It is an abstract cruelty, just like the cruelty of men, of Germans. Gide is not responsible for the cruelty that has raged in Europe for some years now, but he is one of its essential elements, perhaps its most representative.

The Gidean intellectual century's reaction to cruelty is absurd. Passivity, fear, confusion, compromises of every kind. The others, those who fought in the Maquis, in the camps, in the factories, they haven't read Gide and couldn't care less about him. But they have via other routes and other lessons drawn on the same source of cruelty as Gide has. The others—butchers, torturers, sadists—what is their cruelty, if not the same as Gide's? Intellectuals generally believe that things, the facts themselves, remain; they live in the domain of the intelligence alone. They believe that there is a world of reality, of life in common, and a world apart, of intelligence: the intellectual world. They do not know. (Goethe, he knew, and wasn't thrilled about it; indeed, he suffered from it.) They do not have the least doubt that what is intellectual for them is practical for others. A written page, a thought, or an attitude is of the same nature and sometimes of the same quality as the act performed, lived, suffered. Intelligence may have its privileges, but I doubt it. In the face of reality, of practice. There is in intellectuals of all times, even in classical times, a morbidity, even a sadism, that explains and justifies man's cruelty, his actions, his sadism. In modern times, intelligence's cruelty and morbidity are enormous.

And since we're on Gide, let's stay with Gide. He is certainly not responsible for what happened and is happening in Europe in terms of cruelty and sadism; he is one of its elements. His work, his lesson, and his example, too, explain everything that we have seen. We must be clear on this essential point: cruelty does not derive from a lack of respect for man or human life, from contempt for man. On the contrary, it derives from what I would call an abstract, intellectual conception of man.

The Ethiopians are not acquainted with torture; they are not cruel. They are free men, the freest of any men I've known. The director of the Asmara prison used to tell me, in 1939, about making it clear to the magistrates how useless it was to condemn Ethiopians to ten, twenty years for crimes that, prior to the Italian conquest, would have called for a fine. When they knew that an Ethiopian could not live in prison for more than six months at the most. The Ethiopian, deprived of his freedom, dies. Like a bird, like certain wild beasts. I see this freedom as being strictly connected with their complete ignorance of cruelty.

But freedom presupposes not an absolutely abstract concept of man, a pure concept, but a physical concept of the human being (or the opposite, for many?). Man is a living being, and when he is an enemy, it is necessary to take his life. That's it; as swiftly as possible. The Ethiopians cut off the heads of their enemies. (The Gallas, an inferior race, highly impure, which the Ethiopians disdain, cut off genitals and torture. But not the Ethiopians.) They don't torture. They don't understand torture, and what's more an Ethiopian will never talk simply on account of the fact, incomprehensible to him, that he is being tortured, that someone wants to make him talk by means of torture. From a moral point of view, the Ethiopians are a highly civilized people, more civilized than whites, than us. Cruelty is as foreign to them as any sort of metaphysics.

Let's return to Gide. His intellectualism, his morbidity, his cruelty, his aridity (like that of Montherlant, Proust, Kafka, Hemingway, Faulkner, Ernst Jünger, Moravia, the author of *Kaputt*, etc.) are the same as those at the origin of the acts of cruelty with which European history has been full for some years now.

We intellectuals are all more or less responsible for the cruelty that raged and still rages in Europe. André Gide more than any other, because his cruelty assumes a metaphysical aspect, a language accessible to all, especially to the young. It wasn't Gide who invented Gidean cruelty. It was, it is, in the air. All he did was give it its Gidean character; that is, its character of moral necessity. Gide is the high priest of a religion whose sacrificial altars are at Dachau.

March 22, Chamonix. Descending from Planpraz in the cable car, I meet a young French doctor, M. ———. I'm in the middle of telling Georgette M. about the dream I had the night before. The doctor explains the dream using a Freudian argument. We talk about the obsession with corpses that appears in nearly all my writings.

To be honest, this obsession appears in my writings only after my months in prison, my years of confinement. What happened to me, in prison or on Lipari, that drove me to express this obsession that has existed in me since my earliest childhood? Maybe having smelled for the first time, in prison, that corpse smell that every prisoner exudes from his poorly washed skin, from his underclothes, from everything he touches or wears on his person. In any case, it's a fact: in my entire literary oeuvre, save for a few pages in my first book, which is from 1921, the obsession with corpses does not appear.[3]

I explain this obsession with a childhood memory. Around the time of my birth, my mother was haunted by the suicide of her brother, who was mad and drowned himself in a river near Milan, the Lambro. Being pregnant with me, she was disturbed by this event, which caused her to fear the evil effects of heredity.

I was not a normal child, not like all the other children. I was timid, weak, dominated by my imagination, and morbidly sensitive. We lived in Prato, in a house on Via Magnolfi. When I was very small, two years old, I removed a brick from the floor of my bedroom. Having discovered some sand under the brick, I thought this sand was the beach. I would spend whole hours with my ear glued to this sand, to listen to the sea, the voice of the sea. My father bought me a shell, which I used to create the sea in my room, with objects that had nothing to do with the sea, or with the idea that a child has of the sea. My toys, too, were strange.

Chamonix. Françoise M. says to me, "There are people who reproach you for not having deserted the moment you stopped approving of the war. Why didn't you desert?"

I respond that what they reproach me for, at the end of the day, is not having done what Thorez did.[4] How many Englishmen, I ask her, deserted during the Boer War in order to fight with the Boers against the English? Men don't desert. It's too simple, too easy. I stayed, said what I thought, and was arrested and convicted during the war. What do they want from me?

Some of the criticism is quite amusing. I put that down not to the sectarianism raging in Europe, but to coarseness. There's no longer any sense of humor in Europe. In the next war, I will desert, agreed. I will go over to the enemies of my country, will fight with them against my country. But if the enemies of my country are also the enemies of civilization? Well, we'll figure that out later. The important thing is to desert. Right?

Chamonix. There is a kindness in the French people that the French themselves are unaware of. Only a foreigner can see it.

The French people does not love foreigners, but it helps them, welcomes them, gives them work, peace, and security, gives them a *home*. At the prefecture of police in Paris, foreigners are obliged to wait in line for entire days for a visa, a residency permit, an identity card. The officers push and insult them, the clerks bully them, and the poor foreigners feel humiliated, treated like lowlives. Eighty percent of these foreigners do not have their papers in order, do not have the right to live in France. But in the end they all receive their card or residency permit. The rank-and-file French clerk does not deny them what they seek, even if they have no right to it. Something that does not happen anywhere else in the world, except in Italy. In England, in America, etc., a foreigner is, alas, a foreigner. If he's not in order, nothing can provide him with what he seeks. Unless he's Jewish.

This kindness of the French should be praised, and proclaimed.

The Frenchman doesn't love foreigners, quite often with reason. But he helps them. He has a good heart. If a foreigner is a person of quality, if he is worthy of esteem, if he is honest, he quickly feels at home in France.

March 23, Chamonix. I sat on my doorstep from ten at night till two in the morning, barking with the dogs.

At this point they know me, they talk to me. Even Tommy, ——'s dog, who didn't want to respond to me, he knows me now, talks to me, responds to me.

The moon stood poised atop the Aiguille de Blaitière, and the snow had an astonishing transparency; the sky had the same transparency as the sea under the moon. The Aiguille du Midi and the Aiguille du Goûter were reflected in the soft green sky; the stars shone on the glaciers. The dreadful mountain had an astonishing transparency and lightness, as if made of some impalpable material, of sea foam, the same sea foam from which Venus sprung.

Seated on the doorstop of my house, I bark for a long time, and the dogs respond from here, from there, from the chalet above the *téléski*, from the farm before Les Plans: they are the dogs of Roger Demarchi, of Greppon the guide; Mireille and Diane, the dogs of Roger Demarchi's brothers, who live close to me, on the farm past the fountain in Les Plans. It's the dog of Gérard Simond, the beautiful and mad Tex, who responds to me from the Plans house, near the river. I know them all, one by one, and they all know me. They know my voice, and they respond to me; they talk to me. They understand perfectly what I say to them, because I know their language. It is my sole pleasure in life, to call out to dogs in the night, and to talk to them.

I learned how to talk to dogs on Lipari; I had no one but the dogs to talk to. I would go out at night on the terrace of my sad house on the sea, on the Salita di Santa Teresa, near the little church, beside the narrow little streets named Inferno, Diana, Mars, Pluto, Neptune, Proserpina, little streets with lovely ancient names. I would lean on the balustrade of the terrace and call out to Eolo, the brother of my dog Febo. I would call Vulcano, and Apollo, and Stromboli, all the dogs with ancient names; and Valastro's dog, Nicosia's dog, the dogs of my fishermen friends, who themselves have ancient names: Nicosia, Valastro, Amendola, Fenech; Greek names, Phoenician names. I would stay on the terrace for long hours, barking with the dogs, who would respond, and the fishermen of Marina Corta would call me "the dog." They complained to the carabinieri, and I was warned not to bark with the dogs in the night, because the fishermen were afraid to hear me barking with the dogs.

On Capri, too, I talk to the dogs of Matromania, who come to the top of Matromania at night to talk to me, and the inhabitants of Matromania call me mad. And when the Americans went ashore on Capri, they complained to the other Americans; the governor called me and asked if I was the one barking at night. I said yes, it was me. And the Americans warned me not to bark with the dogs in the night. But I complained to the English admiral Morse, who commanded the naval base on the island, and Admiral Morse told me: "You have the right to bark, if you like, because Italy is now free. There's no more Mussolini. You can bark."

In Paris, too, I barked with the dogs, from my terrace on Rue Galilée, but it wasn't the dogs who responded to me; it was the cats, the cat of my concierge, Madame Campio; the cat of the director of *France Dimanche*, M. Max ——, who lived across from me at no. 59; the owner of the Bar Triolet's cat, Corso; and the Hôtel —— cat and the one from Hôtel ——, and I had to stop talking to the cats in the language of the dogs, because the cats didn't want me to, and insulted me.

But here in Chamonix I can bark all night if I want, because the inhabitants are kind, they love dogs, and they know there is nothing that gives greater pleasure to a man who lives alone than barking with the dogs. Ruskin, too, when he stayed in Chamonix, barked with the dogs in the night. It's well known, in Chamonix, that foreigners like to bark in the night with the dogs.

Even so, yesterday evening the big sheepdog from the farm that lies above the cableway, near the rock Ruskin loved to sit on for long hours, gazing at the small glacier at the feet of the Aiguille de Blaitière ("at the feet of the Aiguille de Blaitière there is a small glacier that, in its beautifully curved outline, appears to harmonize with the rocks beneath"[5]), yesterday evening the big sheepdog, Tom, came toward me. I heard his voice come closer and closer, he was asking me, "What's wrong?" I replied that nothing was wrong, but he didn't trust me, didn't believe me, and so he came to see me. He approached me, sniffed me, sat down on the snow beside me, and together we called all the others, who responded from here and from there across the transparent night, in the glow of the wondrously pure snow.

For there is no purer pleasure than to bark with the dogs in the night, on a beautiful frozen night, illuminated by the gentle transparent brilliance of the snow.

March 23, Chamonix. A young North African Jew, F. J. Temple, writes me a charming letter from Montpellier, to tell me that he fought in Italy with the French troops under General Juin, that he is a writer, that he has read *Kaputt*, and that he is indignant about the inane rumors (which I instead find charming) that are circulated about me.

At the same time he sends me a collection of verse, published by Charlot, and a cutout of an article that he published many months ago in a Tangiers newspaper.

Some of the lines in the article made me laugh. "What could be more natural than that M. was acquainted with ambassadors, that he spent time with kings, knowing that the author of *Kaputt* was a diplomat"? Temple will never know how grateful I am to him for his lovely defense.

One day in 1923 I was invited to the Élysée by M. Doumergue, president of the Republic. He wanted to know me because, during his stay in Bordighera, in Italy, someone had told him about me and read him some pages of mine. Doumergue welcomed me with great kindness, in an all-red room. At a certain point he said to me, "I can only offer you a vermouth. I am not a king; the republican label compels my discourteousness. One day you will recount how a president of the French Republic told you there is nothing for a writer to write about a president. We are rather colorless characters. The French people does not like it when one stands out. It hates everything that does not resemble it."

"Monsieur le President," I replied, "the French people does not at all resemble you."

"Alas, yes. Kings are kings of an entire people, while a president of the Republic represents only the little people. And the small occasions. History escapes us."

March 23, Chamonix. Read Charles Du Bos's journal this morning, his conversations with André Gide, Paul Valéry, his trip to London and Stratford-upon-Avon, and his thoughts on Novalis. (In his journal, Novalis constantly reproaches himself for having eaten too much, and observes that overfeeding keeps him far from the thought of death.)

An odd juxtaposition of food and the idea of death. Is there an explanation here for the well-known fact that the idea of death is alien to the French, that reflection on death is a rare thing among the French?

A proposition of Spinoza's came to mind: *Homo liber de nulla re minus quam de morte cogitat, et ejus sapientia non mortis, sed vitae meditatio est,*[6] which made a great impression on me in 1909, during my convalescence from the illness that marked a turning point in my life.

Are the French, who never think of death, therefore free men? French civilization, from which any thought of death is carefully excluded, is a civilization of free men.

I closed Charles Du Bos's journal at the December 1923 page in which he talks about the fascination that the mineral realm held for spirits like Novalis and Gide, and proposes to link this notion to the notion of the crystal in Gide, and to show that in the prose of the early Gide and of Novalis their ideal is precisely that of a beautiful transparent stone.

March 24. Yesterday evening I picked up Charles Du Bos's journal again, at Wednesday, April 26, 1922, where he talks about Shakespeare and *All's Well That Ends Well*.

Referring to the character of Paroles (lines 110–115, spoken by Helen), he compares the attitude of the Englishman and the Frenchman toward cowardice and the cowardly man, and concludes his reflections with this note: "Life, in the eyes of the Frenchman of good breeding, is basically a value without purpose."

There is, in some Frenchmen of good breeding, as Charles Du Bos has it (some intellectuals, some writers especially), a kind of odd pessimism about the Frenchman, about his destiny, about his "position in life"—his position in creation, I would almost say—that never ceases to amaze me. It is, I want to say, the pessimism of Gide, of Montherlant, of Giraudoux too, notwithstanding his words—constantly repeated, pronounced, declaimed—of joy and faith in the Frenchman.

What does Du Bos mean to say with those words, that "life, in the eyes of the Frenchman of good breeding"—I think that "of good breeding" means here a Frenchman who is right wing, well mannered, cultured—"is basically a value without purpose"? Since he is writing these words about Paroles, about the attitude of the Frenchman toward cowardice, toward the cowardly man and his desire to live, to flee ("the Frenchman dumps the coward in an instant: this is part of the intransigence and the beauty of his code of honor"), I am led to conclude that Du Bos means to say that life, for the Frenchman of good breeding, is worth less than honor, that it is without value when it is necessary to sacrifice it for the sake of honor. But then, why "a value without purpose"? Does France's decadence perhaps depend on the fact that the Frenchman of today sees a "purpose" in life? That he, in other words, becomes a Paroles, a coward, someone who clings to life?

I believe the key point lies elsewhere, and think I will return to this topic, which consumes me. Because all of man lies in the purpose-value he assigns to life, and nowhere else.

March 24, Chamonix. M. Cachat, owner of the Hôtel de la Sapinère, came to ask me not to bark with the dogs at night anymore, because his guests can't sleep. They're afraid. They say that I must be mad, or have rabies. M. Cachat is very sorry to have to tell me this, but someone might complain about me at the town hall, and the town council could order that I undergo the Pasteur treatment.

"The injections are very painful," M. Cachat says to me.

"But I don't have rabies," I say.

"I know that you don't have rabies, but my guests want to sleep."

"And if I were a dog, a real dog? Would they complain?"

"No," M. Cachat replies, "clearly not. But they know that you are not a dog and are afraid to hear you barking like a dog."

"I am free to bark at night if it pleases me. I don't do anyone any harm. Tell your guests that I am a real dog, and this will reassure them."

"Oh, no," M. Cachat replies, shaking his head, "Oh, no. I fear you're going to have trouble."

"I won't have any trouble, M. Cachat."

For a little while I won't bark, but in a few days I'll start again. It's my only pleasure in life, barking with the dogs at night. M. Cachat went away shaking his head. His shoes on the snow make a sweet sound, like the steps of the fox that I heard in Crans this winter, from my terrace at the Pas de l'Ours.

Thursday, March 25, Chamonix. The full moon on the mountain. I think about Chateaubriand, this writer of the full moon, who—along with all his disciples, past and present, even the unwitting ones—could see nothing but "moonbeams," but "a sea of diamonds and sapphires" (book VIII, chap. 7).[7]

I read Chateaubriand, his pages on America and the American man, who seems to have "the mission of discovering other universes rather than creating them." Despite everything, a modern Frenchman. His notes on the Americans. On American literature, and on this eighteenth-century writer Brown, son of Puritans, author of the novel *Wieland*, which, according to Chateaubriand, is without a doubt the father of the American novel, up to Dreiser's *An American Tragedy*.[8] Wieland, the hero of the novel, is a Puritan whom heaven has commanded to kill his wife. "I've been brought here," he tells her, "to carry out God's orders: by my hand you must perish";[9] and he seizes her arms. She lets out several piercing screams, and wants to break free: "Wieland, am I not your wife? and you want to kill me! kill me, me! oh! no! oh! mercy, mercy!"[10] As long as she has breath, so she begs for help and mercy. Wieland strangles his wife and experiences ineffable delights beside her "expired corpse" (book VIII, chap. 6). That expired corpse is fascinating. Elsewhere, a good definition of Ronsard, "that old poet adopted by the new school" (book VIII, chap. 5).

Relationship between the art of Chateaubriand and that of Delacroix. How much does French painting, up to the impressionists, owe to Chateaubriand. At Gérard's this evening. The night so clear, the full moon on the Aiguilles, the ineffable lightness and transparency of Mont Blanc, of the Dôme du Goûter, of the Bossons Glacier. Mont Blanc, under the moon, another quality of sky, a sky made from another material.

March 26. Read Chateaubriand. "It was among the ranks of those already proscribed that I was hastening to establish myself; others might perhaps have backed away, but the greatest threat always makes me join the weakest side: to me the victor's pride is insufferable." The lovely portrait in Chateaubriand of his wife, who "has advanced, barren and solitary, toward old age." How a fine phrase can improve the portrait of a man or a woman. Better than a ringlet, a pair of pretty eyes, or a beautiful dress! Passage from book IX, chap. 2 (the end).

April 25. At Royaumont with Padre Bianchi, a Franciscan, professor of theology at the Catholic university of Milan, Bompiani, and Tamburi. Padre Bianchi is a man of great culture. He says things like, "Grace is something that holds no interest for me. I couldn't care less. I want to be saved without the need for grace. Every night I strip myself of everything, I free myself. And every morning I have to recharge. At night I unload. The morning is a reconquest of my faith across the entire day." He says, "Animals are a testament to the animosity that arose between God and men," and explains how, through sin, Adam lost dominion over the animals, over nature. Animals are therefore a testament to this diminishment of man.

April 25. The landscape of the Île-de-France cannot, in my mind, be disassociated from horses and from French painting. It is a landscape, like that of Tuscany, "tied" to painters. The design of the branches that hide beneath the leaves of the trees, of the hills beneath the grass, of houses beneath the color blots of roof and walls, is the same design that hides beneath the leaves, the grass, the red and the white and the green and the blue in painting from Watteau to Manet.[11]

April 26, Paris. We talk about a painter friend of ours. I say: "He's a modern man at any rate, apart from his painting, from what he achieves in his painting." The painter Orfeo Tamburi is less indulgent. He says: "He's a failure manqué."

April 29, Paris. Dinner this evening at the painter Léon Gischia's, with the director Vilar and his wife.[12]

Gerry Gischia is wearing a pretty dress that combines the classic black satin bodice with a tartan skirt. I like her way of opening her eyes wide and smiling, as if something surprising, something astonishing, has struck her.

Vilar's wife is blond, gentle, quiet, the very picture of Shakespeare's "sweet silence." Vilar is young and intelligent.

We understand each other immediately when Gischia asks if I am a Marxist and I answer: "Yes." He understands me perfectly when I say there is a somber beauty in Marxism that fascinates me. I love solitary men. What human solitude there is in Marxism! What despair of the solitary man! Men alone, without God, without friends, without love. We all live in Marxism, even those who are unaware of or fight against Marxism. Gischia is one of the most modern and intelligent men I have met in France. His intelligence is modern not just in the sense of current, but in the sense of reconnecting *Das Da* to what is our past, to what will be our future. He has an uncommon power of understanding.

We talk about the Italian painter Filippo de Pisis, who is in Paris at the moment. I describe for them Ferrara, the city where De Pisis was born, the palazzo his family lived in, the streets that are big, wide, and straight, or slightly curved like Corso Giovecca, the better to display the facades of the palazzi. We find ourselves all in agreement in speaking well of De Pisis, something that doesn't happen often, and makes us laugh. I say: "De Pisis will end up murdered in some debauched crime. I can read his destiny in his face. For that matter, he himself knows he'll end up like that: murdered by a criminal lover."

During dinner we talk about painting, about literature, about the astonishing age in which we live, so suited to research. We talk about Malraux, about his book *The Psychology of Art*. I don't much like the book, which Gischia instead finds admirable. (It's the same word that Emmanuel Berl uses in his *Culture en péril*.) It's a disquieting book, but of a disquiet that is not that of the artist confronting the problems of art. I sense there a disquiet of a nonartistic nature: more moral than artistic. We talk about Fougeron, about his new style, begun upon his return from Italy.

We talk about Stendhal's utter incomprehension of Italian art. Gischia thinks there are only two admirable books on art: Stendhal's and Malraux's. The painter Tamburi agrees with me. Stendhal did not understand Italian art, whereas he wonderfully understood the character of Italians.

We talk about Antonin Artaud, of his death, in that "shitty play where only the fire is alive" (I cite Artaud's own words to —— in *La Table Ronde*). Vilar talks about modern French theater, about *Dirty Hands* by Sartre, about Barrault, whom he admires.

Gischia tells us about André Spire, the old poet who has just married a young woman. The day his previous wife died, his friends found him in a pitiable state. "Look at the state I'm in. To me she was more than a friend, more than a collaborator. What will I do without her? She was everything to me. Look, look at the state she left my work-table in. All these announcements! How will I manage to fill in the addresses? Oh, if only she were here!"

This reminds me of a little story about the siege of Paris in 1870. A gentleman had eaten everything—mice, the house cat, the last of the provisions. All that was left was Fido, his dog. He decided to sacrifice Fido. He killed him, put him in a pot, and invited some relatives over for the occasion. During the meal, seeing the bones of the poor dog mounting on the plates, his master exclaimed in tears: "Ah, all these bones . . . If only poor Fido were here, how happy he would be!"

We talk about Manessier, whom Gischia admires; about his probity, his hard life. We talk about Caputo, his gallery, the sacrifices he makes. Gischia talks about Provence, about Cannes, where he would like to live his whole life; about the Estérel Massif, the orange colors of the rocks that face Agay, the red color of the rocks that face Anthéor. Gischia and Tamburi lament to each other, with little cries of pain, about the impossibility of rendering those black clouds that, at certain hours of the day in summer, weigh heavily on the dark purple, almost black, sea; about this anxiety, tragic nature, the beauty of nature. Gischia describes the area of Provence around Aix-en-Provence: "After —— you enter the land of Cézanne, the paintings of Cézanne. The sky is pure, the perspectives are crisp, the background is not, so to speak, detached from the foreground; these are not the foggy, cottony perspectives of the north, of Holland, Flanders, or even the Île-de-France."

We talk about Avignon, which I know so well.

June. I read an interview with Moravia that he gave to Malraux, in an Italian newspaper. It's rather banal and, like everything Moravia writes, extremely cautious, owing perhaps to the political position assumed by Malraux in recent times.

I've often wondered why I don't feel the need to become better acquainted with the Malrauxs, or the Sartres, or so many others who honor not only French but also European letters today. And perhaps it comes from the instinct for what is false with respect to all men, and especially to foreigners, in the attitudes assumed by a Malraux or a Sartre.

My encounter with Malraux goes back to 1931. In the fall of that year I was living in Daniel Halévy's beautiful house at 38 Quai de l'Horloge. One Saturday afternoon, Daniel Halévy telephoned to invite me to join him, to meet Gabriel Marcel, Malraux, Aron, Dieudonné, and the young Ferrero. To get to Halévy, I had to go down the Quai de l'Horloge, turn the corner at Madame Roland's house, enter the Place Dauphine, and cross the threshold of no. 27 in that same square. So I go down and head toward the Pont Neuf. As I come to the tobacco shop at the corner, a taxi pulls over to the curb. A tall, thin young man, his face covered with tiny red dots, gets out, turns to me, and asks with a half distracted, half imperious air, "if I could give him twenty francs." I rummage in my pocket and hand over a twenty-franc note. The stranger takes the money and, without even thanking me, hands it to the driver, who, after having counted out the change in his hand, hands him the change. I'm waiting at the edge of the sidewalk. The stranger pockets the change and, without a word of thanks, or a smile, or deeming me worthy of a glance, walks away. Amused, I step into the tobacco shop and buy cigarettes, then head toward the Place Dauphine and enter at no. 27.

I climb the stairs and enter the home of Daniel Halévy, who, coming forward and greeting me, introduces me to Gabriel Marcel and the others. Coming to a tall, thin young man I recognize as the twenty-francs man, Halévy says to me, "And this is Malraux." The twenty-francs man greets me in that moment as if he were seeing me for the first time in his life, and asks me a few very polite questions. I stayed at Halévy's until around eight, talking at length with Gabriel Marcel, André Spire, and Malraux himself, who did not say a word to me about those twenty francs, and who left without even thanking me.

How, then, could I pay a visit to Malraux today? I would have the appearance of going to ask him for my twenty francs.

June 9. Mme Cli Laffont has invited me to dinner at her house this evening, to meet Albert Camus.

It's hot out. Paris is wrapped in a shroud of heat that lifts the houses into midair, like in Chagall's dreams.

Mme Véra Korène is expecting me in the bar at the Plaza, to introduce me to some of the Brazilian friends she met during her long and painful exile in Rio de Janeiro. Her Brazilian friends are tall, thin, sleek young women with incredibly small round heads. They have very small noses, eyes larger than life, high and narrow foreheads, very narrow mouths, transparent ears, skin coated with that dull splendor that faces have under the moon. They move slowly, lazily; move their arms or turn their back by swiveling their chest, their head immobile, with the lazy litheness of reptiles. Amid that group of young and very beautiful women, women of strange beauty, Véra Korène looks like a Doric column. She reminds me of a solitary column at Delphi, in the white light of Delphi. Véra's voice is very beautiful, the most beautiful voice in Europe. She calls to me from afar, smiling, her mouth slightly open. Beside her, nearly hidden by the very beautiful Brazilians, is a prince of Braganza, I don't know which, or why he's there: pleasant, smiling, discreet, timid. I've always had the impression, face to face with this species of young and very beautiful women, that they have genitals in their armpits. When they raise their arms, through the black tuft gleams something rosy, deep, and moist that makes me blush, makes me dizzy. I notice that they're upset by my gaze, which slips insistently to the hollow beneath their arms. But I'm upset as well, by possessing them all there, in public, in the bar of the Plaza. There's one, sad and mean, with her eyelashes half lowered, who looks at me with insistence, leaning an elbow on the bar, a glass clutched in one slight fist, the other arm resting along her body. I say to Véra: "I like that girl. Why don't you ask her to raise her arms?" The girl smiles, and slowly, staring at me through half-lowered eyelashes, slowly raises an arm. I have never seen a woman spread her legs with such wickedness. Something rosy, deep, and moist appears among the curly, glossy black tuft. Smoothing her hair against her neck with one hand, she stares, smiling. I say to Véra, "Let's get out of here."

It was already late and Véra hailed a taxi, running after it along the sidewalk for a long stretch. I jumped in the taxi and saw Véra standing at the edge of the sidewalk, solitary and mild. When I got to Cli Laffont's, Albert Camus was already there, seated on a sofa between two young women. I immediately noticed that he was looking at me with hate. He had an unremarkable tie and an unremarkable hate. I immediately strove not to judge him by his tie, but by his books. Not to pay him back in his own coin. I am always sorry to encounter incomprehension, hate, sectarianism. I always strive not to put myself on the same level as someone who stands before me on spurious grounds.

I did not and do not have, nor will I ever have, any reason to hate or disdain a man and a writer like Albert Camus; I have many reasons to be fond, to esteem, and to be grateful for the author of *L'Étranger* and *La Peste*. And it doesn't matter to me in the slightest if he doesn't love me, doesn't esteem me, and perhaps hates me. It's his business.

I was persuaded, in that moment, that he had nothing better to do than look at me with hostile eyes. I had been told he had no affection for me, and that surprised me, coming from a writer like Camus; it seemed to me not worthy of a man of talent to judge a man without knowing him. For this reason, maybe, I went to him with the unconscious aim of winning him over. I was surprised not only that Camus made no impression on me, but that I didn't feel inclined to win his affection.

I recall that, at a certain point, someone having asked me what kind of man was Bottai, the former Fascist minister, etc., Camus said sententiously that such men should be dragged before a court, and then shot. I didn't like this brisk manner of understanding justice, and I asked Camus what made him think Bottai should be shot. Camus, without looking at me, replied that all these men, assassins, etc., should be shot. I replied that not only was Bottai no assassin, he was in fact quite incapable of hurting a fly. But I understood very well that Camus wanted to imply that I too should be shot. This absurd idea made me laugh, coming from a man like him. And I was astonished to see how casually many people judged others without knowing them. I would have liked to respond that, if he wanted to shoot Bottai, let him first try to shoot the many Bottais that exist in France as well. But I kept quiet, not seeing a need to give weight to the words of a man who spoke under the influence of a preconceived hostility, and just to give himself the air of a Saint-Just.

For the entire evening Camus behaved like a man deeply offended by I don't know what, and I thought that that behavior failed to impress even the ladies, and that it was proof of scant intelligence. But since Camus is an intelligent man, I could not attribute such willful severity to anything but a desire to appear pure, intransigent, heroic, resolute, severe, a ridiculous desire if that's what it was. Etc., etc., etc., etc. I would have understood Camus wanting to shoot Bottai, if the latter had been a writer, it being the deep-seated wish of every writer to have other writers shot. But Bottai is not a writer; therefore, he could not provoke a shred of jealousy in a Camus. I thought that Camus, as a writer, wanted to shoot everyone who wasn't a writer, and this idea also seemed strange to me, because we would before very long find ourselves living in a world without any writers, without anyone who wasn't a writer, populated only by a Camus resplendent in his unique, solitary glory. But I abandoned this idea as well, as preposterous. And I concluded that perhaps Camus was alluding to me, only to me, out of jealousy as both a man and a writer. Now, I am a puny writer in comparison with a Camus, and as far as male jealousy goes, I am not such an Apollo as to compete with a Camus. And I settled on the idea that Camus wanted to have me shot to prove to himself his capacity for heroic acts, etc. And I imagined the scene: me blindfolded, tied to a chair or a stake, and Camus alone before me, with a rifle in his hand, a steady gaze, an expressionless face, a bare head. I pictured him taking aim for a long time, squeezing the trigger, and missing the target. And then I would have gotten to my feet, and I would have said to him, etc.

I saw Camus in that heroic attitude that evening, and so I will always see him: armed and alone, ready to shoot a man whom he didn't know, a man who had never done him any harm and who in terms of fashionable rhetoric found himself in much better conditions than him. And I wonder what the hell Camus ever did to have the right to shoot others.

June 10. I am more and more convinced that I prefer real collaborators to fake resistants.

June 15. The image that the French have of themselves is substantially right; namely, as a cultured, refined people, ambitious and in love with glory, without which Europe would be greatly diminished. But what surprises me is what the French believe foreigners think of them. Let's set aside the various foreigners among whom France recruits such a wide clientele: the Romanians, the Greeks, those from the Balkan peninsula, the Jews of Eastern Europe—their judgment is of no importance. Nor let us look to the judgment made by simple folk, foreign peasants, and the peoples that cannot compete with France in terms of civilization and refinement. The simple folk have always considered the French an extraordinary, almost superhuman people, certainly very different from other peoples. I don't know how this idea was born, or why. I know that the Italians, for example—and

I'm talking about the common people here—imagine the French as both fierce and chivalrous soldiers, because what lives on in the people is the memory of the French military invasions, from Charlemagne on. Along the road traveled by Charlemagne to have himself crowned emperor in Rome, in the year 800, still live on poetic legends of that journey, about the grace, strength, magnanimity, and Christian faith of the Carolingian knights. Many of the legends born in the Ardennes Forest were transplanted to Italy, especially to the Spoleto countryside, etc.

June 20. I have not seen Jean Cassou since 1932, on the day before my arrest and sentencing to Lipari.

Then too, Cassou seemed to me what he would later be revealed to everyone as, a man full of a deep and stubborn and savage feeling for life, a writer almost dissatisfied and disgusted by his own profession as a writer, and yet always a *letterato*, a man of letters, and nothing but a *letterato*. Jean Cassou's passage from literature to action does not seem to me to be merely the product of some injury to national feeling, of some injury to a sense of justice and freedom, but almost the revenge of the man against the *letterato*—a natural consequence, because I have always thought and still do that those who pass from action to literature are as dangerous to peoples, and to peoples' freedom, as those who pass from literature to politics are salutary. (No, if anything, the opposite is true.)

It is now very difficult for me to say the good things I've always thought about Jean Cassou, then as now. Since he has become a hero, a representative of the current rhetoric, praising him would appear to me like an act of sycophancy or opportunism. Those who know me—and my entire life proves it—know that I am generally led by my demon to react to the prevailing rhetoric, to the heroes of the moment, to the powerful. All the more so as I believe in noble sentiments only before they become rhetoric; and if it seemed to me right to fight the Germans and the Fascists when they were powerful, today I cannot bear the rhetoric that has been made of the struggle against the Fascists and the Germans, and above all I disdain those who have turned their participation in that struggle into a profitable occupation, and the sole reason for their existence. But Jean Cassou I knew before, I had good relations with him, and no one will believe that I am sycophant if I praise him today, as I praised him twenty years ago. I have no need of Jean Cassou or anyone else, nor does he have any need of me, and I have no idea what my sycophancy could consist of. All the more so as my status as a foreigner relieves me of the obligation to pay compliments or to accept the rhetoric of the French.

I say here once and for all that when I speak well of someone, I do so without calculation, not concerning myself with anyone, needing no one, and well aware that if I needed someone, no one would help me, much less those whom I've spoken well of. This being part of human nature and not just that of the French, who, if anything, in their deep disdain for foreigners, are immediately led to abandon them as soon as these people find themselves needing them. I'm saying, then, that I met Jean Cassou several times, at Grasset's, when he was reviewing proofs of his *Grandeur et infamie de Tolstoï* (Bernard Grasset, 1932), and that my immediate impression was of a man deeply frightened by the new obligations of our time.

August 23, Royaumont Abbey. Last night I strolled in the gardens for an hour with Gadoffre. It was close to midnight; the moon turned the tree leaves pale, almost transparent, turned the sparkling grass to glass.

Gadoffre is a fascinating man. He has that blend of timidity and intellectual confidence that I like so much in the French. As far as what he knows is concerned, he never expresses doubts. He is confident about what he knows. He's a Cartesian (like all Frenchmen, alas!) and has written very sharp, very astute pages on Descartes. I speak to him—with a certain prudence, because I know that I am touching on a *punctum dolens* of French sensitivity—about my idea that Descartes was a catastrophe for France, that Cartesianism is France's weakness. It has robbed the French of all naturalness, all spontaneity, all imagination; made them a people of reasoners, dry, arid, without imagination, without instincts, a prey to reason. The current weakness of France is due to the fact that it finds itself in the midst of peoples gifted with great imagination, whose subconscious life is very active, and predominant, and this in an age in which the subconscious and the irrational play such a large part in man's activity, in his intellectual speculation, in his practical life, in his actions, even in his politics. That Cartesianism constitutes nothing more than a method of studying things, of studying life (and not of understanding it)—this is something a Frenchman will never accept.

Gadoffre defends Descartes with the intelligence, subtlety, and tenacity that are typical of the French. He makes no concessions, because he senses very clearly that France's entire defense is there, in Cartesianism.

I ask him why Descartes had the sensation of advancing into an enemy field = *larvatus prodeo*. Why the need to conceal his face? Why this consciousness of being dangerous, of being an enemy? Descartes transformed the French like Dr. Arnold (with his English school reform around the middle of the nineteenth century) transformed the English. To me Descartes represents the eternal French effort to take over for the "reform," for the Protestant revolution, to take control of the great movement of European liberation that was the Reformation, without, however, repudiating Catholicism, or what the French call Catholicism.

Gadoffre doesn't follow me, demonstrating to what extent Cartesianism has killed all intuition among the French. He seeks to reconcile Descartes and Bergson, just as Maritain will always seek to reconcile Descartes with Catholicism, an effort that to me seems hopeless.

August 26, 1948, Royaumont Abbey. France is not a Catholic country. I strolled in the gardens all afternoon, then I ventured into the forest, sat down beneath Saint Louis's oak, beside the pond. No, France is not a Catholic country. Italy and Spain are the sole Catholic countries in

Europe, countries in which Catholicism has persisted in all its strength and preserved all its irrational elements. Cartesianism and everything that derives from it, all the way up to Port-Royal, Jansenism, and the modern Catholic writers (so subtle, so nearly not Catholic), have made French Catholicism the substitute for the Reformation.

Descartes and Luther—here is the Reformation in Europe. For me, the turning point in French history should be located in the reign of François I, in his wars against Charles V. That's the moment when France missed the opportunity to place itself at the head of the great movement of European liberation (the Reformation). Henry IV got it right. The Edict of Nantes is proof of it. It was Louis XIV who tore up the Edict of Nantes, who abandoned forever the French ambition to take charge of the Reformation in Europe. Since then, Cartesianism has been a last resort, pointing up the failure of French ambitions for hegemony over the continent, *which can only be Protestant.*

What is the point of Cartesianism in a Catholic country? The question might seem useless, but it's not. Cartesianism is the substitute for the Reformation in France. It has profoundly transformed French Catholicism, so different from true Catholicism, which consists in the rational explanation of mysteries, whereas Cartesianism is the method for explaining through the power of reason not mysteries but the phenomena of the perceptible world, of the world of reason. Cartesianism has carried away every element of magic from the French spirit, from French life.

October. The only free peoples are those whose intelligence is not very developed. For example, ——. If the —— were more intelligent, they would not be free. The idea of freedom is a primordial idea, an extremely simple idea. It is intelligence that corrupts this primordial idea. The foolishness of a people is the best guarantee of its freedom.

"We English," says the young Lord ——, who was sitting across from me, beside the old marchioness of F——, "are not fools. And yet we are free."

"You have spent, or squandered, all your foolishness," says M——, "in order to become free. And now you are squandering all your intelligence in order to lose your freedom."

The French, and the Parisians above all, are too intelligent. It's what threatens their freedom's future. One can become a slave to the idea of freedom. That's what happened to the French after 1789. There is no bigger slave than the French people. Because to be a slave to the idea of freedom does not leave an intelligent people any choice but slavery, etc.

"Only foolish peoples are free, then?" says M. Crock.

"Imbeciles and savages."

"Thankfully," says M. F., "we're neither one nor the other."

"You've come up with a very pretty play on words," says the marchioness of F——.[13] "We will all become free, if we go on like this."

October 12.[14] Lunch with Melchior de Polignac at the —— Club, with France, Henry Muller, and Bisquant. I had had a glass of champagne earlier at Polignac's, on Avenue George V. One gaffe after another. Champagne, in the morning, goes right to my head. Gaffe with Deloffre, gaffe with Mme Fernandez. While at the table I describe a conversation with Pope Pius XI, Achille Ratti, a man of good sense who was very fond of me. When, in 1920, I was a young attaché at the Italian embassy in Poland, I regularly visited the Apostolic Nunciature, whose head at the time was Monsignor Achille Ratti, the future pope. His Holiness would talk about Protestants with gruff bonhomie. "Protestants," he said to me, "are the Church's Trotskyists."

October 21. Those who say to you, "Europe is finished, America will be the Europe of the future," are like those who used to say, "Argentina will be the Spain of the future."

October 23. There are those who say to you, "Europe will be to America what Greece was to Rome after the Roman conquest of the Hellenic world. It will be nothing but a set of poor, decadent, refined peoples, without strength, in full moral and intellectual decline."

I concede, with many reservations, that America is Rome. But I propose: "Nothing is less certain than that the Hellenic world, after the Roman conquest of Greece, fell into the greatest moral and intellectual decadence. All of Christian Europe, the entire Christian civilization of Europe, has its origins in the Hellenic world, in the Hellenic culture that followed the Roman conquest. Alexandria was the intellectual center of the ancient world. During the entire Roman Empire—that is, during the five centuries of the Pax Romana—the culture was Greek, and the civilized world's centers of religious, philosophical, artistic, and scientific high culture were scattered within the historical bounds of the Hellenic world. After the Roman conquest, during the centuries of the so-called decadence of the Greeks, the civilization was Hellenic. Greece went through a very serious economic, political, military, and social crisis, one resembling in many aspects the crisis that Europe is going through at this moment (Rome = America, Russia = Persia), but, from an intellectual point of view, Greece was at the head of the civilized world. I wish Europe a similar future: the destiny of Europe has always been and always will be—independently of the fact that other continents are richer and materially and politically stronger—to be at the head of civilization."

November 6. I leave the bar at the Crillon around midnight, having slept there peacefully for an hour. I like to sleep in the bar at the Crillon; I can't sleep in my bed. The hour I sleep at the Crillon makes me happy. It's raining. At the corner of Rue Boissy d'Anglas and Rue du Faubourg Saint-Honoré, a young woman approaches me and asks if I want to buy some American cigarettes.

"For how much?" I ask.

"Come to my place, I don't have them here. We'll work out a price."

I politely refuse, but she insists. I politely bid her farewell and continue on my way. She follows me, step for step. Suddenly she touches my arm and says to me in a low voice, "How foreigners have changed! They don't love France anymore."

"Excuse me?"

"You're a foreigner, aren't you?"

I reply that I am.

"You don't have a foreign accent," she says to me, "but I realized you were a foreigner. You're nice to whores."

So this is what the condition of foreigner has been reduced to.

November 12.[15] Parisians accept strikes in a way completely different from how they used to.

For Parisians in the past, everything was an excuse to laugh. The natural cheerfulness of the little people, with their childlike spirits, their spontaneous laughter, their easy pleasures, would not be upset by any social unrest or workers' struggles. Between the Parisians and the strikers (by *Parisians* I mean the mass of the population, especially that of the lower classes) there once reigned a type of accommodating solidarity, based, as it were, on the politeness of the strikers and the smiling goodwill of the Parisians. One got the impression that the Parisians, while remaining indifferent to the problems caused by social struggles, understood the workers' reasons and supported them with their friendly attitude.

Then, according to what I've been told, during the time of the Popular Front, things deteriorated: the strikes took on the character of social hatred; the Parisians began to grumble; the smiles disappeared from the crowds' lips.

I wasn't in France in those years, I was on the island of Lipari; all I knew of France was the news I got from my Paris friends. But what I see today is truly sad. The faces are sad, the lips mute. This dirty, poorly dressed, poorly fed crowd submits to the strike with fierce detachment, almost with a kind of silent, bleak despair. There is something of the Turkish crowd in this Parisian crowd. The passivity of the Oriental crowds of Smyrna, of Constantinople, this passive acceptance of everything that happens, and which I would like to characterize not as the religious fatalism of the Muslims, but as the fatalism of peoples who no longer live in history. It is clear by now that, since 1918, this historical fatalism, in the Turkish crowds, exceeds Muslim fatalism.

Paris is a Turkish city; France is the Turkey of the West. Turkish crowds are not noisy or restless; they flow past a bit preoccupied, in silence, with just a high-pitched murmur that is the same as that of the Parisian crowds during these days of strikes.

I return home, open *Persian Letters* and the fables of Gasparo Gozzi. The Orient, as it was imagined by Montesquieu, Gasparo Gozzi, or Voltaire, was a very Parisian Orient. Constantinople was a sort of Paris where the *élégants* and the *précieuses* were replaced by eunuchs and odalisques. The harems resembled a sort of literary salon where one discussed politics, society scandals, gossip, or literature, drank coffee or ate Turkish delight. The fact is that, in the eighteenth century, the Orient, even though in full decadence, still believed itself to be living in history, still had a sense of history. The Orient was alive. Let us go to the Orient these days. It's still Paris, but outside history, with crowds resigned to never again playing any historical role. I mean that Paris, like a large part of Europe, is now undergoing the crisis that the Orient underwent in its time, that of passing from the living and acting world of history to the bleak, passive, resigned world of historical fatalism. Europe, it's clear, is in the midst of becoming a great Levantine land, minus the sun and azure sky.

Does the political character of these strikes escape the Parisians? No. Do they know that these strikers are, perhaps unconsciously, the instruments of the enemy, of the foreigner? No. But the French people already accepts the next defeat, the next invasion, the next tyranny. It has not, as certain people believe, given up on Europe. It has, on the contrary, resigned itself to being just one of the many tribes of Eastern Europe. It agrees to submit to the history of Europe; it no longer wants to determine it. What the French people needs if it is to continue in its role as a great people is not only the material means but above all the moral strength.

The French people is ill with what I would call the disgust of history. There is no longer any solidarity between Paris and the strikers, just a sort of resigned complicity. No fraternity in misfortune and suffering, just resignation in the face of violence and others' poverty. I want to say what I think here, and I will say it bluntly. Paris is once again a city occupied by an enemy army, a foreign army. It's as if the Germans, instead of occupying Paris with their troops, had mobilized an army of workers, of unemployed Parisians. There is, somewhere in Paris, a *Kommandantur* heading up this occupation. But this is not a German *Kommandantur*. I walk through this crowd that jostles me in silence, without even looking at me. I have the impression of being a Frenchman lost in a crowd of foreigners.

November 13. How filthy the Parisian crowd has become! This is not just the filth of poverty, it's the filth of moral abandonment, of despondency. Taking the Métro or roving the sidewalks of Rue de Rivoli, of the Grands Boulevards, of the Champs-Élysées even, or in the movie houses, you get the impression that this crowd has forgotten about soap.

When I say filthy, I mean filthy. This is not the filth of Naples, the filth of the saddest and most abject poverty. It's the filth of the crowds of Moscow, the filth of this new "Marxist race" that has invaded Europe over the past ten years or so. At any hour of the day, the sidewalks of Paris resemble the sidewalks of the Tverskaya in Moscow, or of Leningrad's October 25 Prospect,[16] or of the Friedrichstrasse and the Alexanderplatz in Berlin. This is not, I mean, the crowd as it was formed in all the countries of Europe by the decadence of capitalism, the corruption of democracy, communist social sabotage, the contamination of moral standards.

Even those young Parisians who once strolled like flowers in the streets—kind, clean, simply but decently dressed, smiling—are today poorly groomed, poorly washed, poorly dressed, morose, not discourteous but distracted or indifferent, which, for a young Parisian, is a form of discourtesy.

I wonder if it was the Germans who did this. I don't think so.

Something else must have been added to the evils of the occupation. On the one hand, it's the excessive importance that the French give to the occupation; on the other, a sort of masochism, of self-humiliation formerly unknown to the French. They find a sort of morbid pleasure in humiliating themselves. You could say that France's enemies have built a wailing wall in Paris for the use of the French. Go! Go cry at your wailing wall, go, good Frenchmen of 1947, of 1948!

Of course, we have our own "wailing wall" in Italy. Of course we do. But the Italians don't go cry at their wailing wall—they go to piss on it.

November 18. My housekeeper, Mme Antoinette Bacon, says to me this morning that the strike is over. She tells me how the strikers are swine. I reply that they are not swine, because it's not possible to live on a subsistence minimum of 6,000 francs per month.

Mme Antoinette Bacon says that yes, she understands, but why increase the Parisians' poverty and suffering with these strikes? I tell her how strikes in themselves are not immoral, when they are just; that they are a necessary evil, the sole means of peaceful struggle the workers have for improving their sometimes dire economic situation. What is wrong is the Parisians' attitude toward the strike. They accept it as if it were Waterloo, as a defeat for France. "The French," I say to her, "are sick with what the Germans call *Schadenfreude,* the love of suffering. This is the worst consequence of the German occupation of France." I don't tell her the rest of my thought. Here it is: This *Schadenfreude* is a dire sign. It shows that the French people have been Germanized, at least with regard to what is most morbid in the Germans: their love of suffering, their self-humiliation.

November 23. In the papers I read: "Léon Blum said this, Léon Blum did that, Léon Blum thinks..."

I am a foreigner, I don't allow myself to judge the internal matters of France, which has welcomed me, which offers me its hospitality.

But as a foreigner I do have the right to judge French matters to the extent that they concern European matters.

What surprises me is the strange resemblance between current plans and the same politicians' plans in 1936, '37, '38, the years that marked the political and material decadence of France. It's clear that we're facing the same situation today as the one we faced in the years '37–'39.

Little has changed. The men in charge of French politics today are the same ones who were in charge of France in those years. How faithful men are to their nature, to their errors! Here's a good subject for Montesquieu. How faithful, too, is the French people, despite its bitter experience of recent times, to its own nature, which consists of the passive acceptance of history, as if history were destiny. It was very nearly the case that Hitler became the destiny of France.

I have dinner with Paul Reynaud. He paints a strikingly objective picture of Europe today. We will once again have occupations, hangings, acts of destruction, massacres, humiliations. Just like yesterday. This same people that we like to regard as energetic, unpredictable, short tempered, quickly moved to enthusiasm, to anger, to action, gives evidence of extreme passivity. What is it that has changed in France? Nothing has changed in France.

I'm reminded of the situation of the Austrian Empire between 1866 and 1914. This old empire, the longest-standing in Europe, the heir of Charlemagne, had placed itself out of the current of history. Sat down on the bank of the river. Gone fishing. I'm reminded of an anecdote that Sacha Guitry used to tell in his apologist lectures in the Salle Gaveau. In 1940, a few days after the conquest of Paris, Hitler comes to visit Paris. He is shown around the city, from Montmartre to Chaillot. Hitler was on the terrace of the Tuileries, gazing at the Seine. It was six in the morning. A man of the people, fishing pole over his shoulder, passes by on the quay. He gives the group of German officers an indifferent glance. He recognizes Hitler. He doesn't stop, he carries on, he only says, "Huh, there he is." And he continues on his way, to fish from the side of the river. Sacha Guitry sings the praises of this man, saying, "Here is the true French people, here is a good Frenchman, a good patriot"; and the entire room applauds.

For my part, let me say, this man of the people was a wretch. If all French people had been like him, the Germans yesterday, and the Russians tomorrow, would have stayed in France for ten centuries.

December 4. At the home of Melchior de Polignac. His wife smokes a cigar. I see Denise Bourdet again for the first time in fourteen years. We talk about the good old days. Countess Toulouse-Lautrec, etc. The conversation drifts to Mussolini. Melchior de Polignac asks me, etc. The story of the tie, of the tailcoat, of the rose:

[*The text breaks off here. The text that follows is missing its beginning and a date, and its placement here is owed to the fact that it contains, among other things, the "story of the tie" and the "story of the rose."*]

"... also has many flaws. His greatest fault, in my eyes, is to have stained himself with Italian blood."

"Bastard," said Sergeant Cork.

"I often wonder," said Bebe Colonna, "how I would behave if I happened to meet Mussolini again, after the war."

"It's unlikely," said Cumming, "that you would happen to meet him."

"You never know," said Bebe Colonna.

"This time we know how things will turn out. I don't think he'll emerge from this tragedy alive."

"Let's say I meet him," said Bebe Colonna. "I would be disgusted to shake his hand. His hand is stained with Italian blood."

"He would be the one not to shake your hand," said Cumming. "Assassins have a very strong inferiority complex when it comes to their hands. Do you remember Lady Macbeth?"[17]

"In 1931," I said, "I was in Paris. One evening I was invited to the home of André Germain, who at the time lived on Rue Geoffroy-l'Asnier, near the Marais. Do you know André Germain? He's a man of refined tastes, with modern attitudes, and also a bit precious, in the mode of Rainer Maria Rilke. His pages on Germany recall those of Jules Laforgue. No, he's more in the mode of Rilke than of Laforgue. He doesn't love jokes. His snobbery is of an Apollonian nature, like Rilke's. The house where he lives in Paris, on Rue Geoffroy-l'Asnier, is the same one where, in 1913, Gabriele d'Annunzio lived during his years of exile.[18] He had left Italy to escape his creditors, who had seized his villa, La Capponcina, in the Tuscan hills. D'Annunzio called this escape from debts his exile. He lived on the ground floor. The windows of his studio gave on to the courtyard, a small yard with a few meager trees, a few plants, a bit deserted at the far end. It was in these rooms that Ida Rubinstein tried out her dance steps for *Saint Sébastien*. As she danced, covered in long transparent veils, which allowed her bones of ancient ivory to show through the thin veil of her amber skin, D'Annunzio tossed grains of incense into a brazier and recited Pindar's victory odes, in ancient Greek. These were already, on the continent, the years of George V and President Poincaré, of Wilhelm II and the last Russian czar. What there was left of the Edwardian age in Europe was gathered not in London, but in Paris, where Boni de Castellane, Edmond Rostand, and Gabriele d'Annunzio still represented the end of the Decadent movement, of that precious, refined age, which Edward VII had illuminated with his skeptical and indulgent smile. It was in Paris that the echo of Connie Ediss's song from 1900, having died away even in London, survived:

> Oh how lovely to breathe the air
> breathed by people in Grosvenor Square

André Germain lived on the second floor of that quiet and unobtrusive house, on a small, peaceful, secluded street.

Among the guests that evening were the countess and great poet Anna de Noailles; the former minister Joseph Caillaux and his wife; Theodor Wolff, the director of the *Berliner Tageblatt*, who had just fled the threat of Hitler in Germany; the political writer Pierre Dominique; and others, whose names escape me.[19]

Anna de Noailles was stretched out on a sofa, in the style of Mme Récamier, and speaking with Theodor Wolff. She asked him if he was a socialist. "*Are* there any socialists in Germany?"

"Why not?" responded Theodor Wolff.

"I thought there weren't any there, that there could only be socialists in France."

"Ah!" exclaimed Theodor Wolff, very surprised.

André Germain arrived, bouncing on his delicate little feet, and set about discussing ancient porcelains, for which he has a taste and of which he is a very distinguished connoisseur. He described how, in a castle in Baden, Germany, he saw a life-size porcelain woman.

"Was she nude?" asked Anna de Noailles.

"Of course, absolutely nude. Have you never seen a rose absolutely nude, in a garden at dawn?"

"At dawn I'm asleep in my bed," responded Anna de Noailles, who was in a bad mood, hiding her mouth behind a fan made of black feathers. It was a small fan like the ones Pascin painted in his portraits of Romanian odalisques and prostitutes. Pascin was Romanian, like Anna de Noailles, who was born Princess Brâncoveanu. Anna nervously jiggled her little foot, nibbling the edge of her black fan. And I thought that Pascin would have liked her as a model for one of his strange odalisques, with that aquiline nose of hers, that forehead full of wrinkles, those rouged cheeks, those deep black eyes, where genius and old age already contended.

André Germain said that the porcelain woman was nude, that he had never seen a woman more nude. Your gaze penetrated the skin, beneath the shining shield of the skin, into the secret bloody world of the veins, and such was the illusion, so triumphant the lively color of that fleshy rose, that the porcelain was warm to the touch, that it felt like flesh.

"You touched it?" asked Anna de Noailles.

Leaning against the fireplace, Joseph Caillaux spoke with Pierre Dominique about the need to save France from demagogy, about the need for a strongman. He had a huge, strong head, bare and smooth like ancient Parian marble, that ivory-colored marble to which the centuries lend such a marvelous human color. The thick and very black eyebrows bestowed a hard and proud sign on a fair, pale, perhaps too white face, of a shade too fair for his head. His words were short and had a muffled, subdued sound.

"France doesn't need a dictator," Pierre Dominique said.

"It's Europe that needs a dictator to rise in France. Without a strong France, Europe is finished," said Caillaux.

He was older and more tired, but harder and prouder, than fifteen years earlier, when, during the war, he had tried to take control of France's government, to cast himself as Catiline to a France that was tired and disgusted by the long, exhausting war. It was Caillaux who didn't want to surrender, who felt humiliated not to be confronted with an enemy like Clemenceau, but instead with enemies like Herriot, like Briand, like Daladier, whom he considered inferior to himself and to his destiny.

"Did you touch it? Admit that you touched it," Anna de Noailles said in a shrill voice, nibbling the edge of her black fan.

André Germain trotted across the room on his delicate little feet, offering his guests champagne in flutes of fine Bohemia crystal, Moser violet with subtle pink reflections. The champagne was highly amber colored and produced little foam, as is typical of older champagnes, of a noble and rare *cru*.

Anna de Noailles, holding the flute in her right hand, from which her black fan hung like a raven's wing, observed that champagne was tending to disappear from French soirées, replaced by whisky.

She spoke of England, of the slow transition between generations, of the disappearance of a world that had been hers, when the London season didn't have the distant and banal sound it has today, like "The Circle in Hyde Park" or "The Great Exposition," but sounded solely of "sweets and beer." One day the Hon. Dorothy Hood had told her about having kissed the same hand that Victoria, as a child on her first visit to Windsor Castle, had presented to George IV, who said to her, "Give me your little paw." Just think, George IV. The Victorian age had so permeated everyone, young and old, that in 1897, year of the Diamond Jubilee, which marked the peak of Victorian prosperity, when Devonshire House was the scene of the great fancy dress ball, in the photographs of the evening, everyone, young and old, whatever the mask, whatever the costume, retained a Victorian aspect. Was the giveaway the Victorian wasp waist, or something in the hairstyles that recalled Victoria's, or simply, in the eyes, a comforting, composed Victorian gaze? Anna de Noailles spoke of London in her precious, ever so slightly Romanian-accented French.

And seated in a corner, almost fading into the background, a lady listened. She was about sixty but looked younger, with a full, ruddy face, light blue eyes, and short, curly hair (was it blond? was it white?), similar to Mona Williams's hair in 1938, before it turned dark during the war. She listened with bowed head to that remembrance not so much of a city, of London, and of the England of Queen Victoria's last years, but the tender, loving commemoration of a departed age, of a bygone era. It was a golden and happy age. That age had survived longer in France than in England, maybe because the air of Paris is drier, thinner, brighter; maybe because mornings in Paris are longer than in London, as are sunsets; maybe because nights are slower to descend over the Seine than over the Thames.

It seemed like yesterday when the Prince of Wales, later Edward VII, would come to Paris accompanied by the famous captain of the English Eleven, whose photograph was so familiar to readers of the Badminton book on football. His name was Hansell, and when he accompanied the Prince of Wales to Paris, the Parisians would say that "there was more Hansel than Gretel" in the prince's set. It seemed like yesterday when Boni de Castellane descended from his carriage in the Place Vendôme dressed in canary yellow, his bowler hat the color of ashes, and Edmond Rostand and Gabriele d'Annunzio and Debussy were more wooed than a woman. It seemed like yesterday when, on the very eve of the war, a pistol shot unexpectedly brought that golden and happy age to an end, leaving it for dead.

Suddenly the woman raised her eyes, looked at me, and smiled as she stood and came toward me. She spoke a little Italian and, from her face, more than from her accent, seemed American to me. She asked me where I was from. "Ah, I know Florence," she said. Then she added in a low voice, staring at me and smiling, "Botticelli, Giotto, Masaccio." She smiled with a certain sadness. She spoke to me about Settignano, about Prato, about Fiesole. "Come listen to my Sunday lectures on art at the Louvre," she said. "Next Sunday I'll be talking about Pirandello." We spoke about Tuscany, about Pisa, about the uncommonly bright, precise, limpid light of Tuscany.

At a certain point we were approached by Pierre Dominique, who also spoke about Italy; about Umbria, Le Marche, and Tuscany, the three regions where the light is clear and bright. Suddenly the woman smiled at me: "Are you coming, Sunday at the Louvre?" And, saying goodbye to Pierre Dominique, she shook his hand. I expected her to offer her hand to me as well, but she ostentatiously grasped my right wrist in her left hand, and with a slight nod of her head, smiling, took her leave. I noticed that she was very pale, and discomforted.

"Who is she?" I asked Pierre Dominique.

"Mme Caillaux," replied Pierre Dominique.

"Ah, Mme Caillaux, the assassin?" said Bebe Colonna.

"Why, then, did she offer her hand to Pierre Dominique, and not to you?" asked Countess Attolico.

"Because I'm a foreigner, and she was meeting me for the first time. I think assassins are always afraid that people will refuse to shake a hand that has killed."

"You're right," said Bebe Colonna to Cumming. "And I think that, if I were to meet Mussolini after the war, he wouldn't offer me his hand."

"It's possible," said Colonel Cumming, "that he's unaware of the harm he has done. From what I've been given to understand, I believe he's a very vain man. You've seen him up close," he said as he turned to me, "what do you think?"

"I think he is no more vain than we all are, at least in Europe," I replied.

"Men are vain in America as well," said Cumming, "but in another way. Americans are ashamed of being vain. That's already a step in the right direction."

"He was vain like a woman," said Bebe Colonna. "There was much that was feminine about him."

"The first time I saw him up close, and the first time I spoke to him, left me with a rather strange memory. It was 1923. Before that I'd never seen him up close before. In 1923 I was still a young man, not much more than twenty years old.

"I was at home one day when a messenger arrived from Palazzo Chigi with a letter from Barone Russo. Barone Russo is now an ambassador and calls himself Marchese Paulucci di Calboli Barone, but at the time he was head of Mussolini's cabinet in the Ministry of Foreign Affairs.[20] I had met Barone Russo in Paris, in 1919, when he was secretary to Foreign Minister Tittoni, who was very fond of me and protected me. He acted as a protector of writers and artists and had a great deal of faith in me. Paulucci's letter was very brief: it informed me that Mussolini was expecting me at Palazzo Chigi at seven o'clock.

"At seven o'clock sharp I sat down to wait in the Sala del Colleoni, so called on account of a bronze reproduction of the equestrian statue of the famous condottiere. Eight o'clock arrived, and the usher hadn't called me. I waited in a state of anxiety. I was hardly more than a boy, and that sudden, unexpected call on the part of Mussolini, whom I had never seen before, filled me with an anxious hope. Maybe he was calling to raise me to some important post? Or maybe to give me some important task? Who knows? Minister, ambassador? Dictators are like the sultans in fairy tales. You never know what might fall from their generous hands. Maybe the sultan would throw his handkerchief at me. A young man of twenty, as I was at the time, doesn't refuse an honor, or a favor, just because it comes to him from a dictator and not from a minister in a democracy. Be it tyrannical or democratic, a favor is always a favor; and what is always immoral about it, a gift that falls from on high, is the same in tyranny and in democracy.

"But eight thirty arrived and Navarra, the usher, hadn't called me. From time to time functionaries crossed the room, young attachés dressed in the manner of Cirida Cucci or Caraceni, with that amiable style of young Italian functionaries, who wear tweed and flannel to the office, as they would for a weekend in Scotland, in Gleneagles or Saint Andrews, or for a boat trip on the Cherwell and the Isis, or a picnic on Mesopotamia Island.[21] Passing by in silence, or speaking to each other in low voices, they would look in my direction and greet me with a listless air.

"Romano Avezzana, then the ambassador to Paris, passed and stopped to greet me kindly. 'You're here to see Mussolini?' he asked me. And he added: 'I'm very pleased for you.' I was happy and anxious, and I trembled.

"Mario Pansa passed: tall, a bit stooped, his face covered with tiny red spots, his hands thrust deep into the pockets of his jacket. He sat down beside me and said: 'What a drag! No one here ever goes to dinner before ten, sometimes before eleven.' He said that Mussolini suffered from stomach problems, followed a diet, and didn't trouble himself about functionaries who were hungry.

"'All dictators,' I said, 'have stomach problems.'

"Pansa started to laugh. A few days earlier, due to I don't remember what incident, or what misunderstanding (but perhaps it was due to the wicked envy that his colleagues felt for him, to the jealousy that Mussolini's favor provokes), he had left his position as Mussolini's wardrobe attendant, or as they said back then, as Mussolini's '*elegantiere*,' and he was fed up with his brief instant of disfavor. To him it seemed like he was in disgrace. 'It's a very unpleasant feeling,' he said, 'to feel like you're in disgrace; I didn't know such a feeling existed. It wasn't like this in the old days!'

"Pansa was at home in the Ministry of Foreign Affairs. His father was an ambassador, and for the sake of his father's memory, the general secretary of foreign affairs, Contarini, who was Sicilian and had very strong friendships and enmities, protected him, deflecting from his head the thunderbolts that he called down on himself with his laziness, his scant desire to work, his levity, and his graceful and refined immorality as a playboy. Pansa resembled an Austrian diplomat from the time of the Hapsburgs; he was, perhaps unwittingly, of that school, and perhaps one of the reasons for the protection he enjoyed from Contarini was the preference that the latter, a career diplomat, had for the diplomatic school of Ballplatz. In appearance Mario Pansa even possessed the lugubrious air of the Austrian diplomats, the same sad, absent, funereal air of the waltzers and old-school diplomats in Vienna.

"'You don't know what it means to be in disgrace,' continued Pansa. 'No one says hello to you anymore, everyone runs away as if you had the plague. I feel like what Oxenstierna says about the penniless man: a corpse.' He laughed, and soon after he left me. It was past nine. 'I'm going to go have a chat with Lequio,' he said, 'while we wait to go to dinner.'

"I remained alone, and I thought that Pansa had the gift of always understanding things by halves, which is a great quality for a young diplomat, and a sign of great class.

"Finally Navarra, the usher, appeared at the door and gave me the sign.

"I crossed the threshold of Mussolini's office, my legs trembling. It was a large room, an immense room, paved in marble. The room was in semidarkness. Far away, at the opposite end of the room, right up against the wall, behind the table against the opposite wall, sat Mussolini. Next to him on one side was the Marchese Paulucci di Calboli, on the other Mameli, who's now a government minister. Mussolini was signing papers as Paulucci di Calboli handed them to him. He had his head bent over the papers and did not raise his eyes when I entered.

"Mameli and Paulucci raised their eyes but immediately lowered them again, and none of the three of them gave any indication of noticing my entrance.

"On a table at Mussolini's left was a hideous Louis Philippe lamp, its green silk lampshade yellowed by the color of the lamp and by the long-ago-extinguished flame; and that green light turned Mussolini's face livid, sunk deep eye sockets into his pale face, and projected the shadow of his large and fleshy nose onto his right cheek, plunging it into a livid half-light.

"I made my way across the immense room on tiptoes, pausing repeatedly, and when I was in front of the table I stopped, and I waited. (Note: Mario Pansa subsequently took to emulating English diplomats, the young *équipe* of the Foreign Office, of which Anthony Eden is an almost exemplary model, but he never succeeded in imitating the new model. He always remained halfway between Rome and London; he remained in Vienna. Pansa had the gift of always understanding things by halves, etc., etc.) Then passed several minutes of anguish, which seemed to me eternal. My heart raced; my legs trembled.

"All of a sudden, having signed the last paper, Mussolini cast down the pen, threw himself back in his armchair, and looked at me. He stared at me for a few moments with his huge dark, round eyes, and I felt my blood freeze in my veins. Have you ever seen Mussolini's face? At the time he was lean, but the bones of his head were so large that, despite its leanness, it seemed larger than an ordinary head, with something hard and beast-like about it. He had a broad mouth with fleshy lips, a vast round chin, and a large shiny nose; and his eyes, the eyes he stared at me with that evening, were big, deep, and black, gleaming with steady menace. Paulucci di Calboli and Mameli looked at me too, and it was their cold gaze, full of disdain and compassion at the same time (both of them were friends of mine, but in that moment they were two courtiers), that made me understand the threat contained in Mussolini's gaze.

"'So this is you?' said Mussolini after a long stare. 'I didn't think you'd be so young. I thought you'd be different. How old are you?'

"Stammering, I told him my age.

"'What schooling have you had? You were at the Collegio Cicognini? You must have learned very little in your classes. Didn't they teach you not to stick your nose into other people's business?' And without giving me a chance to respond, he added: 'I'd advise you, from here on out, not to concern yourself with me. I don't like that you're a gossip and a malicious type. An intelligent man like you doesn't stoop to innuendo worthy of a concierge. I hope you understand me.'

"A flush of indignation rose to my face. I was too young to hold it back, to remain immune to insults. 'I do not understand at all,' I replied.

"'Ah, so you don't understand?' said Mussolini, leaning back in his armchair and nervously running two fingers between his neck and collar, which he had open, one of those ridiculous stiff collars that are still worn with morning coats. 'Ah, so you don't understand? You want me to explain what it's about? Well, then, I advise you not to speak ill of me, not to criticize my person, especially in public, like you did the other day at Caffè Aragno. Mine is an excellent piece of advice, and you would do well to follow it. You're still young, and this advice, if you follow it, will be very useful to you in life. You can go.'

"'I will not go,' I said, 'until you have told me what my fault consists in. I am not in the habit of speaking ill of people, and I would be grateful if you could tell me when and how and where I have offended you.'

"'I can tell you the place, the hour, and the people present,' replied Mussolini, slightly surprised at my behavior. 'Two days ago, at Caffè Aragno, you told several of your friends that I always wear ugly ties.' Mussolini was visibly embarrassed, and as he spoke he brought his hand to his tie. 'It's a trifle, I know, a bit of carelessness due to your age, but I cannot tolerate being publicly criticized in such a petty way, as if by some gossiping servant.'

"'As a matter of fact,' I replied, 'I did speak about you the other day at Caffè Aragno with some friends. I indeed said that you wear ugly ties. I was wrong, and I apologize. But I had no intention of offending you. It was, it seems to me, an observation made without malice or spite. It's common among young people to criticize the way someone or other dresses. I was wrong, and I am sorry to have unintentionally offended you.'

"'That's better," said Mussolini. 'May this little mishap serve as a lesson for the future. Now go.'

"I turned and headed for the door, which was very far away, at the opposite end of the immense room. As I walked I thought that now it was all over for me. To fall into disgrace with a dictator at the very beginning of my career was to start on my life's path with a terrible, insurmountable handicap. Twenty years old, and I was all washed up. I walked, placing one foot in front of the other on the room's cold, polished marble, and I thought that I was washed up at twenty.

"At a certain point, having reached the middle of the room, I turned and said, 'Will you permit me to say a final word in my defense?'

"'Go ahead,' said Mussolini, looking up.

"'You're wearing an ugly tie today as well,' I said."

"Wonderful!" exclaimed Colonel Cumming. Eleonora, Bebe, and the three young men applauded; the two Sergeant Corks and Corporal Brand applauded too and looked at me in amazement.

"And with that quip," said Bebe Colonna, "you saved yourself. It can't be said you suffer from *l'esprit de l'escalier.*"

"Malaparte's stories," said Cumming, "are made from nothing, but he tells them well. And then?" he asked. "Mussolini forgave you?"

"I don't know," I replied. "He was a man full of bitterness, and never forgave anyone. But what did he have to forgive me for? He was a man who hated wit and witty people, maybe because Pascal said, 'Good wit, bad character.' But that same evening Paulucci di Calboli, whom I had gone to see at the Circolo della Caccia gentlemen's club, told me, laughing, that Mussolini, as soon as I'd left, had started laughing, that he'd had his head usher, Navarra, bring him a mirror, and that, looking at his tie in the mirror, he'd laughed and said, 'I don't understand why Malaparte thinks it's ugly. Isn't this a beautiful tie?'

"'Beautiful,' Paulucci had replied.

"'So what?' said Mussolini. And he caressed his tie."

"I know another story about ties," said Bebe Colonna, "and I would gladly tell it to you, if I knew how to tell stories like Malaparte. One evening Mussolini, not long after arriving in Rome, was invited to dinner at the English embassy. Mario Pansa, who was his wardrobe assistant, had advised him to wear a tailcoat. The dinner was at nine o'clock. At a quarter to nine Mario Pansa discreetly poked his head through the door of Mussolini's office and saw Mussolini seated at his table, in a tailcoat, but with a black tie. Mario Pansa immediately flew home, took off his white jacket, put on a dinner jacket, stuffed two white ties into his pocket, and flew back to Palazzo Chigi. Mussolini was waiting for him impatiently.

"'Is this okay?' he asked Mario Pansa, walking around the table and showing himself like a customer in front of his tailor.

"'Perfect,' said Mario Pansa, 'it's just that, out of respect for the English embassy, it would be better to wear a white tie as the English do.'

"Mussolini touched his black tie and said, 'Why? This isn't English style?'

"'Yes, certainly,' said Mario Pansa, 'it's extremely correct like this as well, but a white tie is more English.'

"'Now it's too late,' said Mussolini. 'Where can we find two white ties?'

"'I brought two,' said Mario Pansa, pulling them from his pocket, 'just in case.' And he swiftly undid Mussolini's black tie, put it in his pocket, tied a white tie around his collar, and did the same for himself. 'There, now it's perfect,' said Pansa.

"'Still,' said Mussolini, 'the black tie didn't look bad.'

"And they left because it was already late."

"It's a delightful story," said Colonel Cumming. "When it comes to Mussolini, I prefer this kind of anecdote, in the style of Tallemant des Réaux or of Suetonius, to stories about his vulgarity or brutality. It's too easy to darken the palette. I love to be told amusing stories, which show him to me as a man, rather than as a demon."

"Mussolini," I said, "is not a man, or a demon. He's an angel."

"An angel?" exclaimed Cumming.

"Please," said Eleonora, "don't get carried away by your own imagination. What does Mussolini have to do with angels?"

"Mussolini is an angel," I said.

"I know what you mean," said Cumming with a laugh. "You mean that Mussolini is not like other men? That he is a superior man, an *Übermensch*?"

"*Übermenschen* are out of fashion," I said. "Mussolini is an angel. There is something morbidly feminine, something *morbidly virtuous* in him, which some people have taken for a sign of homosexuality. I don't believe he is a homosexual, although his adversaries have said this as well. But in Latin countries, when you want to fight a man, you say that he is a jinx, or a homosexual. No, he's not a jinx: he has no influence, neither good nor bad, on men of uncommon spirit and great courage. Unlike the jinx, who strikes precisely uncommon men. His feminine nature is highly developed. He is a cautious, careful man, full of mistrust and fears. He is timid, with something feminine in his gaze, his voice, his gestures, his way of walking. What's surprising to find in him is a certain strange animality. He's a large animal, full of flaccid blood. He's like a goose, an enormous goose. His skin is the color of gooseflesh. It doesn't give the impression of being full of warm red blood. It seems swollen with buttermilk. His complexion is pallid, almost livid, with bluish and whitish zones here and there, especially around the temples. His nose is big and wide, with dilated pores, and from each pore sprouts a hair, which each morning he shaves away with a razor. His lips are large, fleshy, and violet in color, his jaw hard and prominent and wide, his temples wide and bulging. He had the look of a pregnant woman around her ninth month. His head was larger than normal, disproportionate to his body, which with the passing of years had grown swollen and deformed. His eyes were large and dark, with something unusual in the whites of the eyes, such that, when he stared at something, the eye appeared dark, but when he moved his eyes to and fro, rolling them as he often did, turning his head to the right and to the left and looking up as he spoke, sticking out his lips as if he were sucking in the air, the dark orb of the eye was swallowed up by the white, like that of certain animals, gazelles in agony, or certain women in ecstasy. One's first impression was of certain animals full of yellowish blood. Of certain animals painted by Bosch, by Brueghel, by the customs officer Rousseau, whose skin is fatty and delicate, almost transparent, and who are fatty, swollen, heavy, and slow in their movements and gestures, almost bodies in decomposition. Among the many portraits of Mussolini, for me the one with the greatest resemblance is a tempera painting by Massimo Campigli, sketched out on a piece of cardboard in Palazzo Chigi, in 1926, and which the painter showed me one day in Paris. He was protective of it, and would not have cast it off for anything in the world. It was the head alone, seen as if through a magnifying glass. The dominant colors were white, blue, and ochre. The cold harmonies of white and blue, slightly warmed by the ochre tones, gave the head a funereal aspect. You could see the dilated pores, and at the base of every pore the dark root of a hair. But what inspires a sense of repulsion in you is his way of walking: swaying his hips, which are fat and short; the bouncing of his enormous head on his short, thick neck, planted in his stocky shoulders; his cautious, evasive, hypocritical way of placing his feet on the ground, supporting the weight of his body not on the soles but on the external edge of his feet. He must have exuded a strange smell, a smell not common among men.

"Once, in the Roman countryside, in a village Mussolini had visited a few days before, an old hunter told me how Mussolini has the smell of certain wild geese, the smell of wet chicken skin. And he added that his dogs had sniffed him carefully, insistently, then walked away without giving him another glance, notwithstanding his wet chicken smell. 'Dogs don't like him,' the old hunter concluded. 'It's a bad sign, not being liked by dogs.' I said that the smell of wet chicken was the smell of corpses. 'I didn't dare say it,' said the old man. 'It's exactly the smell of corpses. Dogs don't like it.'"

"I don't understand," said Cumming, "why this should make him an angel. Mussolini is a man, in the true sense of the word. A male."

"Oh, he's certainly male," said Bebe Colonna.

"Mussolini is a bastard," said Sergeant Cork.

"Certainly, he's male, but with something feminine, morbidly feminine, about him, the femininity of masculinity in its decadence. His gestures are soft; his voice is deep, full of white [...]; the roots of his voice are in his breasts. Perhaps he doesn't know the meaning of his own gestures, of his own voice, of some of his effeminate gestures that Oscar Wilde would have liked, as would Cocteau and, why not, Shelley too, Nietzsche too. And D'Annunzio too, why not?

"I remember the day when, after a long, grave, deadly illness, he gave a speech from the balcony of Palazzo Chigi that overlooks Piazza Colonna. It was his first time back in public since his illness. He was thin, very pale, his enormous eyes sunken, his lips bloodless. His hands had turned to ivory, like those of an old nun. No, of a dead nun. It was, if I'm not mistaken, March 20, 1925, on the eve of spring. He appeared on the balcony, resting his left hand on the iron railing and bringing his right hand to his face. In this hand he clutched a flesh-colored rose. Mussolini always has a rose clutched delicately in his fist. He doesn't understand the value or the meaning of this gesture, of that rose of his. The day he is shot, I would like to be there to place a rose in his stiff hand. Not to insult him, not to disrespect him—no. I don't like to disrespect the dead. But to be kind to him in death. I know that it would give him pleasure.

"In Jassy the morning after the massacre of the Jews I went to see a hundred or so dead children laid out on the sidewalk of Strada Lăpușneanu. They were Jewish children, murdered. Their little hands were tightly closed, the poor little hands of Jewish children, so small, so white. I went into Kane's grocery, just down the street, bought a packet of candy, and put a piece of candy into the hand of each dead child. There was nothing else I could do for those little dead things."

"You amused yourself by putting candy into their hands, didn't you?" said Cumming.

"No, it wasn't to amuse myself. And it wasn't even because I didn't have any gramophone needles."

"Gramophone needles?" said Cumming.

"Do you remember the Jew in Paul Morand's *Lampes à arc*, the very green dead Jew on the snow? '*Les enfants ont mis sous ses ongles / des aiguilles de gramophone.*' It wasn't because I didn't have gramophone needles. No. It was because dead children like candy. And what if children liked gramophone needles under their fingernails?"

"Don't be cruel," said Eleonora.

The group listened to me carefully, pushing their faces forward. Giacomo was slightly pale.

"With my father," said Giacomo, "when he was on his deathbed, I also put a rose in his hand."

"That's not the same rose I would put in Mussolini's hand after his execution," I said. "No, it wouldn't be the same rose. What I mean is that I wouldn't be moved by a feeling like yours. Oh, no, Giacomo, it wouldn't be the same rose. It wouldn't even be a rose like the one Mussolini clutched in his fist on the balcony of Palazzo Chigi. He would speak, and every once in a while he would bring his right hand up to his extremely pale, bloodless face, breathing in the living smell of the rose. He said, among other things, 'Today is spring, and tomorrow the sun will come out.' When he finished speaking the crowd went wild. Mussolini had to go back out on the balcony three times to greet the crowd. He greeted them with his extended right hand, and it was in his right hand that he had the rose. The third time he went out on the balcony, he breathed in the living smell of the flower, and tossed the rose to the crowd."

"And what did the crowd do?" asked Bebe Colonna.

"The crowd ate the rose," said Cumming.

"Yes," I said. "The crowd ate the rose. Crowds love roses. The delicate, living flavor, the feminine flavor of rose petals. I was in the middle of the crowd, and when the rose fell from the balcony onto the crowd, I blushed. I felt ill at ease. That gesture à la Oscar Wilde, Byronian in a sense, that decadent gesture, made me ill at ease. It was the same unease I felt one day in Finland, at the red-painted fingernails of Marshall Mannerheim; the same unease I felt the day I joined the crowd waiting outside Palazzo Venezia for Neville Chamberlain. It was the eve of the war, the man with the umbrella came to Rome to negotiate with Mussolini to secure European peace. I was in the first row of the crowd, and I had an umbrella in my hand. Not because the weather was bad, but because I too carried an umbrella in the English manner, as the French carry canes. At a certain point a police officer, quite elegant and proper, approached me and took the umbrella out of my hand. 'Are you mad?' he said, 'going around with an umbrella on this of all mornings? It's tactless, don't you understand?' I felt ill at ease, just like when, after being in the Regina Coeli prison for several months, one day the prison chaplain came to visit me. As we spoke he suddenly asked, 'Do you mind?' and crushed a bug on my forehead. The same unease I felt that day in Turin, as I danced with the princess of Piedmont at the Borgognas' ball, and at a certain point I realized that one of the princess's shoes had become unbuckled. I bent down to buckle it, and as the princess gave me her foot she unintentionally kicked me in the face. The same unease that I felt when I walked handcuffed through the crowd at the Rome train station, on my way to Lipari, among the carabinieri. I had a cigarette between my lips that had gone out, and I couldn't, handcuffed as I was, relight it. A railroad worker approached me and lit my cigarette. And as he brought the match toward my lips he looked me right in the eyes and said: 'Imbecile.'"

December 19. Dinner at the Italian embassy, with Stanislas de La Rochefoucauld and his wife, as well as the Austrian minister, ——. Ambassador Quaroni tells us about Afghanistan, where he lived for five years, before being posted to Moscow in 1944. He tells us about Soviet Russia, which he knows wonderfully well (his wife is Russian). Anecdote of his visit to Pope Pius XII: Ambassador Quaroni, returning from Moscow on his way to assuming his new post in Paris, goes to visit His Holiness. The meeting is cordial and intelligent. Pius XII asks Ambassador Quaroni to describe in a few words how life is in Russia. "Well," says Quaroni, "whenever I enter the Vatican, I always feel like I'm entering the Kremlin. The atmosphere is the same."

Earlier, the Pope had spoken about the USSR. "There are only two universal powers in the world, the Church and the USSR. Whichever way we turn, everywhere we go, we clash with the USSR. And the USSR clashes with the Church. The true struggle is between the Church and the USSR."[22]

UNDATED ENTRIES

DINNER at the home of my friend G.J., with Paul Reynaud, Annabella, Mitou, Léon Bailby, Jean-Pierre Aumont, Duhamel, and others. I tell them about the poor Duchess di N., who began crying yesterday evening because I said Pascal is cruel. The theme of cruelty is not as familiar to the French as it is to the Germans, the English, the Russians, the Americans, the Italians, the Spanish. The French remain outside cruelty, without crossing its threshold. It is the only animal side they have left, this unconsciousness of their own cruelty. They are perhaps the only human species, at least in Europe (with the exception of certain Calvinists, certain northern Lutherans, in Finland), who are unconscious of their own cruelty.

Paul Reynaud says the French are not conscious of anything unless they have a concept of it, their nature being entirely intellectual. I like this definition. Do the French, then, have no concept of cruelty? I cite Descartes, who has a concept for everything, from whom the French have inherited a concept for everything. The form French cruelty takes, in my view, is Cartesianism. What abysses of cruelty there are in Descartes!

The other day I found myself at the home of the Marquis de P. I told him the following story from the Spanish Civil War, which had been told to me in Helsinki by Count Augustin de Foxa, the Spanish minister in Finland, and which would seem to have surpassed the limits of the worst cruelty. The story is very Spanish; that is to say, dry, simple, gray. The cruelest story in the world, thanks to its bonhomie, simplicity, ingenuousness.

In a small Spanish city one morning at dawn, two Civil Guards are escorting a prisoner (Francoist or Red, I don't know) to his execution site. It's winter, and a freezing-cold north wind blows from the sierra. The prisoner is a poor wretch with nothing but a canvas jacket on his back, only espadrilles on his feet. The two Civil Guards are cold as well, covered with only shabby, tattered overcoats. The prisoner, walking toward the site of his torment, his teeth chattering, complains bitterly about the terrible cold. He has flipped up the collar of his jacket and walks with his hands in his pockets, shivering. The execution site is two kilometers away, on the bank of a little river. The prisoner curses the cold aloud: "This damned cold!" One of the Civil Guards says to him: "You're complaining? Think about us, we've got to come all the way back!"

The story provoked the protests of the countess of Toulouse-Lautrec, sister to Louise de Vilmorin Pálffy, who exclaimed that I could not compare the cruelty of the Spanish with the supposed cruelty of Descartes or Pascal, in whom, what's more, she didn't see anything cruel.

Of course, we have to agree on what cruelty means. Dickens is cruel. Flaubert is cruel, much more than Baudelaire. There is a French cruelty that is completely intellectual, and which can't be compared to anything else. I'm talking about cruelty as a quality that is very developed among women. When the corpse of a drowned person is fished out of the Seine, or out of the Tiber, the female spectators outnumber the male ones.

There is also a particular species of cruelty revealed in the manner of presenting certain foods. I remember having lunch in a little restaurant in Thebes. The city, which frequently experiences earthquakes, is like many cities in Greece (Sparta, for example) made up of wooden shacks with roofs of sheet metal. I was served a mutton soup. The tureen sat in front of me, I plunged the large spoon in, and imagine my fright when I saw, floating up in the soup, a head and eyes, a head still covered in its flesh and skin. The eyes looked out at me from the bottom of the tureen with an expression of such pitifulness, such supplication, that I cried out, overturning the tureen. It was the head of a sheep, which in Greece is served whole in the soup.

Naturally, one can't compare this type of cruelty to that of Pascal, to the particular cruelty of Port-Royal, to certain crystalline cruelties of Racine, to certain complaisant cruelties of Proust.

One must never tell the French the truth. One must say to them: "You are what you think you are." If you say to them: "Why do you fear the future? France is immortal, it will still be the first nation of Europe," they think that you're not saying what you think, that your words are a polite way of saying to them: "You are more unhappy than you think." If they complain about the men and events of 1935 to 1939, of the Popular Front, etc., and you say to them, "What are you complaining about? Your men of 1935, of 1939, are still around, they're in power, they're still doing the same things they did in 1935, in 1937, in 1939, they speak the same language, and so what, then?" they look as if they think you're reproaching them for the calamities of 1940, when all anyone is doing is reproaching them for the calamities of 1948.

The French are a proud and sensitive people, with the grace not to understand history. They are completely resistant to its comprehension. In this regard they resemble the ancient Greeks. The Latins understood history; the entire history of Rome is full of historical sensibility; it is history made and lived by men who knew themselves to be at the center of history. The French feel themselves to be at the center not of European history but of European attention—which is not the same thing. Now that this attention is distracted from them, they feel excluded from history. A strange and fascinating people. They are unaccustomed to calamities.

In French literature nature constitutes the literary *plafond* that Charles Du Bos has spoken of with regard to Théophile Gautier, rather than the living substance, the subject of art. Du Bos, on the same occasion, likens Gautier to Venetian painters, Titian, etc. Instead it seems to me that in French literature nature is seen as having something gothic about it, as Dürer would have seen it, or a Frenchman of the twelfth century. It's made from a dry material, one that smells of old wood, of the old bones of the ancients; with Ronsard it quickly became a shiny, precious material, gold, silver, or diamond; it became crystal in the sixteenth and eighteenth centuries; cotton wool, with Rousseau and the Romantics; and finally an opaque, tender, delicate material, the same as how the impressionists rendered nature. In Proust it's made of paper; in Gide it finally becomes a lithograph, thereby returning to what it was in the beginning, to what it had of the gothic to start with. But the role of nature in French literature remains ornamental, a *plafond*, or something distant, detached, foreign, whose function varies. This reminds me of those Versailles nobles who, having become exiles from the countryside and from nature, of which they no longer retained any memory, called the countryside "the place where birds are raw." In French literature, all birds are cooked.

A young student, Jean Rosenthal, comes to visit me. He's tall, thin, pale, bent. His voice is low and deep; he speaks as if his voice were older than he is.

He asks me why I seem so obsessed by cruelty, whose role in human life seems to him accidental, entirely external, an illness, unhealthiness, rather than a fundamental element of our nature. On the subject of cruelty I am cautious. Nonetheless, I think that cruelty is proper to man, that conscious cruelty is found in man's nature alone.

Animals and plants possess only unconscious cruelty: it's not thought out, it's just instinctive. They derive advantages from it (in hunting, nourishment, or procreation; for example, among praying mantises), but no pleasure, sensual delight, or enjoyment.

In man, cruelty is conscious. Man is cruel in everything, even in his pity. In his Christian pity, in all his most noble sentiments—generosity, altruism, courage, pity—there is a *background* of always conscious cruelty that perhaps has its origins in the fact that man is the only animal who is conscious of death, who knows that he must die.

Animals know that they can die. Death, for man, is an inevitable end, an inevitable result. For animals it is only a possible accident. Animals' fear of the dead, including the dead of their own species. Watch a dog when it encounters the carcass of a dog. How scared it looks as it walks, with its tail between its legs, its ears glued to its head, its eyes full of terror. Watch the death of an animal, a dog, a horse, a fox, a cat: This "why" in their gaze, this mute pleading for help. The air of asking: "What is happening to me?"

Man's awareness of inevitable death leads him to look closely at suffering, agony, and death, "to see what it is," to avenge himself, in some way, for the fact of having to die, to pass through this same suffering, this same agony. The extreme pleasure—always conscious, even if he is unconscious of being conscious—that he takes in making others suffer, or watching others suffer, or taking pity on the sufferings of others.

Man can have no idea of God or eternal life without cruelty. I add that cruelty is a metaphysical fact, that it is bound to the metaphysical concept of God. The cruelest peoples are metaphysical peoples. The origin of the famous Oriental cruelty is in the metaphysical nature of their religion, of their belief, of their conception of man's life and destiny. And the crueler a people is, the more intellectual it is, and its culture distances itself from nature, becomes abstract and intellectual.

In Europe it is Christianity that has developed man's cruelty. The cruelest peoples in Europe are those who have developed a metaphysical conception of Christianity; for example, the Germans. The Nuremberg trials neglected to hand down indictments against Kant and Hegel, against all of German metaphysics, a source of cruelty comparable only, perhaps, to the metaphysics of the Jews. To accuse the Germans of being barbaric because they are cruel is, to say the least, naive. They are cruel because they are a metaphysical people, and their culture is metaphysical, and even in their realism (Dürer, Cranach, Matthias Grünewald, etc.), there is an underlying layer of abstraction, which is characteristic of everything that is gothic, that makes something gothic. The ancients (the Greeks, the Latins) who had a naturalistic religion, who had nothing metaphysical in their

religion, or even, I would say, in their culture—aside from Pythago-
reanism and Platonism, which together encompass the metaphysics
of the ancients—were not cruel. "Achaean man," who remains one
of the highest exemplars of humanity, was fierce, not cruel. There is
nothing cruel in Homer. But some subtle cruelty in Dante, Shakespeare, Dickens, Racine, Corneille, etc., etc., etc., Shelley, and Keats,
etc., etc. Sometimes I think that Cartesianism can become a source
of cruelty.

I went to dinner at A.'s, at the far end of the Muette neighborhood. I
leave A.'s house around two in the morning. I walk down to the Seine.

The night is clear. A warm wind blows from the west, sweet and
laden with the smell of the Sèvres and Saint-Cloud woods. I recognize
the fresh smell of the woods, the scant smell of the birches, the somewhat sickly sweet smell of the chestnuts, the smell of the hazels. I
walk slowly along the Seine toward Chaillot, inhaling the breath of
the Seine. A dog barks in the distance, on the other bank.

Trucks rattle as they pass. A bicyclist comes toward me with tires
looped around his chest in a figure eight resembling (O Cocteau!)
the eight wrapped around Mercury's caduceus. The Eiffel Tower
winks at me with its lofty eye, in the azure meadows of the night sky;
the stars bob in the wind like primroses. In this limpid, luminous
December sky, there is something springlike that recalls May winds.

Some verses by Omar Khayyam come to mind, the verses that sing
the meadows of the Asian high plateaus bent under the east wind. I
feel young, free, and happy. My canine nature returns; I start to bark
like I do on the beach in Forte dei Marmi, or on the rocks of Capri,
at night, when I feel young, free, and happy. The dogs on the other
side of the Seine respond to me. I speak their language. I bark as I
walk, the long, passionate barking of dogs in love.

Under the bridge of the Grenelle Métro a policeman approaches
me and says, "Is monsieur a guard dog?" I offer him a cigarette; he
looks me over with a smile.

"I love dogs very much," I say.

"Has monsieur lost a dog?"

"Yes," I say, "he was my brother, and he died."

"Killed by the Germans?"

"No," I say, "the Germans didn't kill dogs."

"My dog was killed by the Germans," he says, "on the very day of the liberation."

"Dogs are better than men: they don't betray their friends."

"It's true," he says, "dogs are faithful friends."

"I would like to be a dog."

"Oh, it's very difficult to be a dog," he says.

"In Paris, is it prohibited to bark in the streets?"

"No, it's not prohibited. If you've paid the tax."

"Will you allow me to bark? It's my sole pleasure."

"Go right ahead, monsieur," he says.

I shake his hand; we smile at each other warmly. I walk away and start to bark again. A dog from the other bank replies. Halfway between the Pont de Grenelle and the Palais de Chaillot, I see men on the bank of the Seine. They're armed with barge poles. Something is floating on the current and they are pulling it to the bank. I stop, observing the men's gestures. The black form floating on the current approaches the bank. It's a corpse. I approach.

"What do you want?" a man asks, looking me up and down.

"Is this your corpse?"

"No."

"So let me look at what's not mine either."

It's a man of forty or so, dressed in black. A three-day beard darkens his face. His eyes are open, the head limp, floppy.

"He's been dead for a few days," says one of the men. "Look at his beard."

"Beards," I say, "don't grow on the faces of drowned men."

"Who told you that?" the man asks me.

"I know it. Hair grows on the faces of dead men, but not on the faces of those who drown."

"That's strange. I didn't know. Do you think he's been in the water for a long time?"

"I couldn't say. My impression is that he hasn't been in the water for more than a few hours."

"He's not wearing shoes," says the man.

"It's common for drowned men to lose their shoes," I reply. "The foot contracts and softens, and the shoe slips off."

"You're a specialist," the man says to me.

"I've lived on the seashore," I tell him. "During the war, the sea would throw back the corpses of drowned sailors onto the shore below my house, so I have a certain experience."

"Look at him. Do you think he was murdered?"

"I couldn't say. Ask the dead man."

"He doesn't respond, monsieur."

"No? He doesn't respond?"

"No, monsieur, he doesn't respond."

"He's a rude fellow. The dead are impolite."

"We need to notify the police."

"There's a policeman two hundred yards from here, toward the Pont de Grenelle. Go call him over."

"I'll go. You'll wait for me?"

"I'll keep watch over the dead man," I tell him. "I'll wait for you."

The man walks away. I remain alone beside the corpse. The dog from the opposite bank barks. I reply. A dialogue is established between me and the dog. The dog asks me what's going on. I reply that there's the corpse of a drowned man on the riverbank. The dog asks me who it is. I don't know. I don't know him. And anyway, all corpses look alike. The dog laughs. I laugh too. "What a funny idea," the dog says to me, "all corpses look alike!" "Yes," I reply, "all corpses look alike."

Finally the man and the policeman come down to the bank of the Seine.

"Ah, it's the gentleman who acts like a dog," says the policeman.

"You're the one who's barking?" the man asks me.

"Yes, that's me. Why?"

"Oh, no reason!" says the man.

The policeman looks at the corpse. "He must be taken to the morgue," he says.

"Right," says the man, "he can't be left here all night. There are a lot of mice around here."

"I'll go telephone the police station," says the policeman.

"I'll come with you," says the man.

"Why don't you want to stay with me?" I say to him. "Are you afraid of the corpse?"

"I'm afraid of you," says the man.

"You're afraid of this gentleman?" says the policeman.

"He barks like a dog," says the man.

"So?" says the policeman.

"He scares me," says the man.

"Aren't you afraid to leave me alone with this corpse?" I ask him. "Dogs eat corpses."

"Oh," says the man, "today would hardly be the first time a Frenchman ate a Frenchman."

"I'm not French," I tell him. "I'm a foreigner."

"You're a foreigner?" says the policeman.

"I'm Italian."

"Ah, you're Italian?" says the policeman. "Show me your documents."

"Here they are."

"Good. Malaparte, Curzio. Yes. I'm sorry, monsieur, but you'll have to come with me to see the police chief."

"Of course," I say.

"You never know with these foreigners," says the man.

"Will you follow me?" says the policeman.

"Of course, you never know with these foreigners."

Lunch at Mme de B.'s, on the Île Saint-Louis. The smallness of the rooms, the low ceilings, the smell of the wood, the small windows that look out onto the misty landscape of the Seine, the cries from the barges and the tugboats, and the skimming flight of the seagulls (are they seagulls?) over the gray water, remind me of my little apartment at 38 Quai de l'Horloge, on the Île de la Cité, near Pont Neuf.

Mme de B. welcomes me with her broad smile, which resembles the smile of Italian women (of the Milanese women Stendhal loved so much, of Angela Pietragrua, who made him suffer so much before disappointing him), and leads me into the drawing room. Claude Bourdet and Gérald Van der Kemp, curator at the Musée de Versailles, talk to me about Italy, about great Italian architects, "of which the greatest," I say, "were those from the Marche, like San Gallo, Sansovino, etc., Bramante, etc."

Van der Kemp talks to me about French architecture, which he calls the most beautiful in the world.

"You mean the architecture of the cathedrals," I say to him.

"No, I'm talking about the Louvre colonnade, for example, or Les Invalides."

"How can you admire," I say, "the Louvre colonnade?"

"I understand what you mean," Van der Kemp says, "but you'll agree with me about Les Invalides. It is the pinnacle of human architecture."

"Explain to me why."

"That dome, which is without a doubt the most beautiful dome in the world, and the gigantic triumphal arch that occupies the entire facade. Is there a building anywhere in the world that more solemnly expresses regality, dignity, triumph?"

"Nothing," I say, "surpasses Brunelleschi's dome in Florence. Michelangelo himself, after having built the dome of Saint Peter's, recognized that he fell short of Brunelleschi. The dome of Les Invalides cannot be compared with either that of Santa Maria del Fiore, or with the dome of Saint Peter's. As far as the arch of the facade, it reminds me of the arch of Tamerlane's mausoleum, in Samarkand. The style is Persian. Do you know Tamerlane's mausoleum in Samarkand?"

"I'm surprised," says Van der Kemp, "that you don't admire Les Invalides. It is, I repeat, the pinnacle of architecture. Men will never be able to outstrip this example."

"Let's set aside Les Invalides," I say. "Talk to me about Versailles."

Van der Kemp talks to me about Versailles. He tells me that the sum spent to build Versailles is no greater than that spent every year to maintain the châteaux of France. Comparing it with today's prices, the Château de Versailles cost very little.

The conversation continues at the lunch table. Claude Bourdet talks to me about the Resistance. I ask him why his newspaper *Combat* persists in slandering me. "For Italians, I was part of the Resistance; why, in France, would you have me pass for a collaborator? You'd think that the French were the only ones to have resisted, in all of Europe."

"You find it odd to be a target in my newspaper," says Bourdet.

"Of course," I say. "What would you say if I wrote in an Italian newspaper that you had been a collaborator?"

"I would say that you slander me."

"That's what I say about what you're writing about me."

Claude Bourdet seems to be getting annoyed. If he had any powers of observation, he would see that I couldn't care less what he says about me. Yes, it's a foregone conclusion, the only ones who carried out a resistance were the French. Everyone else was a collaborator.

Van der Kemp tells me he would like to go to Italy, at the beginning of next year. I give him addresses in Florence, Rome, Capri. We talk about Versailles. He talks to me about Versailles with a love and a delicacy that charm me. Bourdet listens to us in silence.

"Versailles," he says at a certain point, "is the heart of the French monarchy."

I expected him to say that Versailles is the heart of the French Resistance. You never know. Van der Kemp asks me what my current personal situation is in relation to Italy.

"It would be more accurate," I say, "to ask what Italy's situation is in relation to me."

Van der Kemp laughs; Bourdet wrinkles his brow. No one realizes it's possible to regally disregard such things. Why should I care what the Italians think of me? The fascists used to hate me; now the antifascists hate me. So what? It's very revealing that they show such an interest in me, one side as much as the other.

We get up from the table, pass into a small sitting room. One by one the guests leave.

"Stay," Mme de B. says to me.

I stay; there are three of us: Mme de B., a lady of a certain age who, during the entire lunch, had not said a word, staring at me all the while, and me. At a certain point Mme de B. leaves the room. I remain alone with the lady.

"Does this apartment not remind you of anything?" the lady asks me. She has dark hair, with some silver at the temples. Her face is pretty, if lined with wrinkles. Her mouth is tired, soft; her forehead reveals her age. I look at her, trying to remember where I have seen that face before.

"It reminds me of my apartment on the Quai de l'Horloge."

"Your apartment was very beautiful," she says to me.

"Did you know it?"

"Of course. I was there several times. You don't remember me anymore?"

I look at her, scrutinizing her face, her mouth, her eyes.

"I loved you very much," she says in a low voice.

I look at her.

"You were cruel to me," she says in a low voice, "and quickly forgot me. Your love did not last a month. I suffered very much when I read that you were in prison. Why didn't you respond to my letters?"

I had never received those letters. Prisoners did not receive letters, especially those coming from abroad. I take her hand, feel her tremble.

"I've terribly changed, haven't I?" she says.

I close my eyes. Fifteen years have passed since I left Quai de l'Horloge, Paris, France.

I say to her: "Speak to me, say something."

"I am dead," she says.

Her voice resounds through the wind of those fifteen years, a distant voice, the voice of a stranger.

She stands and offers me her hand.

"Goodbye," she says.

I clasp her hand between my own. I close my eyes. I feel her warm and trembling hand slip from mine. I hear soft steps move away, a door that opens and closes again.

France gets upset because I say that the Resistance is a European phenomenon, and that certain French people believe the Resistance happened in France alone. It's absolutely true!

An Italian comes to France: It is immediately thought and written of him that he is pro-German (because Italy was in the Axis), that he's a fascist (because there was fascism in Italy), that he's a collaborator. He demonstrates that he was anti-German, antifascist, that he was in the Italian Resistance. His denial goes unheeded. He's Italian; therefore he is what he's believed to be. In getting upset, France demonstrates the truth of what I say. How hateful and petty the nationalist spirit is! Try to tell someone in Paris that there was also a resistance in Germany! And yet there weren't just Jews in the German concentration camps. There were also Germans there. Yes, but... Enough said.

Lunch at Taillevent, with —— . I find myself among intelligent, cultured, sensitive, smiling men and women.

How different from Italian lunches, where, if you're not of the same opinion as everyone else, they look at you with a sullen, ridiculous, and cowardly hate. I say *cowardly*, because as far as the courage of sectarians goes, there's much that might be said.

The lunch is, alas, in my honor, and since I don't care for ceremonial meals, I would find myself at a bit of a loss, if the conversation were not of such exquisite taste and discretion. I observe that there is a great deal of curiosity about me. They look at me, question me, study me, but with considerable grace and restraint. It's not a lunch of judges but, let's say, of doctors. The culprit—I mean the patient— is me.

So much has been said about my cynicism, my cold cruelty, that

I amuse myself imagining that the worst is being thought about me at this table. If they only knew the truth. But why speak the truth? Why defend myself? Why take away their delusions, which they love? Little by little I understand that they too think I am a collaborator, and that they all consider themselves sublime resistants. I sit here before them like a bloody collaborator. "Let them believe what they want about me, it doesn't matter," Gide would say, "I'm writing *Paludes*."

Little by little I amuse myself in misleading them. It's so simple to seem what others want you to seem. I am a citizen of the Axis, an Italian, so it's very easy and very comfortable to deduce from that that I am a collaborator. How my Italian friends would laugh, if they were here. There are no resistants anywhere but in France, it's obvious. But why doesn't it occur to them to wonder whether I might not be a collaborator? Why doesn't it enter their head to ask me whether I am a collaborator? Out of politeness, they don't ask. And out of politeness they offend me, they insult me, with their looks and their veiled allusions.

I'm seated next to a very pretty, very intelligent young woman, whose wit, intelligence, and literary talent I would later have the opportunity to appreciate: Claudine Chonez. She tells me she was in Italy as a French officer, with the rank of lieutenant. She tells me this as if to say: "And you, dear sir? Where were you then? With the Germans?" This amuses me. I would like to say to her: "But I too was an officer at the time, on the Cassino front with the Allies. What's so special about you, etc.?" But I'm amused to see her pretty face so full of irony, her smiling at me as if she had caught me out.

I would have liked to say to her as well: "Did the Germans arrest you in 1941? I say 1941, and not 1943, with good reason. So, I was arrested by the Germans in 1941, and I was sentenced to four months, for my war correspondence from the Russian front. If, in 1943, the Allies had arrested you for your war correspondence, it would have meant you were a collaborationist. If the Germans arrested me in 1941 for my correspondence, it's because I was a resistant. How can you be Cartesian, and not understand logic?"

But I keep quiet, because the conversation takes an interesting turn. They ask me whether Mussolini is hated in Italy. Of course, I respond, from the moment he fell. If you don't want to be hated, you'd better not bite the dust. They look at me as if I've said something cynical. Dear God, I don't understand anything anymore. But Marshal Pétain, was he not hated after he fell? Thus is the human heart made, that woe betide anyone who falls. And the higher he falls from, the more he'll be hated. Everyone goggles at me, and I laugh to myself, because the entire conversation is based on an amusing misunderstanding: they think that I'm an Italian collaborator and that they're the only resistants in Europe.

It's at this moment that my demon whispers an amusing idea in my ear, a truly amusing idea. "Think," I say, "what would have happened if Mussolini, in September 1943, instead of getting himself rescued by the Germans, had gone underground, only to set himself up as the head of the Resistance that didn't exist yet? He would have become the leader of the Italian Resistance against the Germans, who had occupied the country." Everyone looks at me in astonishment; voices rise in protest around the table. Me, I enjoy myself and laugh. Why not? If Marshal Pétain, in November 1942—at the time, that is, when collaboration officially began—had become the leader of the Resistance against the Germans, think what would have happened! The hero of Verdun at the head of the partisan army that's fighting the Germans! But everything I say is interpreted in a strange way, as the words of a collaborator. What can I do, dear God? It doesn't matter, I'm writing *Paludes*.

Only Claudine Chonez seems to have grasped my irony. She smiles. She looks at me askance, but she smiles. Descaves, too, has a suspicion, a very slight suspicion. She keeps quiet and gives me a strange look. It's a lunch in my honor, of course. Alas, all the Attic salt, all the *humor*, all the irony of my words is lost. For them I am nothing but a collaborator. A talented writer, of course, but a collaborator. Whatever I say or do, I am judged. Alas, irony is dead in Europe. No one knows how to judge anymore. Nonetheless, it would be easy to ask me: "Pardon me, monsieur, were you a collaborator?" But I can't answer a question that isn't asked me. *Excusatio non petita, accusatio manifesta*.[1] All in all, I'm amused.

I'm dining with Paul Reynaud when he asks me: "Do you have faith in the future of your country"?

I answer that I have full faith.

"Why, though?"

"Because Italy is not a state. It's a people."

"Nevertheless, it's a people in terrible conditions, just like the French."

"Yes, but it's not a state. It's a people. In Europe, the future lies not with states, but with peoples."

I run into Max Dorian. It's been fourteen years since I saw him last. He invites me for a drink at Fouquet's.

We were good friends in 1931 and 1933. He worked at Denoël, doing press service for L.-F. Céline's books. Now and then he would come over to Grasset. Then I was arrested, sentenced, confined to Lipari. During my confinement he wrote to me often, sent me newspapers and magazines. Then came the war, and I lost track of him. When *Kaputt* appeared in France, he published some stupid, nasty lines about me in a Nice weekly, *Midi*. I responded harshly to him, and so did Henry Muller, in *Carrefour*, who had been singled out by Dorian for no reason whatsoever. After this incident, he wrote to me very amicably. I didn't harbor any bitterness toward him for his idiotic and cowardly words, I'm so used to being betrayed by friends!

We sit down at a table in Fouquet's, as if nothing had happened. We talk about the rain and about the nice weather. He tells me that he has to leave for America, where his wife is waiting for him.

And suddenly he says to me: "Do you know why I attacked you in *Midi*?"

I reply that I don't know.

"Because you were happy," he says.

I look at him in astonishment. "Are you sure I was happy in Paris in 1931 and 1933?" I ask him.

"You loved a woman, she was beautiful," he says. "She came from Italy to join you here; when she left she was crying. She was very pretty and very kind."

"I was not happy in Paris in those years," I tell him. "I felt what was about to happen to me, I had a presentiment. I would often cry for no reason. Just ask Daniel Halévy, or Pierre Bessand-Massenet, Guéhenno, Henry Muller, Sabatier, my friends from then. Ask them if I was happy at the time."

"I don't know what it means to be happy," Dorian says to me.

"And anyway, it's not a crime to be happy," I say.

"She was very beautiful," he says. "She loved you very much. You were happy."

A long moment of silence. Fouquet's is deserted inside; everyone's out on the terrace. The voices come through the glass as a gentle hum. The voices are foreign: Romanian, Italian, Spanish, American—foreign. But Dorian's voice is French. I don't like hearing all those foreign voices in Paris. I would like Dorian to talk to me in his rapid voice, his French voice. Despite everything, I love him. I am faithful to friendship. When a friend betrays me I remain faithful to the memory of his friendship. I can't hate him, because his friendship was dear to me, because the memory of his friendship is dear to me.

"Why did you hurt me?" I ask him. "Why did you slander me? You know well that everything you said about me was false."

"Yes, I know," he replies. "But you were happy. And you didn't see that I was unhappy."

"You're mad," I say.

"Who says I'm mad?" he replies, staring at me and blushing. "It's true, I risked becoming completely mad. It's not my fault, I didn't do it on purpose. My wife wanted to leave me. You don't bear a grudge against me?"

"No, I don't bear a grudge against you, I understand you."

"Do you want to come to dinner at my place tomorrow evening? The Troubetzkoys will be there. I'd like you to be my friend again."

"I am your friend. You know that."

"No. You don't love unhappy men."

I run into Marion in the Place Vendôme. She's working at Schiaparelli's. She's Swiss, and kind. "Where are you going, Charlotte?" She's going to Bettina Bergery's. I like Bettina Bergery very much. I remember when I first saw her enter Élisabeth de Gramont's drawing room, in Rue Raynouard, sixteen years ago. She was blond, tall, slim, and smiling, with that smile stuck to her red lips like the smile of the cat in the blue air, on the green branches, in *Alice in Wonderland*.

I like Bettina very much. She was smiling, kind, blond, and white, like all American women in Paris when they're smiling, kind, blond, and white. She would look me up and down, entering Élisabeth de Gramont's drawing room, with the eyes both curious and disdainful of women when they meet a man of the day (I was then a man of the day), of American women in Paris when their eyes are curious and disdainful. Beside and a bit behind her, a bit removed, was Gaston Bergery: blond, with the slight frame of a cat, blue eyes, thin lips. He had just lost his electoral battle in Mantes. He had half-closed eyes, a sleepy look, a bit like Chateaubriand, fallen asleep and from his horse on the road to Damascus (book ——, chap. —— of *Memoirs from Beyond the Grave*).

"I'm going to Bettina's," Charlotte tells me. A beautiful young woman, Charlotte. Blond, pink, smiling, a bit masculine, but full of ovaries up to her neck.

Élisabeth de Gramont was telling us the story of Rue Raynouard: where Montesquiou lived, and Jacques-Émile Blanche. I remember Jacques-Émile Blanche in Daniel Halévy's library, in 39 Quai de l'Horloge, sixteen years ago. How quickly time passes when you're far from Paris.

Seated in an armchair, his legs crossed, his hands crossed on his stomach, his head slightly bent toward his chest, his myopic eyes twinkling behind the filmy reflection of his pince-nez, he looks at me without speaking, with the gentle disdain of a goat. I feel that he disdains me, and I don't know why. I feel that he disdains everyone and everything around him, Daniel Halévy, Marianne Halévy, and Françoise Joxe, who tiptoes lightly by at that moment. He stares at his portrait of Marianne Halévy: she is beautiful and pale and smiling, with long red hair, against a drab and gloomy background, a species of night, which the painters of the Falières period would use, like an underlayer of gold, as the background for their canvases. He stares at the sketches, drawings, and paintings hung on the walls with the obstinate, greedy gaze of a goat. I wouldn't leave him alone like this in a room; he's capable of eating everything, of grazing like a goat. I see him, Montesquiou, and Marcel Proust, these three sacred goats, walk up Rue Raynouard, grazing on everything in their path. The other day I crossed Rue Raynouard, and they had left untouched only a strip of sky between the houses at no. —— and those at no. ——, at the corner of Rue ——. But you could see in this untouched strip of sky the marks of a strong set of teeth, without a doubt Montesquiou's.

"He had strong teeth," Boldini would say about him, in his Ferrarese accent. "When I did his portrait, I held the brush in my hand like a club, ready to strike him on the neck if he'd tried to bite me."

Yes, that smile on those beautiful and strong teeth. People with strong teeth. Goats with strong teeth. That's why I wouldn't leave Jacques-Émile Blanche alone in my drawing room: he would graze on everything, even the harpsichord.

And suddenly—I'll remember it for the rest of my life—Bettina, too, began to laugh, displaying her own strong teeth, the white teeth of a young goat, and I was afraid. Élisabeth de Gramont, too, began to laugh, like a goat; around the table, everyone was laughing like goats, and at the far end of the table, between two still-young women, Max Jacob, with all his beautiful, white, false teeth, was laughing like a billy goat. And a billy goat smell, strong and sweet, emanated from his old laughter, rose to the ceiling, suffused the blue stagnant-water reflections of the large Venetian mirrors.

Marion walked beside me with her long, springy stride, and when we were in the Place de la Concorde, I said to Marion, "Look at that green cloud up there." The cloud was a raw green, a cloud of fresh grass, and it floated above the Seine like an upside-down meadow. A green light bathed the Place de la Concorde. It's like walking in a transparent forest. The bronze of the fountain statues is green. I remember the "singing fountains" in *Fantômas* (and the suddenly childlike face of Jean Cocteau when I reminded him, the other evening, about the singing fountains in *Fantômas*, the singing fountains of the Place de la Concorde), and I smile kindly at Marion and say to her: "It's as if we were walking in a transparent forest, a forest of glass." And Marion smiles at me kindly, looking across at me with those wide, slightly oblique eyes that mountain women sometimes have. I don't know why the women from mountainous countries, the women of Ramuz, the women of Giono, have long, wide, slightly oblique eyes. Perhaps it's due to the valleys, because mountain people live without a horizon in the valleys, and their gaze shifts from right to left in the corridor of the valley, or perhaps for the same mysterious reason that goats and chamois have the same long, slightly oblique eyes and wide pupils.

Marion looks at me and smiles, tells me how Mme Schiaparelli sometimes walks along the Seine, or spends hours in the middle of the Place de la Concorde, looking at the Paris sky, the color of the trees and of the water of the Seine, seeing the colors of her fabrics, discovering the folds of her designs in the clouds. Everything is mental for Mme Schiaparelli; she thinks of a new color without seeing it, thinks of it at night in her bed, in a completely abstract way, in a way I would call Cartesian.

This reminds me of the director of a large perfume house, who would say to me, "I first think of a perfume. I don't smell it, I think it, I conceive of it in a mental, abstract way, as if I were thinking of a number, as if I were performing an arithmetical operation, adding two numbers, or multiplying them. I think, and the result is the new perfume, which I don't smell, whose odor I cannot perceive. I think it, and it's an abstract perfume: I have it in my head, in my brain, not in my nostrils. Then, in the laboratory, I translate this abstract idea of the perfume into a smell, as if I were writing down a number, the result of an arithmetical operation. For me the perfume is first of all an idea, not a smell."

We cross the Seine, cross Boulevard Saint-Germain, enter the Place du Palais-Bourbon, enter Rue de Bourgogne, enter the door at no. 29, climb the stairs, and on the first-floor landing meet a gentleman who respectfully asks us if we know what floor Mme Bettina Bergery lives on.

"No, I can't remember," says Marion. No one can remember; the porter's lodge was empty; we'll end up guessing.

"I forgot it," the gentleman says politely. "I always forget everything. My memory is very, very weak." He has a light South American accent, maybe he is South American, with his smooth face, fair eyes, pleasant voice, polite manners. At last Marion says, "It must be here." We ring the bell, they open, and we enter: it's here.

The polite gentleman has already forgotten us. He shakes the hand of every woman twice. Bettina Bergery stands smiling before me, and Gaston Bergery is there smiling too, and I suddenly remember the young woman we met on the stairs, when we were looking for Bettina's door. A young woman dressed in black, in black velvet, I think, because I remember the soft reflection of her dress on the ivory white of the stairway walls and on the brown of the wooden steps. A young woman with a smiling face and a large black velvet hat à la Rembrandt, who said to me as she passed, calling me by name, "How are you! Don't you recognize me?" Yes, of course I recognized her. She was a known face, a face that was familiar but from the past, oh, from the distant past, like a face that emerges from a painting, a face from a painter's canvas. Marion says to me, "It was Leonor Fini." Ah, Leonor Fini, it's been sixteen years since I saw her last, how much *blanc de plomb* has dried in its tin tubes since then, with the white label and the words *blanc de plomb* from Lefranc, Paris, 1931. I remember the day I climbed the stairs of her new apartment, on Boulevard Saint-Germain, I think. It was a new apartment, which she was setting up. Workers passed to and fro through the small rooms—painters, carpenters, joiners, plumbers—and Leonor Fini sat across from me, drawing my portrait, a portrait of a young man that resembles Holbein's *Duke of Southwell*, which is in the Uffizi, in Florence.[2]

Dear, dear Leonor, always young and fresh, with her beautiful, insolent, and tender mouth, with the eyes of a woman who does not believe that women have a common destiny. Stanislas de La Roche-foucauld is here as well, sitting on a sofa between two young women, as is his wife, ——, and the countess ——, and a tall blond Englishman, slightly bald, with mustaches that were fashionable among cavalry officers in the Chelsea barracks before 1914, the same style that Harold Nicholson continued to uphold after 1914. And seated in an armchair, her intelligent face slightly bent over her shoulder, Mme Schiaparelli looks at me with her dark eyes, where the intelligence sometimes rests, and sometimes rises up, threatening, like a beast in a cage. I see reflected in her dark eyes furniture, people, glasses set on a large table, but all upside down, like in a crystal ball, and suddenly I see something emerge amid all this upside-down furniture in the eyes of Mme Schiaparelli, and I say to myself with a shiver, "It's her," and I turn, and it's her.

Tall and slender, her forehead high, narrow, immense, the forehead of an Etruscan statue, the oblique eyes of an Etruscan statue, the mouth of an Etruscan statue. All the noise of the sea envelops her, and the smell of the sea follows her, and the blue and green light of the sea surrounds her, and I see again her naked foot on the sands of Forte dei Marmi, I hear again her blue and pale green voice perch atop the crest of the waves like a white gull.

In the room the street noises die down little by little, like the distant noise of the sea. The noises die in the ears of the young women sitting in deep sofas, like the sound of the sea in a conch shell. And Bettina has pink ears, and Marion white ears, and —— blue ears, and —— has green ears, and —— has silver ears, and —— gold ears.

And when I stand up, the night has already fallen over the roofs, the sidewalks glisten from the light autumn rain, the Place de la Concorde is like the Naples sea when the fishermen emerge with their glowing lamps, which you can see swinging in the distance on the waves. "Right here," I say to Marion. "This is where I met Jean Giraudoux for the last time." Giraudoux would turn from time to time to call his dog Puck, an invisible dog that followed him everywhere, and he would say to me, "Isn't my Puck a handsome dog?" And I would reply, "Yes, your Puck is a handsome dog," and I wouldn't see a thing, because the dog Puck wasn't there. He was at home, in his dog bed, but Giraudoux liked to take walks in the evening, followed by his invisible dog, whom he would call from time to time in his deep voice: "Puck, come here. Puck, watch out for the car." It was the last time I saw Jean Giraudoux. And Marion says to me: "Goodbye, see you tomorrow?" I tell her: "Of course we'll see each other, Marion. I'll come to get you at Schiaparelli's." She says to me: "Till tomorrow." Yes, till tomorrow.

She crosses the street, enters the Crillon. She enters the Crillon with her long, agile stride. I head for Rue Gambon, enter the Hôtel de Castille, and go up to my room. Jean Giraudoux is there, and he says to me, "Have you by any chance seen my dog Puck?" No, I haven't seen him. "That's strange, I left him here. I come back, and I can't find him anymore." Maybe he went out for a walk with Jean Giraudoux. "Ah, yes," says Jean Giraudoux, "that's right, he must have gone out for a walk with Jean Giraudoux." Because my room at the Hôtel de Castille is the same one in which Jean Giraudoux spent the last days of his life, and now he's here, I know he's here. May I turn off the light? "Yes," he says to me, "you can sleep. I'm going to wait for Puck to return."

Goodnight, Giraudoux. Goodnight, my friend. And here begins the dream, with its clarity, its precision, its realism, and everything is exact, everything is true, everything is precise, real, until I awake, until I plunge back into Paris, which is so sweet, so unreal, so similar to this dream that is life.

I meet Colette Clément at the Crillon. She is fascinating, elegant, smiling. An old friend, since 1936, Constance Coline.[3]

I'll always remember when she visited me in Italy. She told me she was in the Resistance, and looked at me with an ironic smile, as if to say: "You, on the other hand…" It's extraordinary, the idea the French have of the Resistance. There's only them, in all of Europe; the rest are collaborators. Why deprive her of this illusion, which makes her believe she is a heroine in my eyes? I've seen so many of them, heroes and heroines, that I will never pose as a hero. I've had enough. I did my duty as a resistant, at the front from 1943 to 1945, on the front lines with the Allies. I have a commendation from the Allied general headquarters—I'm indifferent to what people think of me. I have opted to behave like a foreigner, and a foreigner must have a great deal of tact, a great deal of discretion.

If I were to say, "But I too am a member of the Resistance, a hero, like you!" the whole effect would be lost. Why ruin their little effect? I'm a foreigner, I don't have the right. And I calmly reply, "I know. You were brave. I am happy to know that you were very brave." It's the truth. Just based on a lie. On the lie of what she thinks of me.[4]

De Pisis and I leave the house of Juliette Bertrand. We cross the Pont de l'Alma toward Rue Galilée.

De Pisis walks with a light step, cane in hand, and turns his head to the left and to the right, sniffing the fresh night air. He says, "Ah, how good it is! How good it is!" He licks the trees, the clouds, the red reflections that rise from the Place de la Concorde, the white clouds that float on the surface of the misty sky, like a child licking barley sugar. He turns his face toward things as if sniffing a tasty dish, a nice beef bourguignon, a nice fish à la provençale, a nice Normandy stew. "A painter," he says, "has to know how to eat, has to know the art of cuisine. You can't appreciate Delacroix, Degas, Géricault, Picasso himself, if you don't have a taste for good things, for good food."

I remember a visit I paid him in 1931, in his apartment at 7 Rue Servandoni. He was painting a fish, a beautiful silver and blue trout. As he painted, he spoke to me about the Place Saint-Sulpice, about Rue Servandoni. "Have you seen," he says to me, "the stores that sell religious articles? The Virgins, the Baby Jesuses, the Saints, all made of wax? The flowers and crosses made of silver? Don't they remind you of the Borgo, in front of Saint Peter's in Rome? The shops here smell of provincial cooking, of old provincial dishes." He looked at the trout with gluttonous eyes, the eyes of a painter who tastes his colors. An Italian friend, the publisher and painter Longanesi, having come to visit him on Rue Servandoni not long after, tells me how De Pisis invited him to lunch. "I'll cook," said De Pisis, and he put the fish he was painting into a pot. The fish, like everything De Pisis paints, was not fresh, and smelled slightly. It smelled like flowers.

In the Métro taking me to La Motte Picquet, a lady approaches and asks me if I'm Spanish. I answer no, that I'm Italian. She looks at me in silence, then says, "Are you the one who killed my son?" I answer her that I have never killed anyone. "My son died in 1940, in Belgium," she tells me. I tell her that her son was probably killed by the Germans, since there weren't any Italians in Belgium. "It's all the same," she says, "you killed him." At a certain point I'm afraid she's going to start yelling, because she gives me a very strange look. "Excuse me, Madame," I say, "but the Italians are not Germans." "Oh," she says, "they're very similar." She looks at me, then she starts laughing. "It's not true," she says, "I don't have children, I didn't have any children killed in the war." I ask her why, then? She says: "To see the face you'd make." "What face did I make?" "I thought that if I'd had a son killed in the war, and that you had killed this son, you would have made that same face." When I leave the Métro she says goodbye to me and smiles. What a strange encounter.

The sun is out this morning, a bright, warm sun pervaded by the drone of invisible insects. The leaves on the trees, burned by autumn's lazy fire, strangely glimmer. The water of the Seine is green, swollen with earth, and with the sky; enormous white clouds, slashed with blue, tumble in the current, shatter against the bridge piers. The flag over the French parliament makes an Utrillo-esque blot. I enter the

Tuileries Garden and sit down on a bench, joining a young mother already seated there.

A young boy romps in front of her; he runs, stops, lifts his head, closes his eyes, calls out, "Maman." Moments later the child comes toward me, runs into my knees, stops, stares at me with fear. "He's blind," the mother says to me in a low voice. I touch the boy's hand, clasp it between my own. "Who's there?" asks the child. "I'm a general," I answer, "dressed in red and blue, with a hat full of feathers on my head, a great sword at my side, and my horse is waiting for me at the end of the path."

The boy starts to laugh, then he says to me, "I'm the horse."

"I know, you're my horse. Gallop!"

The child sets off at a gallop, then returns to me.

"Why are your ears red?" says the man.

"I'm the king's horse," the boy says.

"Yes, I am the king," says the man. "I'd forgotten that I'm the king today. Do you want to call my soldiers for me?"

"Yes," says the boy, and gallops away. He turns around, comes back, stands at attention in front of the man, and says, "I'm the army."

"This morning I declared war, we must fight. Go and win the battles."

"Yes," says the boy. He kneels, takes aim with an imaginary rifle, and fires. He makes the sound of a cannon, a rifle, a drum, a trumpet.

"You're dead," the man shouts at him.

The child falls, with a high-pitched cry, and his dog runs up to him, whining, licking his tiny master.

"What do you see?" the man asks.

"I see the Virgin," says the pale child, "and the Saints."

"Do you see Christ?" says the man.

"I don't see Christ, I see Napoleon," says the dead child.

"Do you see your comrades who died for France?" says the man.

"I see all my dead comrades," says the dead child.

"How are they dressed?" says the man.

"They're dressed in red, green, and yellow. They have eyes that twinkle like two stars, they're very happy to be dead."

"Now return to the royal palace," says the man.

The dead child stands up and returns to the man.

"Let's go to the theater," says the man.

"Oh, yes," says the boy, "I really like the theater."

"Let's go," says the man, and he sets off, holding the boy by the hand. They take two steps, then slowly return to sit down on the bench.

"They're playing *Cyrano*," says the man.

"I really like *Cyrano*," says the boy.

"Quiet," says the man.

The two stare in front of them, following with their eyes the show on the invisible stage. From time to time the boy applauds, overjoyed.

"Oh, he's such a good actor!" says the man.

Suddenly it begins to rain. The drops are fat and warm and raise a small cloud of dust from the gravel paths of the garden. A light mist veils the trees of the Champs-Élysées. The man stands, saying, "It's raining. It happens every time, when they perform *Cyrano*: it rains. Let's go."

He takes the child by the hand, calls out "Mouton." The dog approaches. The man attaches a leash to its neck and the three slowly set off, the dog turning from time to time to look at his masters. I follow them with my eyes, without understanding.

"They're both blind," says the woman sitting on the other bench. "They used to come here almost every day; for the last few weeks they've been going to the Luxembourg Gardens. But they like the Tuileries."

"They were born blind?"

"Yes, they've never seen things. The world they imagine for themselves is very strange. They play at seeing each other, in color. Do you understand?"

I returned the next day. They weren't there. Two days later I saw them. They played war, describing aloud the soldiers' uniforms. I understood that what they depicted were not facts, characters, or roles, but colors and forms. When, after their game, they got up to go, I approached the man and, doffing my hat, asked him if I could accompany them under my umbrella. They thanked me, and we set off. The boy asked me what color my umbrella was. "Black," I answered. The man turned his face toward me and I noted a slight tremor in his lips. We walked in silence. Beneath the arcades of the Place des Pyramides, the man thanked me and lifted his hat. Then he said to me in a low voice: "Why deceive us? There are no black umbrellas. Your umbrella is red. Why lie?" And he went away, holding the boy by the hand.

An undefinable sadness strikes me in the streets of the Rive Gauche, once so dear to my heart. A feeling of wretchedness, of sadness, of illness, invades me little by little. Only the French flag, the little tricolor trophies on the doors of town hall offices, police stations, and barracks, creates the mood of an Épinal print, evokes something of the naivete and grace of the people's placid good humor, now lost. The memory of Utrillo, perhaps, and of Apollinaire. Just these two. Victor Hugo falls outside. The dark streets of Baudelaire fall outside. Balzac too. As does everything and everyone. Just Utrillo and Apollinaire.

And this sky of blue paper, of thick blue paper, stretched over the roofs of the houses, over the gray slate of the roofs, over gray and yellow walls, and over this invisible layer of pink that enlivens the dull tones of the yellows, the blue, the gray, the green. But only at the end of Rue Saint-Dominique, of Rue de Grenelle, of Rue de l'Université, toward Les Invalides, beyond Les Invalides, where the Seine's reflection gradually invades the sky, does it turn the Paris sky into a gray-blue lake, traversed by the light breeze that descends from the banks of the river, Meudon, Sèvres, Saint-Cloud.

A sky full of green and blue water, a Manet sky in places. Oh, but did Manet go so far inside this Paris sky as to be able to see the invisible pink and green and yellow that is mixed in with the visible blue? Courbet flew through the Lazio sky like an angel. Like one of those Etruscan angels that flew through the Roman sky to watch over the

Holy City. Courbet drew his landscapes with a pencil, and there was pink, green, and yellow in his gray pencil, in his black pencil. And Manet's blacks, his Goya-esque blacks that, in his Île-de-France landscapes, so strangely depend on the greens and pinks. The whole Rive Gauche retains the memory of these blues, these greens, and these pinks that were the colors of eighteenth-century Paris, the colors of Watteau and Greuze.

The people in the streets are a Parisian people, in which the few Sidis who come from the banks of the Seine preserve their Second Empire complexion, and the few bougnats to have arrived in recent times contribute a gray note.[5] But the workers, the merchants, the men in the doorways of the bistros, of the bakeries, of the groceries, the housewives with their shopping bags hanging from their arms, even the cats asleep in the shopwindows, have preserved this Parisian sky since 1789, this children's sky all pink, all gray, all blue, this sky made of the thick blue paper used for wrapping sugar in. The shouts, the voices, the sweet screech of the wheels, weave a lattice of sound, a pink arabesque in the sky above the roofs. The birds, invisible, sing in the folds of the sky as if in the folds of thick blue paper. And when they beat their wings, something falls from the sky, a blue powder that covers the windowpanes, that settles on the windowsills, on the ridges in the plaster of the facades, a powder that is a green rain, a blue snow, a pink ash.

This woman at the window who shakes her hair, who sinks a shiny comb into her hair, a shiny white comb of old bone, the polished, shiny, smooth bone of a cat, why does she speak, and to whom? The house across the street has its windows closed; this woman is not speaking to anyone, or else she's speaking to her own image reflected in the sky.

Cat bones, white, smooth, and shiny: are the crosses I'm looking at in the window of this funeral parlor in Rue Saint-Dominique not perhaps made of cat bones?[6]

Soldiers pass by in the streets, silently laughing, like the soldiers who pass by in Degas paintings. And this horse that rears up at the corner is a Delacroix horse, with its black satin coat, its swollen mane, its small hooves like women's feet.

By now this tenderness is all that remains in Europe, this tenderness of the Parisian people of the Rive Gauche, the tenderness and the sweetness of these sweet voices, of such a tender pink. The sky like a leaf, where the shouts and the voices sketch the green veins of young leaves, of new leaves. A somewhat pleated sky over there, toward the dome of Les Invalides, toward that gentle rippling in the sky. No, it's not the sky of Utrillo, or of Apollinaire, or of Baudelaire, or of Verlaine; it's not that sky but another sky, one without sadness, without remorse, without love, even. A sky of a tenderness that knows nothing of love, feelings of sadness, or even the somewhat vagabond joy proper to these poets and painters.

But the deep, dark, and mysterious sadness of Manet's blacks and pinks, where nude women, Olympia, dissolve in the air like a drop of honey in water.

Rive Gauche Paris, Paris as a dead young girl, a young model all pink, all blue, made of dust; the Paris of houses made from the smooth and shining bones of white cats; thick-blue-paper-sky Paris; Paris with its silent funerals, funerals redolent of cat fur, blue and pink and gray and yellow funerals; closed-window Paris; the Paris of gray slate cobblestones, of roofs of pink leaves, of corners where the Seine flows and rises up to see the bus pass when the gentlemen on the upper deck have removed their tall hats so as not to touch the green branches of the yellow trees lining the new boulevards.

How pleasant it is to rediscover the Rive Gauche liberated from this Balkan rabble, from these transatlantic drunkards, who had changed even the name of the Rive Gauche, to the *Left Bank*. It's a Rive Gauche that's been deserted, inhabited solely by the indigenous population, by the petty bourgeois, by the modestly well-to-do ruined by the war and inflation, by ministry employees. But it's the Rive Gauche again, not the *Left Bank*.

Paris, along with Florence, is the city where the tedium of life hangs heaviest in the air.

It's easier in Paris than elsewhere to hate life. And that arises perhaps from the fact that the effort required to live there is greater than elsewhere; not for the usual and minor material reasons, but because Paris does not offer the sense of eternity that nature offers, and that is offered by some cities, like Athens or Rome. The sense of Paris is fugitive, ephemeral, fleeting, provisional. The spirits there are intent on seizing the transient moment, on seizing its meaning, its individual raison d'être.

This is why French literature is so very subtle, the opposite of Italian literature, for example, or Spanish, which is sensual and rather coarse, because it's happy with what can be seen and touched, and doesn't worry about getting inside things and feelings. French literature is analytical, introspective, fastidious, highly astute in seizing the most ephemeral and delicate feelings and thoughts, and binding them to the French philosophical system, which is more a method of thought than thought itself. The Parisian spirit is light, elegant, brilliant, impulsive; it is interested only in what sparkles, and is thus essentially feminine.

I thought about all this, with admiration and sadness, as I listened to Anouilh's play *La Marguerite*.[7] There is a clear effort there to react against an elegant and ironic tradition, to laugh bitterly at what ordinarily provokes a gentle, fleeting laugh. Teaching the French to hate life seems to me the secret aim of a good part of literature, especially since Baudelaire. Not with romantic poses but with nastiness, a nastiness of which there is hardly a trace in French literature until *Les Liaisons dangereuses*, a nastiness that is perhaps more Parisian than French, and that in the upper class, and not among the common people, achieves a kind of perfection not found anywhere else. By *nastiness* I don't mean, of course, frivolity, fickleness, maliciousness, and the other defects found in all elegant high society, but nastiness true and proper, with which Paris teaches hate for what in life is not frivolous, or fickle, or malicious.

Perhaps it's necessary to not be French to grasp this Parisian sadness, this ravishing cruelty.

Tolstoy, *War and Peace*. How the Russian people imagined the French, during the retreat from Moscow. "They're white as birch trees," says one soldier. And further on he says: "But here's something that doesn't make sense, you guys: a farmer near Mozhaysk told me about how, when they started to carry away the fallen soldiers, where the battle had been . . . Guess what? He told me that, think about this, their dead had gone unburied for a whole month. And that, he said, some of them lay there, clean and white as paper, and didn't stink at all."

"What, because of the cold?" asks a soldier.

"You're so clever! Because of the cold! It was hot then. If they had been frozen, ours wouldn't have rotted either. And instead, you went up to one of ours, and you found him all teeming with worms. So we covered our mouth and nose with a handkerchief, and we turned our face away as we carried them off, we couldn't stand it. And their dead were white like paper, and didn't stink at all."[8]

The recent message from Pastor Niemöller in Lausanne, in the little church of S. T., disappointed many followers.

Everyone expected a story about how the famous anti-Nazi pastor suffered in the German camps; everyone was surprised not to hear the word *suffering* ever uttered in reference to himself.

The theme of the message was German and European nihilism, whose influence is increasing among the young people of Germany and of Europe. Everyone was surprised not to hear him bring everything back to Christ, to make Christ the only possible cure for this nihilism. I heard someone wonder if, for Pastor Niemöller, as for the young people of Germany and Europe, Christ was no longer a source of hope.

Pastor Niemöller is a German who knows perfectly well, beyond his role as pastor, the value of Christ in the real life of the German people. He knows perfectly well that for the German nation, for the German spirit, Christ is a very different notion than for us Latins. That Christ takes forms and is presented under aspects that are not those under which we are accustomed to seeing him, to recognizing him.

German nihilism is a form of Christ, one of his aspects. And though I know that many readers will be scandalized by what I mean to say, it's nonetheless necessary that I say what anyone who knows Germany is certain of: that the famous German cruelty, like that of the Spaniards, is a cruelty of a metaphysical nature, which presupposes a habit, if we want to give it this banal name, of bringing everything back to metaphysical problems. With this difference, however: that Spanish cruelty is of a theological nature, that in every act of cruelty in Spain there is an act of faith; that Christ is as a consequence tightly bound up with the notion of cruelty.

It is not possible to accept the German Christ without accepting the cruelty that underlies this notion of Christian life. And Pastor Niemöller very much put his finger on the problem when he recalled that many Catholics and Protestants in Germany refused the collective responsibility of the German people expressed in the Stuttgart Declaration, for everything that happened in Germany, and in Europe, from 1933 to 1945. He both marveled at it and lamented it. For the French who don't yet know the Germans, who don't want to know them, this refusal can seem like new proof of German duplicity.

Are the Germans, as Christians, responsible? That's the question, in all its gravity. They are responsible as citizens, and as men, but not as German Christians, because among Germans a sense of responsibility is never associated with a sense of sin. It's independent. It's too easy—and this is what Germans, even German Catholics, reproach Latins for—to have a sense of responsibility as a consequence of a sense of sin. What constitutes the value of a sense of responsibility is the belief in one's own innocence, in one's own purity and rightness. The (free) sense of responsibility can have value only for those who believe they are right, who believe they are on the side of truth.

A Swiss I was traveling with the day after Pastor Niemöller's speech, on the train that goes from Martigny to Sion, said to me: "As Pastor Niemöller rightly pointed out, these Germans are incorrigible."

I was scandalized by the idea: Why incorrigible? Were they never guilty? (Because you're guilty only if you have a sense of your own guilt.) Did they never have a sense of their guilt? They believe they are right. They believe they are on the side of truth. Christ is with them, or at least so they believe. And it's enough to believe it for it to be true.

Why would Christ reproach the Germans for their cruelty, their nameless acts of violence? What would he interfere for? It's not in their *own* interest that the Germans suffer and make others suffer. It's in the interest of truth, of justice, of—in a word—Christ. They are (they believe themselves to be, and it's enough to believe it for it to be so) civilization against barbarity, *Kultur* against the savage state of inferior or condemned peoples. Trying to explain to them that they are guilty, to persuade them, is a waste of time.

They lost the war: Is that proof? I shiver writing these lines. Is that proof? Are they not free, free men, free Christians? Can a free man err? No, because freedom goes hand in hand with the privilege of truth. When it comes to explaining and understanding the Germans, this fundamentally important point should never be forgotten. A free man is always a just man. And the Germans are free men, the only free men in Europe. (They believe it, at least, and it's enough to believe it for it to be so.)

Forgive me this refrain, it's indispensable. I wouldn't know how to continue writing if I had to give up singing softly through my teeth this horrible refrain. Does the fact that they lost the war constitute decisive proof? Christ himself lost his earthly war. He lost it at the level of the chronicle, of the history of facts, not at the level of the history of the spirit, naturally, right? The German people is Christ. It was crucified. *It has risen to heaven*. What remains of the German people on earth is the numberless army of the defeated, witnesses of the fact that Germany—Christ—has risen to heaven. It's left to others now, *to the Romans* (the Allies), to take the Germans' place on the battlefield, to take the place of Christ who has risen to heaven. The future will tell us if the Romans can tough it out and defend the legacy of this defeat, and of this victory. As for the German people, they limit themselves to their nihilism.

Is this nihilism a specifically German fact? Certainly not. The nihilism that Pastor Niemöller laments is a European fact: it is as French, Italian, English, Spanish, Romanian, etc., as it is German. I defend this nihilism. I would so like to give it an acceptable face for French readers, to strip away its horror, its sadness, its solitude.

Undoubtedly, Pastor Niemöller must himself be tormented by an obsession with this nihilism; he must be a nihilist as well. How could he lament it if he too had not been beset? Nihilism, this nihilism, our nihilism, is a form of Christianity. It is the modern, contemporary form of Christianity.

After 1914–18, men went in search of order, of hierarchy, of an architecture of order. They sought and sometimes found it in fascism, in communism, in Catholicism. After 1945, men seek nothing but solitude, freedom, and a sense of innocence. They reject every former order, vomit up any architecture, don't know what to do with the capitalist, communist, or Catholic order. They don't want to serve any church. They don't believe in anything anymore. They are perfectly right not to believe in anything anymore.

Does Pastor Niemöller have the air of reproaching them for no longer even believing in God? Yes, he has the air of reproaching them for the crime of no longer even believing in God. He is wrong. God has nothing to do with it. On the contrary, it could be said that nihilism is a form of complete faith in God, of abandoning oneself to God. God doesn't know what to do with earthly architectures, with order on earth. He does without them, and splendidly so.

What is amazing about the German spirit is this repugnance at representing God in human form, at representing his interests in the form of human interests. At the core of the German spirit, of the

German Catholic spirit as well, lies the notion of the absolute disinterestedness of God in human interests. Whatever man does, for better or worse, God loves him—if we can say that God loves men!

During the war, I saw Germans fight; I also saw them kill off the battlefield. I never, I repeat never, observed the Germans acting out of blind obedience to orders received. I never perceived the Germans to be automatons, men without personal freedom, acting in such a way because they were ordered to. On the contrary, I observed complete self-assurance, complete freedom, complete understanding of what they were doing. I never saw moral doubt brush against their souls. I never saw a German hesitate and say to himself, "Is it possible I'm an assassin?" or, "Am I in agreement with God's laws?" or, "Is it possible that I'm offending God?" On the contrary, I've always observed in them an awareness of performing a rite, a sacrifice to God. The slaughter would leave them calm, confident, and serene, as if they had killed in God's honor.

The nihilism that Pastor Niemöller complains about has its origin in the feeling that morality is not bound to divine laws. We know what a man is for a German. Before all else, he is a German. Then he is a man. He never addresses the question of whether he is Christian or not, Christianity for the Germans not being that mawkish philosophy of kindness, compassion, and forgiveness that it is for other peoples. It's a virile Christianity, they say; it's a pagan Christianity, others say. It's a metaphysical Christianity, I myself would be tempted to say. It is certainly not a Christianity subjugated to Cartesian reason. That's it: the Germans reject Cartesian reason; their Christianity places Christ outside the feelings and the interests of Cartesian reason.

Western Europe is seriously worried about what Pastor Niemöller calls German and European nihilism. Speakers from England, France, and America cross Germany to preach fraternity, European solidarity, and hope. Be reasonable, they say, don't turn toward Russia; above all, don't be nihilists. Believe in something, then. The Germans, especially young Germans, smile at such lines of reasoning.

The only feeling that is common to all the peoples of Western

Europe is pessimism, an atrocious pessimism. One shouldn't be suspicious of pessimism, no matter how atrocious. In my opinion, Europe is gradually returning to the pessimism of the ancient Greeks, which is the essence of their Hellenic civilization, joy itself. Europe is de-Christianizing.

The phenomenon is naturally more visible in Germany than elsewhere, because Germany is where it started. But de-Christianization is no less underway in France, England, or Italy. The Catholic countries fight back a bit more, but they are already giving up. Everywhere we are witnessing the return of a kind of primitive Christianity, imbued with the pessimism of the Greeks, the pessimism of ancient realism.

In Europe today, Christ is no longer anything but a method for seeing clearly into what Christianity has obscured since Rome and Greece. Men and peoples no longer believe in the destiny of man. Man having a distinct destiny in nature—that's what men no longer believe in. Man is merely an animal endowed with a different reason than that of other animals. He is destined to live and to die, and that's it. Think about Homer's famous simile of the leaves.[9] What Christianity has superimposed on the ancients' concept of man is falling away, little by little, layer by layer. Man is returning to what he was at the dawn of Christianity: he lowers himself, loses the dignity that Christianity had given him. Nothing is more unsettling, and under a certain aspect more beautiful, than this gradual regression of European man toward his old form, his ancient image. Everything in him is simplified.

For a long time Plato was considered a kind of pagan prophet of Christ. There was a desire to see him as the messenger of the soul, virtually the discoverer of the human soul, or even of the Christian soul. It's strange to see Plato and the intellectual cult of Plato reemerge every time that Christianity is in crisis. The Renaissance made him into its new Christ, a philosophical reincarnation of Christ, at the moment when Europe was rediscovering the deep meaning of Greek civilization. Plato has been dressed up as a cultured Renaissance Florentine, as a Protestant, as Melanchthon. The Church has, with a vigorous shake, thrown off the Platonism of the Renaissance, point-ing to it as one of the intellectual justifications of the Reformation.

I don't believe that, in the indisputable regression of man toward his own ancient Greek image that was the Renaissance and the Ref-ormation, Plato has had the importance that one wished to attribute to him in the time of Marsilio Ficino, or of Melanchthon and Erasmus. It was an intellectual pretext that did not act in the depths of men's hearts, in the breast of the masses, but only in the breast of the intel-lectual elites. What influenced the masses, rather, was weariness, disgust with the great labors and immense suffering of the Middle Ages; the great wretchedness of those centuries of war, famine, pes-tilence, and massacres; and the hope inspired in the hearts of men by the transformation following from the evolution of production meth-ods and of the economy.

In Savonarola's cry of anguish, rage, and menace, one grasps the impotent fear that the economic and thus political transformation of society at the close of the Middle Ages, at the dawn of the new age, produced in the ruling class of the period, above all in the Church, which feels threatened every time the faith and hopes of peoples change form, direction, or object. What is endangered in periods of European transformation, evolution, or transition is Christ, in the sense that Christ is not only a religious figure, bread of the spirit, but also the image of a certain form of moral, political, and economic life.

It's clear that the Renaissance betrayed Christ, that to a certain extent it renounced him.

The Church's whole reaction during the fourteenth, fifteenth, and sixteenth centuries demonstrates that if, on a political level, it reacted against the princes—that is, against the new spirit of the states— nonetheless, on the moral (and consequently also political) level, it conducted an implacable, at times subtle, at times cruel and violent, war against the masses, the populations that later (employing an ancient word in a new, polemical sense) were called the proletariat.

Being unable to separate the masses from their princes, or to bring the princes back to their former submission to its policies and temporal interests, the Church sought to establish a kind of tyranny over the masses, one that would play a role in its dealings with the princes. The Church became democratic, in the sense that it made an effort to control the masses, to turn them into an instrument of its policy toward the princes, the states. To this end, the first thing it did was to create the modern instrument of mass control: the police.

The Society of Jesus brought nothing new to the Church, if not the concept of controlling the masses by means of the police. It's the GPU, the Gestapo, in its primitive form. These days we've lost the sense of what the Society of Jesus was in the seventeenth century, the period of its omnipotence. The masses' moral situation with regard to the invisible, omniscient, always everywhere present power of the Society must not have been much different from that of the urban masses of Soviet Russia with regard to the GPU. (In the countryside the GPU, police of the state, has less strength, and less need to make itself felt.) If you read the memoirs, the chronicles, the diplomatic reports, priests' homilies, the trials, investigations into uprisings, etc. of the seventeenth century in every European country, you realize the atmosphere that reigned in Europe among the urban masses (petty bourgeois and proletarian alike) was the same atmosphere of mute fear and invisible oppression observable today in the big cities of the USSR and observable yesterday in the totalitarian countries (Germany, Italy, and now Spain). In this atmosphere, Christ was nothing but an object of fear.

When Christ seems to fight his own children, his own believers, to frighten them into obeying his ministers, the masses detach themselves from the true Christ, the flesh and blood of every believer. Religion becomes a kind of external practice, of official ritual, a state religion. The de-Christianization of the masses actively continues into the eighteenth century, across Protestant as well as Catholic Europe, despite—and I would say even thanks to—the fear inspired by both the Church's and the princes' state police. Little by little the masses fall into a sort of passive acceptance of the external rituals, of the apparent authority of the Church; at the same time, the Church turns toward an image of man that eighteenth-century philosophers called liberty. I would say instead that this is an image of the free man living unconsciously, an unexpressed, unformed memory in the hearts of men, the image of man alone on the earth, without heavenly assistance, relying on his own resources.

It has long been debated whether or not Marxism is a form of Christianity. I think that Marxism is instead a form of the de-Christianization of European man under the pressure of economic necessity.

I am taking great pleasure in rereading Chateaubriand. I too have returned to Paris after a long exile. Fourteen years! And what an exile: Regina Coeli prison, Poggioreale prison in Naples, the prisons of Messina, of Milazzo, of Palermo, and being sentenced to five years' confinement on Lipari. Then the war, and finally here I am again in Paris, like Chateaubriand returning from America in 1792 and being surprised to no longer find *Le Réveil d'Epiménide* in Parisian theaters, but *Charles IX*, and to see pastoral scenes replacing wit and mirth. I wonder if Sanson, given the time, wouldn't play the part of Colin, and Mlle Théroigne de Méricourt that of Babet.[10]

I have lunch with ——, editor of the newspaper ——, stroll in the Bois with ——, editor of ——, have dinner with the editor of ——. And I wonder why these men, being so full of resentment, malice, and hate, boast of being the mildest-mannered among us. They talk about virtue, honor, France, glory, peace, justice; take children gently into their arms to show them the *horsie* harnessed to the cart carrying victims to their execution. They sing of nature, peace, justice, honor, forgiveness, charity, and innocence, and have their neighbors' throats slit so delicately, for the greater happiness of the human species.[11]

The Paris that I rediscover is a Paris between two revolutions. I am a foreigner, writing this diary so that it can be published not in my country, which lacks the spirit necessary to understand and ap-

preciate certain things, but in France. And I must not—I owe it to
my French friends, to the French whom I respect and honor, whom
I love—I must not say things that could hurt them. Even if truth,
and sincerity, sincerity above all, seem to me necessary in Europe,
above all in France and from the lips of a friend.

The war of 1940 was wretched, very nearly causing the loss of
French honor. It did not succeed, despite efforts both external and
internal, in causing the loss of the honor of the French people, who
redeemed themselves through sacrifice, courage, suffering, and revolt.
The next war will be terrible; in it the French people will risk losing
their honor, their reason to live, their glory, their freedom. The first
revolution, the one that went by the name of Liberation, risked killing the spirit of justice in French hearts, elevated civil war to a system
of government, perpetuated the crime of the collaborators (informing
on others) and elevated it to the status of a national merit. The next
revolution risks lowering the French people to the level of Spain, a
decadent, dispirited, lost Latin nation. The French fail to understand
that the revolution of 1944–45 (the Liberation) is merely the prologue
to the one that will reduce France to slavery.

What amazes me about the French as I rediscover them after my
long exile is not their unconcern for the future, which they visibly
worry about a great deal, but their incomprehension of the future.
The French are not good prophets. They lack the divine gift of proph-
ecy. They don't recall the future, and they don't foresee it. In politics
they give America more credit than America gives to Europe or to
France. They believe they are being helped, when they are the ones
being asked for help. They believe themselves out of the game, when
the entire game of Russian and American policy in Europe is based
on France. They don't even know how to set their past against the
future. They simply shower themselves with praise for the Resistance,
when the Resistance already belongs to the past, when it is but a
prologue to a series of events contrary to the national spirit of the
Resistance.

Every time that I, a foreigner, say to them, "The spirit of the Resistance is killing you, it's leading you to ruin," they take me for an

enemy of the Resistance. They look on me as an enemy. They believe they themselves invented the Resistance, that it's a French idea, like the Revolution of 1789. They don't know that the Resistance is a European fact, presenting two principle aspects: the aspect of a spontaneous revolt against the German oppressor (Poland, Norway) and the aspect of a revolt organized externally, with leaders coming from outside, with foreign arms, provisions, uniforms, and money. It is this second aspect that applies to the Italian, French, Dutch, Danish, Belgian, Yugoslavian, etc., etc. Resistance. The first aspect is Polish and Norwegian. As a consequence, both in France and in other countries, the Resistance has nothing to do with the intellectual, historical, etc. traditions of France. It's an instrument of war created by foreigners. Thus the future of France cannot be entrusted to the "spirit of the Resistance." It would be ridiculous; it would be fatal. The spirit of the Resistance in Europe today is communist. It is created, paid for, armed, and organized by foreigners.

Be warned, my French friends. Scylla was the spirit of collaboration, animated by foreigners (Germany); Charybdis is the spirit of the Resistance, armed by foreigners (England, America). Be warned: here are your two mortal dangers.

Chateaubriand (book I, chap. 2) calls beauty a "serious trifle," and adds: "It remains when all the others have passed away." What are these trifles that pass away because not serious? I believe that M. de Chateaubriand never had a very definite idea of feminine beauty.

Chateaubriand has quite a strange idea of pity. He calls himself a Christian and paints others as pagans. He travels to Brussels and passes through Namur (book X, chap. 2). The women of Namur helped him, took pity on him, welcomed him, brought him bread, wine, fruit, milk, broth, and blankets. They showed him, in short, an absolutely disinterested Christian pity.

"The women of Namur," he says, "helped me climb into the van, commended me to the driver, and obliged me to accept a wool blanket. I noticed they were treating me with a kind of respect and deference. There is in the nature of the Frenchman a certain superiority and delicacy that other peoples recognize." So suspects any foreigner who is asked for charity by a Frenchman. The fear that the mendicant will judge him not full of pity, but struck by this certain superiority and delicacy, which Chateaubriand believed to be a uniquely French quality.

I'm at lunch with Mme de la F. She's a woman like Mlle de la Môle doubtless was after the death of Sorel, roughly forty-five years old. Haughty but with perfect manners. Her apartment on Rue de St.-D. on the Rive Gauche is small but perfect. An exquisite sense of taste that reveals not only her instinct, but an erudite memory, an artistic education shaped by good books—a sense of taste, I would go so far as to say, educated by the Goncourts (I would not be surprised to learn that Mme de la F. is related to the Goncourts)—has presided over the decor of this apartment, the choice of furniture, paintings, bibelots, fabrics, carpets, the book bindings that gleam on the shelves of a Louis XIV bookcase that belonged, Mme de la F. tells me, to Mme Roland.

We are alone in the little room. It's a lunch offered only by former mistresses to an old lover rediscovered, after long years of separation and forgetfulness. Mme de la F. is very devout; she tells me about certain colored candles that she used to buy in Assisi. She asks me if in Assisi it is still possible to buy these candles, "made with the honey of bees raised by Saint Francis."

"Honey?" I say. "You mean wax."

"No, honey."

I'm astonished. She has the candles brought. She licks them.

"Taste," she says, and I lick one of the candles. It's sweet, in fact. The honey flavor is very faint, nearly faded, spent. "It's the flavor of

Italy," she tells me. For the first time in my life, I learn that the flavor of my country is this honey flavor. "The flame is sweet as well," she says. She lights the candle. "Taste," she says.

In this small gesture I rediscover the old honeyed flavor of our old love. I look at her and smile. Only the French know how to preserve the sweetness of a memory with such intelligent fidelity.

Chateaubriand (book XI, chap. 1) says: "As I believe in nothing except in religion, I distrust everything: wishing ill and speaking ill are the two distinctive qualities of the French spirit; derision and slander, the reliable result of a confidence."

How easy it is to be wrong about one's own people, when one judges them with passion! I know the French people; they're the European people I know best after the Italians, and though France is not my second homeland, the French people are nonetheless my dearest brother. I have but one homeland, but one brother. Whenever I've thought about a people to live among in freedom and serenity, my thoughts have flown to France. And I marvel to find such an opinion in Chateaubriand, which can be excused only by the circumstances of the time, and by the passions that they provoke.

In periods of revolution, war, famine, epidemics, and other scourges, all peoples turn nasty, very often against their own nature. What happens to individuals happens to peoples: evil, misfortune, and hunger turns them into wolves. But with the return of serenity, nature regains the upper hand, and goodness and kindness return.

The opinion cited above is from 1822 (revised in December 1846), a time when, covered with honors, Chateaubriand, ambassador to London, could well have forgotten the wrongs received, and judged his old passions with a more impartial eye. The Frenchman does not wish ill of others, even if he does love to disparage. His excess of spirit leads him to distrust, to derision, at times to slander. But he is not wicked. His essence is impetuous and fickle, but not malicious. If the French people had been malicious, they would not have been for so many centuries the most civilized and the most generous people in the world.

That foreigners have sometimes attributed their combative spirit to a vain and fatuous love of glory, and of what follows from that socially, and not to a generous nature, is an explicable fact. For centuries the Frenchman fought for everyone. With incredible generosity he squandered his blood and his money in the service of a politics that appeared nationalistic, but which essentially obeyed his historic destiny to promote the progress of humanity. Every time a population turned to France, France responded.

And if a certain shabbiness is also to be found in the French spirit, that cannot be put down to the fact that it is (as Stendhal, disgusted by the "purge," etc., would say) "*un peuple de vaudevillistes*," but to the fact that the petty bourgeois, which dominates today, is shabby, not only in France but in the whole world. It's the defect of a class, not of a people. Today it's the petty-bourgeois spirit that's causing the decline of European civilization, and of France itself. Not the nature of peoples.

Thoughts. I am reproached for having dedicated my book *The Skin* to the American soldiers who "uselessly died in the cause of American freedom." It's the word *uselessly* that strikes critics. We're no longer accustomed to the words *useless* and *uselessness*, to their meaning, which to me seems admirable. Everything in this century is useful, necessary, advantageous, profitable, etc. The contrast between the word *useful* and the word *necessary* seems to me much less important than in the time of Voltaire, who said of the Jesuits: "To ensure that the Jesuits are useful, it is necessary to prevent them being necessary." We could reverse the phrase, and it would suit our century perfectly. My dear and detestable and sometimes ridiculous René[12] was acquainted with the word *useless*, in the same sense in which I attributed it to the American soldiers. Did he perhaps not say, about the death of the Chevalier de La Baronnais, fallen at the Siege of Thionville: "Noble, useless victim of a lost cause"? These days, in France as elsewhere, everything is useful, even necessary. When the French people realize that they are no longer useful in Europe, that they are useless, then they will once again be necessary.

I too, like René, have been "the Dutch dog on the vessel of the Legitimacy" (book IX, chap. 14).

I have never managed to understand what the French really feel in the face of death.

Do they fear it? Are they indifferent to death? They never talk about it, never paint it, don't sing about it, never sculpt it. They don't have that sacred horror of death, that macabre taste, that lies at the base of the Spanish soul, and of that of the peoples of southern Italy.

The French do not love the dead. They hate corpses and are horrified by them. They do not express this horror, because they never express their passions, or their feelings. But everything that is dead oppresses them. They do not, as the Germans do, have the metaphysical cult of the dead, of dead bodies. They are too refined to appreciate the insipid, sweet, and greasy smell of corpses. Before a live, wounded body, a body crippled but still alive, the French are capable of anything. But as soon as that body is lifeless, they respect it.

One day I saw a dead woman on the corner of Pont Neuf and the Quai de l'Horloge, where I was living then. She was a young woman who died, as I later found out, of a heart attack. A prostitute and a drunkard. She was dead, and no one dared approach her. I was the only one trying to pick her up, not believing she was dead. During my struggle with the poor corpse, one of the wretch's shoes slipped off her stiff foot. The next day, that shoe was still there. And yet Pont Neuf is frequented by vagrants, paupers, tramps, beggars. But that shoe smelled like death, and the French are horrified of death.

In French literature, death does not take up much space. Yes, of course, Villon, Baudelaire, Lautréamont, to cite only the purest, most gratuitous examples. "O death, old captain." Death appears to the French as a young woman with blond curls and a smile on her lips. French gallantry, even with regard to death. They are a young people, despite the petty-bourgeois spirit that invades and ages everything. If I had to identify a French painter comparable to the German painters of death, I would name Watteau.

De T. comes up to me in Rue de la Paix and asks me to join him at the café bar in the Ritz. We go. De T. is a youngster no longer in the bud of youth. I'm grateful to him for the postcard that he sent to me on Lipari in 1934.

I like Chateaubriand, even if he doesn't resemble me. I like his constant contempt for the new men; this fidelity, entirely illusory, to the old ideas, to the customs, tastes, pleasures, sufferings, and sentiments of old France, in which, despite what he says at every opportunity, he no longer believes.

I like this hidden love for the new ideas; for the new France, the new glory. However, nothing material binds me to this old France (this old Italy, this old Europe) that I have seen—that I am seeing—die.

I do not pine for privileges, or honors, or anything. From the old Europe I received nothing but beatings and prison. I will not receive anything better from the new Europe or the new Italy. What I like nonetheless about the old Europe is my youth, my life, the pains and the pleasures of my life.

And I strive like Chateaubriand—who believed himself to be a man of the past century, of the old France, and who was a man of the new France, of the new century—I strive like he did, I say, to grasp in this transformation of old Europe into the new that which is eternal in our race, in our civilization. From one Europe to another, one France to another, I delight to see, like Chateaubriand, "merely a transformation of virtue" (book IX, chap. 10).

Chateaubriand (book XXIII, chap. 7): "At Coppens' house, a gala dinner (in Gand), which I was compelled to attend, lasted from one in the afternoon to eight in the evening. I counted nine courses: they began with preserves and ended with cutlets. Only the French know how to dine to a plan, as they are the only ones who know how to compose a book."

It is this *compose* that says everything.

The instigator of the massacre of the young girls at Verdun was the minor poet and regicide Pons de Verdun, relentless against his native town. What the *Almanach des Muses* furnished in terms of agents of the Terror is incredible. The vanity of suffering mediocrities produced as many revolutionaries as the wounded pride of runts and amputees: appalling analogy between the infirmities of the mind and those of the body (Chateaubriand, book IX, chap. 16).

In Italy I have often been compared to the Cardinal de Retz, to Benvenuto Cellini, to Aretino, to this or that writer of the Renaissance. For my prose, for my spirit, for my irony, for the classical accent of my style, for I don't know what mix of ancient and modern that constitutes the most evident aspect of my prose.

A romantic side to my soul, which undoubtedly comes from my paternal family's Nordic origins, has nonetheless rather surprised my Italian critics. They don't know how to connect it with my classical learning, which I owe not only to the excellent instruction I received at the Collegio Cicognini, in Prato, but also to the long attachment I had in Prato, between the ages of twelve and sixteen, to the poet Bino Binazzi. His grasp of classical Greek and Latin was accompanied by a very modern taste and a deep knowledge of modern literature, especially modern French literature. The excellence of my readings, the conversations between Bino and his Florence friends (Louis Le Cardonnel, Giovanni Papini, Ardengo Soffici, etc.), conversations in which, being a child, I did not take part, but which I listened to with passionate interest and love, shaped my learning and character as much as my unhappy adolescence did.

I've never said so—I say it now only against my will—but I feel closer to Chateaubriand than to any other modern writer. The very course of his life resembles mine. In Chateaubriand's imagination, his irony, his sense of the novelistic, his feeling for nature, his broad interest in men's lives, his interest in history, his inclination to personally participate in the events of history, to get intimately mixed up with the events of his time, I discover my own tastes, my spirit, my feelings, my inclinations. His profound melancholy, which can be upsetting at times in its overly superficial self-satisfaction, is familiar to me. As is his pleasure in not telling the story of anything else—in everything he writes, even in his novels—but his own life, but the facts that concern him: all this brings me closer to Chateaubriand. And the observations of a few French critics who spotted this resemblance have given me much more pleasure than all the Italian critics' praise put together.

Also, Chateaubriand's behavior with regard to Napoleon, this Mussolini not of his time but of his life, is not without surprising parallels to my behavior toward Mussolini.

But if I had to limit myself to Chateaubriand's style and my own, just reread *Atala*, *René*, and a few passages of the *Mémoires*, and you will see that I'm not mistaken. I was thinking of this this morning as I reread the passage from book XI, chap. 1, in which Chateaubriand sketches his self-portrait. That page on the Siege of Thionville (book IX, chap. 15) and on Libba, the deaf and dumb German girl on the battlefield, "sitting on the grass that was staining her dress with blood."

In short, without wanting to make too much of my similarity to Chateaubriand, because I nonetheless have an ironic awareness of my own limits, I dare to assert, with a bit of truth, in my opinion, that there is something in Chateaubriand—in his life, in his style, in his behavior toward men, events, the story of his times, and the profound transformation in the society of his times, which so resembles something in ours—something in which I recognize my life, my feelings, my behavior; in which, in other words, I recognize myself.

It's due to Chateaubriand that I sometimes feel French. Not to Descartes, whom I abhor, or to Pascal, Montaigne, or La Fontaine; but to Chateaubriand, in which I find, as if resolved, smoothed out, and justified in a profound melancholy, in a sentimental irony, full of feeling, all the problems of French classicism, all the problems of the European spirit in its passage from ancient to modern times. All the problems of Italian and French culture in relation to modern— German, English, American—culture.

It's from Chateaubriand, as I've said, that comes a large part of the most essential nineteenth-century French painting, from Delacroix, Géricault, down to the impressionists; and of literature, from Musset, Baudelaire, Barrès himself, down to certain fundamental cadences of Apollinaire, Mallarmé, Valéry, Proust himself. There is nothing in Chateaubriand (his sense of cruelty, for example) that cannot be found in the moderns.

I drew on Chateaubriand, where he speaks of the "cruel gaiety of Cervantes," for the phrase that I placed at the beginning of *Kaputt*, a "gay and cruel book," for which so many American critics reproached me. (The Spanish critics compare me to Cervantes, the English critics to Swift. This is also the thrust of Aldous Huxley's opinion of me in his letter to Baltus.)

Chateaubriand begins his *Mémoires d'Outre-Tombe* with these words: "If ever the Bourbons return to the throne, all that I shall ask of them as a reward for my loyalty is to make me rich enough to join the edge of the surrounding woods to my property" (written October 4, 1811).[13]

One can imagine a politician, writer, or regular citizen these days yearning for his political party, or his king, as a reward for his loyalty, to make him rich enough to satisfy the secret wish of even the purest of men. Every political militant, anyone who works for a political or human cause, thinks it—but doesn't say it.

To be rewarded with money for one's loyalty: here is the secret desire of even the purest of men. Today as in Chateaubriand's day. There are some who do not think this. Such men are admirable and rare. In general, though, men's motives are low. Such was the correct opinion of La Rochefoucauld, who considered men's motives very low indeed.

Leaving Saint-Malo for America on Captain Desjardins's ship, Chateaubriand wrote, seeing the land of France recede and disappear into the night: "I went away equally unsure of my country's destiny and of my own: Who would perish, France or I?"

When Mussolini was arrested he was wearing the uniform of a German soldier. Napoleon, en route to the island of Elba, wore the uniform of an Austrian official. Calamity has always worn the uniform of the victor. What is surprising about this? The victor ends up wearing the uniform of the vanquished.

I know Africa, Europe, and Asia. In no country in the world have I ever felt as free as in France. Is it the nature, the sky, how the houses are laid out? Is it the men? The French? Is it the water, the wine, the bread, the air, the light, the color of France?

What do I know? The fact is that I always feel free in France. And yet I am neither persecuted nor exiled. Every time I cross the French border, I breathe more easily, I sleep, I feel calm and safe. Gone are the fits of anguish that would wake me in the night, in my bed on Capri, in Forte dei Marmi, in Rome, in Florence. Here I don't feel surrounded by the petty cowardice of the Italians, by their jealousy.

I'm sorry to say it, but I can't live with Italians anymore, not in Italy. It's a wretched country, where individuals are defenseless and count for nothing. And the law? The famous Roman law? What nonsense. In Italy, the fact is you're at the mercy of informers, the police, and the judiciary. You can be accused of any crime or offense and be arrested and put in prison. And if you don't have powerful friends, there's no way of defending yourself. Italy is a wretched country reduced to slavery by a gang of professional and amateur informers.

And there's no way to save yourself. What I'm saying here is not just applicable to Italy today. Things were the same during Fascism, and long before Fascism.

At the heart of Italian life, there is injustice: a state hostile to the private citizen. Everything is ready to pounce on the private citizen, to persecute him. There is no tranquil sleep to be had in Italy.

And the dangers that threaten the Italian citizen also threaten foreigners, if a bit less.

The great jurist Mortara used to say to his students: "If you're accused of stealing the Milan Cathedral, don't laugh it off. Defend yourself." He would also say: "If you're accused, especially if you're innocent, try not to get yourself arrested. Run away. A man in prison in our country is a lost man."

One day I showed up for a trial in Naples. I was accused of fighting a duel. I had fought in sixteen of them, but it was the first time the magistrate had summoned me. I brought with me my friend the marchese Antonino Nunziante, a Neapolitan, and Marghieri the lawyer, son of the great jurist Senator Marghieri. We waited in a large hall in the courthouse, where thin, pale men dressed in black sat in silence. At a certain moment a door opened. A robed lawyer appeared in the doorway and said loudly: "I need three witnesses." A man stepped forward, greeted the lawyer, and asked him what he needed. "Three witnesses for my trial. Homicide." "All right," said the man, and he signaled to three men. They rose from their seats and came forward and bowed to the lawyer, down to the ground. The lawyer looked at them and asked their names, which he wrote down on a piece of paper, then started to instruct them. "You were in such and such a café on such and such a day. It was four o'clock. You saw a man"—he described the man—"come out of the door that's across from the café, and the man shouted: 'Finally, I've punished him!'" "All right," said the other man, "I saw this and this," and he repeated the lesson. The second was supposed to have seen, passing by on such and such a street, a man running away and throwing down a bloody knife. The third, etc. When the instructions were finished, the lawyer gave each of the men a 100 lire note cut in two, of which he kept one half. Then he went away. I was shocked. "Do the magistrates know about this trade in false testimonies?" "Of course they know!" the lawyer replied. "For them, though, the essential thing is that the trial, from a formal point of view, is perfect, correct; the rest doesn't count. I don't want to say that all..."

Why do the Italians not love Corneille, Racine, and in general what in France is classical in the sense of Greek and Roman? Because we have our classics; because, when you have the colonnade of the Temple of Neptune in Rome, and the temples of Paestum, Agrigento, Selinunte, etc., you can't love the Louvre colonnade. Because in Italy we have such a familiarity with the Greek tragedians, that we can't prefer Racine or Corneille to them. And finally, because we don't love translations, and all of French classicism is nothing but a translation of Greek and Latin into seventeenth-century French.

Personally, I love the French Grand Siècle very much, and particularly Racine, or Poussin in painting, Claude Lorrain, Le Nain, because I love Tasso, and everything that is not an "ironization" of classicism (like Laforgue, Giraudoux, Cocteau, in a certain sense Valéry) but a Romantic vision of classicism, a development of what can already be found in certain classical authors of antiquity: in Virgil, Homer, and Sophocles, principally. I see the heroines of Racine dressed like the heroines of Tasso, or, if you prefer, like Ismene arriving on a horse, at a gallop, in the last act of *Oedipus at Colonus*. I love such pathos in Racine, pathos that is proper to Tasso and to the other great Italian authors of the century of *Jerusalem Delivered*, this predominance of the feminine spirit in heroes as well, like Pyrrhus, Orestes, etc., etc.

The French seventeenth century is the great French Romantic century, or even, I would say, the great Romantic century of all of Europe, in Italy as in Germany, as in Spain, as in England. And the fact that the scenography, the passions, and the language are those of antiquity, or of imitations of antiquity, means nothing. It's not possible to disassociate French painting of the period from the poetry of Racine, of Corneille, etc. Poussin painted Doric columns choked with Latium green. The heroes and heroines of Corneille and Racine are like Poussin's Doric columns, choked by the sentimental greenery of the Grand Siècle, sentiment whose pathos is Romantic.

This is what bothers me about the traditional scenography of the Comédie-Française: in its place I would like to see a scenography à la Poussin, a Cornelian or Racinian scenography. And instead of those costumes copied from the ancient Chaldeans, Phoenicians, or Babylonians, which belong to the Greek world in the way that the Volsci costumes in Shakespeare's *Coriolanus* at the New Theatre of Stratford-upon-Avon (a costume copied from the legendary and conventional costume of the Gauls who invaded France) belong to the Latin world, I would like to see costumes à la Tasso, as the seventeenth-century poets imagined them, in Italy as well as in France. The costumes, in a word, worn onstage by the heroes and heroines of Corneille and Racine in their time. What romanticism, what pathos, what sweet and strong emotions in such costumes!

I think that in Italy they wouldn't put up with the staging of Corneille or Racine; as they don't put up with Metastasio. They put up with reading them, because reading benefits from the scenography of Roman and Italian antiquity. Read Racine while sitting on the steps of the Temple of Neptune in Paestum; hear the whisper of the tall grass come toward you, and the sweet whisper of the waves on the deserted beach, and from time to time your gaze rests in its scan over those sacred ruins, those mountains, that shore, that sea. Read Racine or Corneille in Paestum or among the marbles . . .

For centuries accustomed to looking at themselves in the mirror of the world, to considering themselves the center of Europe and of the civilized universe (even as the Tartars, the Chinese, the Japanese, and other vast peoples did not trouble themselves about France, or about

Versailles), the French do not know how to adapt themselves to the changes occurring in recent years in the relations among the nations of the world.

What is happening to them now once happened to the Italians, and, toward the end of the Renaissance, to the republics and grand seigniories of Italy. The French of today struggle to free themselves from their political ideas, to give up their supremacy over the civilized world. In the face of America, of Russia, in a Europe that has been discouraged, devastated, reduced to a state nigh on barbarism, deprived of any moral prestige or political strength, they develop an idea of their condition that is much worse than what it really is.

They believe they've been stripped of their authority, whereas they are only exhausted. They believe they've been deprived of what they retain to be their right to govern the world, to be the first in Europe, at least, when they are merely out of the game temporarily, on account of their education, their political class, their political class's narrow-minded ideas. They no longer have sufficient faith in their intelligence, in their genius. They've lost faith in the supremacy of intelligence.

I say to all my friends: "I am a foreigner, I look at you with the eye of a foreigner, and I don't see you looking as bad as all that. You're ill: heal yourself, take care of yourself. But your illness is not fatal; to intelligence the world will inevitably return. Everything that is military strength, material strength, economic prosperity all that is ephemeral. The world will return to the intelligent nations, to France first of all. But you must have a broader vision. If you do not accustom yourself to having a broader vision, Europe will seem small to you. And it's big, it's immense. Stay French. Take our eyes, take the eyes of us foreigners, to see more broadly, but stay French. For centuries it's been the best condition in the world for a man in Europe, for a people in Europe."

Chateaubriand [book XII, chap. 5], in London in April 1822, wrote that "all of England can be seen in a four-league radius, from Richmond, above London,[14] down to Greenwich, below." And he creates a little topographical portrait of this little England contained between the village of Richmond and the village of Greenwich. Below London he places the England of industry and trade; above London, agrarian and pastoral England. In London itself, to the west, he places the aristocracy; to the east, democracy, the Tower of London, and Westminster.

The whole of France, too, can be seen in the space of two leagues, from the Porte d'Italie to Saint-Denis, with the aristocracy in the west; democracy, the Bastille, and the Arc de Triomphe in the east. But is it truly all of France that can be seen in this small space, or not perhaps all of Europe, in a moral sense? The French, the Parisians of our time, simply see Paris as all of France in a political sense: MRP, RPF, PC, SFIO, CGT, etc.[15] They show you a map of Paris and say to you: "This is MRP country. This is PC country. Here's where the RPF are." They talk about invasion, as if the north of Paris, the banlieue, were from one moment to the next supposed to cross the border and invade MRP country, SFIO country, etc. They don't realize that all of Europe is here, that its parties are the different countries of Europe, that in our age every national element is a foreign international element, that there is no longer *a* France, in the political sense, just as there is no longer *an* Italy in the political sense, or *a* Sweden, *a* Holland, etc.

The nations of Europe are governed by foreigners; the different political parties are all, even without knowing it, sold to foreigners, or rather, instruments of foreigners. This is what constitutes the slavery of the nations of Europe, including France. The remedy will not be found in political struggle, which is stupid and useless, but in the terrible bloodletting that looms. Europe will be liberated from its contaminated elements, as in the fifteenth century, as in the sixteenth. We have returned, because of Marxism, to the wars of religion. So those who do not follow the true religion must die. So much the worse for them. They asked for it.

Chateaubriand [book XII, chap. 5], describing how he spent a part of the summer of 1799 in Richmond, says Henry VIII and Elizabeth died there, and adds: "Where can one not die?"

Here is an astonishing example of the aberration and the ridiculousness to which certain French authors of the period, and of our own, can be led by the vice of expressing oneself in maxims. Montesquieu's "How can one be Persian?" reveals a century's spirit, its sense of humor.[16] Chateaubriand's "Where can one not die?" exposes French Romanticism's lack of a sense of humor.

Romanticism cannot bear wit or humor. It is a gloomy, sad movement. To cheer it up with quips and witty sayings, as the French have done, is to degrade it. It ceases to be Romanticism.

Women have always been unlucky for France. What I mean is that each time French state policy has clashed with the policy of an enemy state governed by a woman, it has brought misfortune to France. Two very persuasive examples: Queen Elizabeth of England and Maria Theresa of Austria.

Talking about England at the end of the eighteenth century, Chateaubriand [book XII, chap. 5] writes in 1822: "On the same sidewalks where one now sees grimy faces and men in frock coats, little girls in white cloaks passed by, their straw hats fastened under the chin with a ribbon, a basket containing fruit or books on their arm; they all kept their eyes lowered, all blushed when one looked at them. 'England,' says Shakespeare, is 'a swan's nest in the middle of the waters.'[17] Frock coats without a jacket underneath were so unusual in London in 1793 that a woman, weeping bitterly over the death of Louis XVI, said to me: 'But my dear sir, is it true that the poor King was dressed in a frock coat when they cut off his head?'"

Where in present-day France are the "passing generations of flowers" that Chateaubriand spoke of with reference to England at the beginning of the last century? The Marquise de V., with whom I'm having lunch, says to me: "This Fourth Republic, so poor in beautiful women."

I look around and, indeed, do not see any beautiful women.

"French women," says the old Count de B., "have their own particular beauty, a beauty based more on liveliness of spirit than on facial features. Look at Watteau's women, or Boucher's, the women painted in the eighteenth century. They're enchanting, not beautiful. Quite different from the English women painted by Lawrence or Gainsborough."

I'm amazed at this language, and I say as much.

"Dispense with your good manners and courtesy, be honest, and tell us, where in France can we find women as beautiful as the Italians, as the Spanish?"

"It's another kind of beauty," I exclaim. "Women's beauty corresponds to the genius of a nation. The French genius is clear, subtle, lean, sparkling, witty, Cartesian. The beauty of French women is clear, subtle, lean, sparkling, sober, witty, Cartesian." The word *Cartesian*, applied to feminine beauty, makes the old Count de. B. laugh.

"What do you mean by Cartesian beauty?" asks the Countess de V., who is one of the beautiful women of Paris.

I answer her indirectly, describing the women painted by Italians (Raphael, Ghirlandaio, Botticelli, etc.). They're fat, well fed, sensual. They don't have any Cartesian spirit, that intellectual light that in French women mortifies the flesh and sensuality, subordinating them to the spirit.

"But, the women of Stendhal?" the Marquise de V. says to me.

"Exactly," I say, "the Italian women as seen by Stendhal are beautiful, if you can even say that Angela Pietragrua or the Duchess Sanseverina are beautiful. I've seen Bartolini's portrait of Countess Guiccioli in the Palazzo Pretorio in Prato, my native city.[18] Her beauty was sensual, contrary to the French manner. The women in France are not lymphatic; they possess an intelligence that they know how to use in love as well. They are the first women of Europe. They are much better than men.

"What strikes a foreigner in France is the place that women even today occupy in every area of French life, in the economy, etc. You're speaking with an industrialist? He invites you to lunch to talk about business. At four o'clock he leaves to visit his mistress: 'Talk to my wife about this matter.' You're always having to deal with a woman. They have a very strong character. Without them, France would merely be another Latin country submerged in confusion. If Spain or Italy had had women like the French, they wouldn't have fallen so low in their political decadence.

"French women have a sensuality that is always wary. What I admire most in France is the great solidarity that exists between men and women. They mutually adore each other. They think there are no other men and women on their level in the world. This reciprocal adoration, this sexual nationalism, moves me. Even in love the French believe themselves to be unique."

"Perhaps we are unique," says the Countess de V.

"It's a great strength, to believe oneself unique. I belong to a people that always doubts itself; a people that, despite its pride and self-regard, doubts itself. I belong to a jealous people.

"'The beauty of the French woman no longer agrees with modern times. Her century is the eighteenth. A time dominated by reason, by cold intelligence. We are now in the full flowering of the subconscious. Ours is a romantic age, the age of the irrational. The French find themselves ill at ease in an age inclined to outbursts of passions and instincts, of the irrational forces that smolder in the depths of human beings."

"Have you never fallen in love with a French woman?" the Marquise de G. asks me.

"No, never. I don't know why, but I never have. I'm too timid to love a French woman."

"Timid? What does timidity have to do with it, in this sort of thing?"

"The French woman is always very sure of herself. She is the most confident woman in Europe. Not because she knows, as the American woman does, that the law always agrees with her in everything. But because she knows that men always agree with her out of gallantry. I am not so gallant that I always agree with a woman, even if she is French. That's why I only ever approach a French woman with the idea that she's wrong, something that makes love impossible."

During the war French women alone defended the interests and honor of France, much better than the men. Don't tell me that the men were heroic, etc., in the Resistance. It's the least they could do. They were the ones who had lost in 1940; they were the ones who had to make up for it. Without the women, though, what would have been left of France? During the war various publications about France appeared in Germany: combatants' newspapers, articles by journalists, books of war. All these books, which the French know nothing about, because they know nothing about anything foreign (didn't Maurras say that "everything that is not French is foreign"?), speak with considerable respect and admiration about French women.

One day in Lapland, on the shores of the Arctic Ocean, a German soldier spoke to me about France and French women. "They're wonderful," he told me. "They never forget that France did not lose the war. Whereas the men either think of themselves as victors, or think that they're all washed up. The women, though, they know that France neither won nor lost the war; that France is what's at stake in this struggle, because the struggle is for supremacy in Europe, and a Europe that is dominated without the consent of France is nothing, is a failure. We hear that they look on us as enemies. We don't go to bed with French women, except with prostitutes, who have no nationality. We feel inadequate, guilty, in the presence of French women. They handle all the business, while the men play politics."

I recall that men, when they're not petty, are proud, which is laughable. French women have perfect manners. They treat us with a cold courtesy, which humiliates us . . .

France is a police state that respects the liberty of its citizens.

It's with the French Revolution that states become police states. All of them, democracies and absolute monarchies. In a democracy, a republic like France or Switzerland, and in constitutional monarchies, the police state respects the liberty of its citizens; in an absolute monarchy, it does not.

The French do nothing but moan and complain and cry about their misfortunes.

If you ask them, "What are your misfortunes?" they answer: "Ah, France was occupied for four years. The occupation was terrible. We came out of it ruined. Oh, what a terrible misfortune the occupation was!" etc., etc.

One marvels at their laments and wants to laugh at their tears. They believe the occupation was an irreparable misfortune, etc. And the northern departments that were occupied from 1914 to 1918? Did they die of it? Were the French of the north and the east hopelessly ruined? Ah, how France is shown to be a privileged country, which has always benefited from liberty and national independence; which has not, since the fifteenth century, been occupied in a permanent way by foreigners!

What should the rest of us say, then, we Italians, Flemish, or Germans? Italy has been occupied for centuries and centuries by foreigners, including France. Italy is no worse off for this. Germany has been invaded and occupied by French armies for centuries. Did Germany die from it? The German occupation of France from 1940 to 1944 is nothing but a fleeting incident, a misfortune like so many others, from which a people does not die.

A people dies from corruption, from pettiness of spirit, from internecine struggles; it doesn't die from foreign occupations—which develop the pride, the courage, the vitality of a people. As can be seen, for that matter, in France itself. The Resistance has this going for it: it brought the French people out of that state of ignominy, of cowardice, into which it had fallen after 1935, in which it still was in 1940. Without the Resistance—that is, without the occupation—France was lost.

For the Frenchman, love does not mean possession. The Italian man wants to possess a woman, to make her his property. He no longer has anything else to possess; for him love is a substitute for everything that he has lost: preeminence, an empire, glory, etc. For centuries the Frenchman possessed everything that a man could desire to possess. He possessed the world. Still to this day he possesses an empire; the memory of his omnipotence is still alive in him. He considers women as instruments of pleasure. Women know this and make themselves elegant at every opportunity.

For the Spaniard, too, as for the Italian, love means possession. I think this sentiment developed in him after the collapse of the Spanish Empire and of Spain's power in the world. I think that as soon as a people becomes the ruler of an empire, its women become the women of everyone.

The Italian, like the ancients, considers history as the whim of God. The Spaniard, as the will of God. The English, as a fact of nature, a geographical notion. Likewise the Russians, in part. The Germans and the French, as a fact of the will of men. History as man's creation; history without any extrahuman concept. No precise design. This French and German notion is the cause of Europe's decadence. They are responsible for the decay of Europe.

France has had two universal ideas in its history: monarchy and liberty (the French Revolution). Chateaubriand says that the French love equality more than liberty, and that they are "attracted to government." Here are Chateaubriand's precise words: "Daily experience shows that the French are instinctively attracted to power; they have no love for freedom; equality alone is their idol" (book XXIV, chap. 6). He adds: "Now, equality and tyranny are secretly connected."

It is no less true that, in addition to the monarchy, France's universal idea has been liberty, or, if you will, the Revolution, with everything that the word entails (equality, liberty, democracy, etc.).

*

Cartesianism is not a French universal idea, sharing as it does in both the idea of monarchy and the idea of liberty (Revolution). It is not in itself a universal idea.

I close Montesquieu's *De l'esprit des lois*, and naturally my mind starts to reflect on the causes of the decadence of peoples, and of states. I think that the decadence of a people begins when it fails to stay loyal to its Weltanschauung, its conception of the world.

From this point of view, Christianity has an enormous responsibility for the decadence of the classical world. Decadence that began in Rome, with the adoption of foreign gods, evidence of broad-mindedness and tolerance among the Romans, or of weakness and uncertainty. The Jews remaining faithful to their one God. The Latin-Christian world remaining faithful to the Church. The universal idea of the French: the monarchy; of the Italians: the Church (their own monarchy). The French Revolution signals the abandonment of the unitary conception, in favor of the diversity and multiplicity of gods, and of idols (democracy). The Germans remaining faithful to their unity, to their German unitary conception of the world (racism, the German god of philosophers, etc.). Decadence of the Church, decadence of the Latins. Reform, the decadence of the Latins, since it signals the rupture of the unity of the Catholic world.

What might be the Latins' universal idea today? No universal idea. Not even capitalism. Capitalism is becoming a racist idea of the Anglo-Saxons, their principle of moral and intellectual unity, of social unity, etc. Communism, the universal idea of the Slavs. To my mind, individualism is, or could be, the universal idea of the peoples of Western (i.e., Latin) Europe. Apart from individualism, no salvation, no resurrection for the Latins. Man as the center of the Latin world.

Return to the ruling idea of the ancients, above all of the Greeks: that man is the center of the world. Return to Aristotle, Ptolemy, stoicism, (original) Christianity.

*

Everything that is not individual is not human (for us Latins).

The ruling idea of the French Revolution (liberty, equality, etc., rights of man, etc.) is man, the individual. Decadence of this idea in bourgeois democracy (the idea of class replaces the idea of man, of the individual). Revolution—return to classical ideas, to the rhetoric of the republican virtues of the Greek and Roman world. Evidence.

I like the way that Véra Korène is French. It is not only an intelligent way (it's easy, even too easy, to be intelligent in Paris: if this nation had been just a little less intelligent, just a little more foolish, it would still be the first nation of Europe, the first nation on earth), but above all an affectionate way. She loves France in a way that justifies the love of her poets for France, from the ancients to the moderns, up to Giraudoux, Valéry, Cocteau, Morand, Éluard. It is the ancient, traditional, classical way to love France.

There are some French people who, in their love for France, forget that to love France one needs manners, good manners. It's not possible to have bad manners and love France. One needs courtesy to love France, and dignity and wit, and intelligence as well, because intelligence is not yet forbidden in love for France, as it is in so many other things, in so many other sentiments. One needs a sense of honor. Loving France is not so easy as they would have you believe. It's not as easy as loving England, Germany, Spain, or Italy. Not everyone is allowed to love, to know how to love France. Because to love France is already to be French, at least a little.

Véra Korène is French in a way that is not only intelligent, witty, and courteous, but also dignified and severe, almost inflexible. In her way of being French, in her way of loving France, she leaves nothing to chance. Every love for France is a pact, an alliance, a pact that is as little human as possible. Everything that is inhuman in its spirit, in its culture, its literature, and its arts; this whole blend of wit, courtesy, and glacial impassivity; all this snow, all this blue, all this white, all this steel gray, all this cold, gleaming glass; everything there is of Descartes, Pascal, Montesquieu, Voltaire, and Valéry in the soul of France is carved into this pact between France and whoever wants to love France.

On the Théâtre-Français and Racine: according to some critics, Schlumberger among them, Racine's heroes are "diminished by tragedies of a private nature." In this view, Racine is merely "a court poet skilled at creating gallant adventures for mythological heroes." Audiences of the time criticized Racine's heroes for their violence, for their threatening, deranged manner. Certainly, Racine would respond, these heroes have not read "refined" novels. Racine, according to the Germans, is the poet of *Selbstvernichtung*, of self-destruction.

The audience at the Théâtre-Français. Gérard de Nerval's *Sylvie*: the parterre packed full of connoisseurs; boxes garnished with old-fashioned coiffures and clothing, or else an animated, tremulous hall, crowned at each level of boxes by flowery outfits, sparkling jewels, and radiant faces.

Disquieting: "*unheimlich*" (Kafkian term).[19]

At every moment one encounters marvelous beings who bear all the suffering of the world.

I know of no greater, or more hateful hypocrisy. They seem to reproach you for living, for laughing, for loving, while thousands of men suffer far away from you, while the happiness of so many human beings is in peril. The suffering of these marvelous beings is not religious or moral in nature, but political. To bear all the suffering of the human race is not their mission—it's their politics. This political type, exploiters of the suffering of the human race, is completely new. Its origin is Anglo-Saxon: English yesterday, American today.

Europe will not be cured of its ills until we have the sincerity to return to our traditional sentiments: a fondness for misfortune that is not political, and that doesn't prevent men from living and being happy. I begin to tire of suffering for others. I can't take it anymore. My personal suffering, my own suffering, is more than enough. I have very good reasons to suffer for myself. I pay no mind to the professed fondness of others for me. I even begin to have had enough of suffering for myself. No one helps me carry my burden. There are some who enjoy kicking me as I weep. Let others suffer for themselves; I'll suffer for myself.

Padre Bianchi was saying to me yesterday evening: "We must not reduce Christ to the measure of man. It's men who must measure up to God. Christ did not come to stop poverty, illness, and suffering. He knows his job, he doesn't waste time stopping tears from falling. May the tears fall, may men cry and suffer: it's necessary. And may all men start to suffer for themselves, to know how to suffer for themselves. There's always time to suffer for others. But the most difficult thing is to know how to suffer for oneself. I repeat to you: Christ's job is not to cure men of their sufferings. But to teach them to suffer, as the true Christian must suffer."

I ask him, "Is it men's duty to suffer for others?"

"Pray, first for yourself, and let it be your prayer. Pray for others as well, but let it be your own prayer. And bear your own suffering. And repent of your own sins. Let all men weep for their own sins. And bear their own suffering. The rest is nothing but Christian hypocrisy." He then adds, "The rest is nothing but what I call Christian atheism."

Because there is a Christian atheism, which calls for a Christ commensurate with man, a man more or less like any other. I love finding this cruelty of the ancient Greek gods in Christ. And I'm sorry that it's fashionable to suffer for humanity. It may make for good politics, but I distrust politics, especially good politics. Maybe it's right that the human race suffers; it surely is right. I'm not the one who makes them suffer. They'll say that I'm an egoist, etc. Enough with these stories! There is no one who truly suffers for others. And very few who can suffer for themselves.

A woman put a question to me the other day: How should a man whose wife has been unfaithful behave toward the child born from the adultery, who bears his name but is nevertheless not his child? The woman, as she said this to me, trembled slightly, revealing a kind of anguish filled with hope. I was surprised by her pallor, by her anxious gaze.

I tell her, "If this man is strong and just, if this man does not want to be hated by this child, he must send this child away, conceal himself from him, conceal even his existence from him. Because this child will be his worst enemy. If this man is truly strong and just, he must do away with this child. If he doesn't do so, the child and its mother will establish a secret complicity in their hate for this man. They will persecute him with their hate, attempt to do away with him using the worst means, which are not physical means. We must beware of children who bear our name and who are not of our flesh and our blood."

The woman starts to cry softly. She says, "How right you are! And how horrible."

I tell her, "Women know this well. They know well that when they are unfaithful to a man, the child born of this infidelity will be the betrayed man's worst enemy. So why cry?"

She answers, "Women love to bear the child of a snake. It's our curse, and our only revenge, our only joy."

The Countess de ——, who is without a doubt one of the most charming women in Paris, said to me yesterday, "Have you noticed that female characters have become less important in French literature in the last few years? The emphasis has been on men. There are no more heroines in the French novel. Montherlant started a trend."[20] The culprit is certainly not Montherlant's influence. It's that these are men's times. Europe's current problems are manly ones. As women gain importance in social life they lose it in literature. Men are less and less bound to problems of love. By now François Mauriac may be the only one left cultivating women in his greenhouse. But these women are more and more formulaic and old-fashioned. The true hero of modern literature, like that of Greek and Roman literature, is man.

My friends write to me from Italy, marveling at my silence, at my reluctance to assert, against various too-facile slanders, my Resistance credentials, which are certainly not inferior to those of a François Mauriac, a Camus, a Sartre, etc., etc., just to limit myself to writers. I did not only write against, I did not only conspire. I paid with prison, before and after the war; I fought on the battlefield, in full light; I've exchanged gunfire with the Germans and the Fascists. At the same age, more or less, as Sartre and Camus, the age Mauriac was in 1940. Aside from the fact that my Resistance credentials—seeing as how I have no political ambitions—have value only for my conscience, I have not come to France to assert my Resistance credentials in the eyes of the public. But neither have I come so that I might be called a collaborator, so that I might be slandered. Let this be said once and for all, and as clearly as possible: If you don't believe in the authenticity of my Resistance credentials, all you have to do is make inquiries.

One by one I find my old friends again. The friendship of a Frenchman is a very delicate feeling, of which he takes great care. The friendship of an Italian is a fruit; that of a Frenchman, a flower. The Italian is much warmer in his friendship. He offers you that fruit with pleasant generosity. But the fruit spoils quickly, without even dropping from the tree. The flower that the Frenchman offers us is a pure flower, whose fragrance is subtle, delicate, and faint. It never fades. I return to France after fourteen years and the flower of friendship is still there, fresh and alive, and the air is filled with its faint, delicate fragrance. The friendship of a Frenchman doesn't satisfy one's hunger. It doesn't nourish the body, if I can put it like that. The friendship of a Frenchman is a flower. That of an Italian is a fruit. That of a German a drink, that of a Spaniard an orange, that of an Englishman a fine slice of meat, that of an American, the same in a can. But the friendship of an Italian has to be cultivated, if you don't want it to turn to hate. The friendship of a Frenchman does not fade, and it's not at all necessary to cultivate it. The Frenchman is not unfaithful. As a point of honor? Surely not. Out of courtesy.

I've always wondered what was behind the French people's proverbial love of cats. There is certainly no natural affinity. Nor a commonality based on memories of war, of hunting, etc., as with dogs. There must be something more subtle. Montherlant's aversion to dogs has always moved and disgusted me. His "Chienne de Colomb-Béchar" seems to me a page unworthy of the man—and the Christian—Montherlant claims to be, believes himself to be, and is.[21]

The Ball of Count Pecci-Blunt.[22] In the summer of 1938, I was in Forte dei Marmi, just days after being released from internal exile, not seeing anyone, living alone with my dog Febo behind the high walls of my garden. Little by little, cautiously, my friends tried to push me out onto the stage of the world again. I had been kept away both by the cowardice of men, who don't like the defeated, and by my own repugnance at resuming the social intercourse I'd come to despise.

Among my faithful friends, Countess Laetitia Pecci-Blunt was the most faithful, the most generous, the most humanely discreet. A niece of Pope Leo XIII, who was a Count Pecci, Laetitia had married a captivating and yet very rich, not to say too rich, man, an American citizen by the name of Blunt, whom everyone loved for his charm, his generosity, his repugnance at pushing his way through the world or too openly enjoying his wealth. There was nothing about him of the rich American; instead he seemed like a well-bred European. He had picked up his manners in Paris and Rome, and these manners were discreet.

Laetitia, who had connections inside the Vatican, had obtained for her husband the privilege of bearing his wife's title and adding Pecci to his name. He had converted, calling himself Count Pecci-Blunt, and his wife had become Countess Pecci-Blunt. His conversion and entry into the Roman nobility were greeted warmly by Roman society, who continued to frequent his palazzo in Piazza d'Aracoeli in Rome and his residence on Rue de Babylone in Paris, two of prewar Europe's most Proustian places. Laetitia was one of the most beloved hostesses of Rome and Paris, for her intelligence, her learning, her passion for the arts and literature. She had founded an art gallery in Rome, La Cometa, that quickly became the intellectual center of Rome, where you met the cream of Roman artists and the less provincial elements of the city's gilded mob.

Everyone loved Laetitia and her husband, and everyone rushed to their luncheons, balls, and parties. The Vatican sent the best in purple hats and hose, the Italian aristocracy everything that in their girls' profiles, turquoise eyes, white foreheads, and coral red lips most closely resembled Perugino, Leonardo da Vinci, Donatello, and Raphael. Lombardy sent the still living models of its Mantegnas, its Dolcis; Tuscany, its Donatellos and its Botticellis; Venice, its Titians and its Tiepolos; Naples, its Riberas; Turin, its ——; Rome, its Raphaels and its Giulio Romanos. Palazzo Pecci-Blunt, at the bottom of the immense staircase of Ara Coeli, at the feet of the Campidoglio (from the window of Laetitia's room you can see the Tarpeian Rock and Marcus Aurelius on his horse of bronze), was in the years leading up to the war the best attended in Rome, a kinds of Domus Aurea where Elsa Maxwell and —— obtained the material for their columns in *Vogue* and *Harper's Bazaar*, as well as the finest names in the Roman Social Register.

Every season in Rome opened with a traditional ball at the palazzo of Count Pecci-Blunt. There was the autumn ball, the winter ball, the spring ball. The beginning of summer was celebrated at La Mar-

lia, the marvelous villa that Laetitia had inherited from Elisa Baciocchi, Napoleon's sister, in the hills near Lucca, in Tuscany.[23] Every
year, all the Italian nobility gathered at La Marlia to celebrate the
outbreak of summer. La Marlia is perhaps one of the most beautiful
villas in Italy: in its vast gardens, modeled on the gardens of Versailles
(where Le Nôtre's art was obscured by the Medicis' gardeners), everything that Italy at it most generous can offer in the landscaping
arts is arrayed with an incomparable abundance and rhythm. The
labyrinth (modeled on the labyrinth of the Minotaur on Crete), the
lake, the theater, and the Doric colonnades made of greenery had no
equal in Italy, or in Europe. At every turn of the gardens' paths,
embellished with rare exotic plants that seemed straight out of the
verses of Tasso, one discovered a Da Vinci landscape, with the rocks
covered in green moss; a Botticelli landscape, with foliage of a tender
green, white clouds floating on the surface of an ethereal, deep blue
sky; a Piero della Francesca landscape, with dark, almost black trees
closing off a horizon in the delicate shades of pink and blue that female
flesh has in that hard and smooth painter's work. And, at the feet of
the hill that bounds the park on the side of the Apennines, packs of
gray and white greyhounds, and the "pink coats" of the beaters, created splashes of white and gray among the green of the trees, like in
Politian's *Stanze*.

Each year, around a hundred little tables scattered in a clearing in
front of the green theater, Count Pecci-Blunt's ball would open with
a dinner that brought together four hundred guests chosen from the
nobility of Italy and Europe. The best singers from La Scala and from
the Royal Opera in Rome entertained guests with the performance
of an act by Cimarosa, or Paisiello, or Rameau, or Gluck. Naval
battles took place on the lake's surface; at battle's end, fireworks were
set off from the hill to announce the start of the ball. And from behind
a row of cypresses and laurels the best orchestras of Paris or London
would suddenly shake the leaves in the park with the violent clamor
of their savage rhythms. The dancing went on through the night,
until the milky river of dawn flooded the sky. And the return at dawn
was beautiful, toward the sea of a tender green color somewhere

between the leaves of grapevines and the moist green of the Luccan countryside.

The day before the Marlia party, Princess Jane di San Faustino Bourbon del Monte called me from Rome. As everyone knows, Princess Jane was American by birth.[24] Over seventy years old at the time, she was tall and slender, dressed always in white (she wore white mourning for her husband, the Prince Bourbon del Monte di San Faustino), her white hair styled à la Mary Stuart. With a haughty expression and full of wit, she was cruel, courageous, and wicked. I was very fond of her, and she had a cruel and bitter affection for me. I distrusted her, because I was distrustful in those days, but I knew she was doing everything possible to bring me back into the world. In her hands I was an instrument of her treacherous revenge against the society that had long scorned and isolated her, a young American without means who had had the fortune to be liked by the Prince di San Faustino.

"Are you going to La Marlia tomorrow evening?" Princess Jane asked me on the phone.

I replied that I didn't know yet, that I had no desire to be among so many people, that perhaps I would write to Laetitia with my apologies.

"You too?" Princess Jane asked in a tone of disdain.

"What do you mean, me too"?

"I never thought of you as a coward."

"I don't understand."

(The return at dawn was beautiful toward the green sea, while over our heads, from one tree to another, the nocturnal cicadas passed their song to the cicadas of the morning.)

"What! You don't know anything?"

"No, I don't know anything."

"Wait, don't write to Laetitia, I'll drive over to you tonight and tell you everything. And tomorrow we'll go to La Marlia together."

Around ten in the evening a car stopped in front of my gate and Princess Jane entered the house. She sat down in the library and said merely, "Cowards."

I knew the Princess Jane, and I smiled.

"Don't laugh," she said, "it's not worth it."

And she told me that Laetitia had sent out her invitations for the ball at La Marlia fifteen days ago, that everyone was preparing for the big event, that the best singers from La Scala were already at La Marlia to sing Monteverdi's *L'Orfeo*, when, two days before the big event, Count Ciano received an order from Palazzo Venezia not to go to La Marlia. Count Galeazzo Ciano, who was an intimate friend of Laetitia's, had telegraphed that affairs of state prevented him from going to La Marlia. His affairs of state were the racial laws promulgated a few days earlier. Countess Edda Ciano, who was particularly fond of Laetitia, telegraphed that she was gravely ill. Which could hardly come as a surprise to anyone, given that all the young diplomats of Palazzo Chigi, who usually constituted the most select group at La Marlia, had fallen ill at the same time as Countess Ciano. From one hour to the next, a strange epidemic had struck Roman society, which usually enjoyed excellent health. The epidemic had rapidly spread across Italy, suddenly striking the nobility of Milan, Florence, Turin, Venice, and Bologna. What didn't fail to surprise impartial observers of this strange pestilence, though, was to find out that the epidemic had also struck the foreign diplomatic corps at the Quirinal and the Vatican, and that the pestilence had also struck Laetitia's invitees in Paris, in London, and even in New York.

In the past two days hundreds of telegrams had arrived at La Marlia from all corners of the world, announcing the illness of an aunt, an urgent affair of state, a sudden bereavement, and in the various telegrams the illness put forward seemed everywhere to present the same symptoms.

"Cowards!" said Princess Jane.

"I didn't know anything," I said, "and I'm as disgusted about it as you are. Tomorrow evening I will accompany you to La Marlia."

"I was sure you'd accompany me," said Princess Jane. "We'll both go and kindly wish Laetitia and her husband a good evening like nothing happened."

The next day around seven in the evening, Princess Jane came to pick me up in her car, and we set off for La Marlia. From Forte dei Marmi to La Marlia it's about fifty kilometers. During the trip, Princess Jane did not say a single word. We arrived at La Marlia around nine. Princess Jane entered the villa with her haughty air and asked the servant who had opened the door to announce us to Countess Pecci-Blunt.

"The countess and count are in the middle of dinner," said the servant, and asked us to wait a moment. Only then did we hear coming from the gardens the sound of an orchestra and a female voice singing the famous aria from Monteverdi's *L'Orfeo*. Princess Jane looked at me in silence, slightly pale. Then she crossed the threshold and made for the gardens. I followed her in silence. Suddenly, at the end of the path, we saw the illuminated stage of the green theater, and onstage the singers. The little tables in front of the theater were empty. At their center, we saw, seated at a table, Count and Countess Pecci-Blunt having dinner. The majordomo and some servants stood beside the table. Laetitia was in a ball gown and the count in full evening dress. A large bouquet of roses illuminated the table with its pale, fleshy reflection.

Princess Jane took me by the arm and said to me in a low voice, "Let's hide." We hid behind a bush, and waited. The notes of Monteverdi rose, flawless, into the moist evening air, the voices of the singers interwove in the air with the birdsong, and the lament of Orpheus and Eurydice seemed like the lament of winged beings, the lament of the evening, the lament of the wind among the leaves of the trees. Count and Countess Pecci-Blunt, sitting at the table alone and in silence, smiled at each other as they listened to the divine harmonies of Monteverdi, and smiled as they leaned in over the table from time to time to exchange a few words. Hidden among the cypresses, Princess Jane and I watched the two solitary tablemates in silence. Princess Jane clutched my arm and cried silently. The tears rolled slowly down her cheek, and the moon rising behind the hills made her tears sparkle.

All of a sudden the music stopped, and the count and countess turned toward the stage, applauding. Then the count rose and bowed to the singers (we couldn't see them from the place we were hiding), who had come downstage and were acknowledging the two solitary tablemates. Then the count offered his arm to the countess and the pair moved away toward the lake. We followed them at a distance, hiding behind the laurel and cypress hedges: we watched them take their places on cushions laid out on the grass beside the lake, at an elevated spot from where the lake appeared in all its expanse. The count raised his hand and made a sign, and the naval battle began.

At first a trireme advanced, propelled by oars over the surface of the lake illuminated by the rising moon. The rowers, bent over their long oars, rowed at a steady rate, without strain, marking the rhythm that the navarch, standing astern, prescribed by beating a leather cymbal with a little silver hammer. In the vast silence of the deserted park, the blows of the silver hammer generated muffled echoes among the trees, and the birds, who had approached in flocks to listen to the music of Monteverdi, rose into flight with frightened little cries, coming to rest on the branches of the pines covering the hill behind the lake. The trireme was in the middle of the lake, when several gondolas emerged out of the shadows and set off to board the vessel.

The battle began. Archers wearing light silver hauberks, ranged along the flanks of the trireme, gracefully launched arrows adorned with ribbons. After tracing graceful curves through the air, they fell gracefully into the water, or continued on to wound the maidens, dressed only in light Amazon tunics, who stood in the flower-decked gondolas, themselves garlanded with flowers as well, and hurled their javelins, or rather long flower stalks, against the young archers of the trireme. Soon the entire surface of the lake was covered with gondolas; with small triremes of the same graceful and arbitrary form as those painted by Watteau; with wounded swimmers who, with sweet laments, sought to reach the shore; with the remains of sunken gondolas and floating garlands of flowers. The battle raged sweetly; the combatants' cries, which a hidden music that seemed to spring from the very bottom of the water sustained and accompanied with its amorous melodies, became ever louder when they saw, emerging from the branches of the weeping willows, which covered the lakeshore at the point known as the tomb of Narcissus, a gigantic shell containing Botticelli's Venus Anadyomene rising from the sea. The battle stopped at once. A sort of happy stupor seemed to drain the life from the combatants, who, leaning out over the sides of the trireme and the gondolas, their faces illuminated with joy and a sort of religious admiration, watched the triumphal procession of Venus. The music, which until then had seemed to spring from the depths of the water, rose up and seemed to descend from the starry sky like melodious dew. Standing in the shell—pulled by Tritons and driven with silken reins by a young Neptune armed with a trident, his forehead adorned with a golden crown—and smiling gracefully, her large open eyes the color of mother-of-pearl, her face immobile, Venus watched Countess Laetitia Pecci-Blunt sitting on cushions on the lakeshore. When Venus passed before her, Laetitia bowed her head and smiled; Count Pecci-Blunt bowed as well, his radiant face turned toward his consort. Laetitia was slightly pale, her smile dull; I noticed a shiver of cold course through her naked white shoulders.

As Venus's procession, followed by the trireme and the gondolas, disappeared between the branches of the weeping willows bent over the water at the far end of the lake, and the music fell silent, Count Pecci-Blunt rose, held out a hand to his wife, and affectionately led her, hand in hand, toward a nymphaeum: a fountain surrounded by laurels, rosebushes, and cypresses, by marble statues depicting Diana the hunter with her nymphs and her dogs, in pursuit of Actaeon, transformed into a stag; Apollo the archer, or killer of mice, armed with his terrible silver bow; and Hercules, who from afar watches this scene and the goddess and the gods. Around the fountain there were white marble benches. The countess sat down on one of these benches and raised her eyes toward the summit of the hill that rose across the lake, meanwhile gracefully fanning herself with a fan made of ebony and mother-of-pearl. Count Pecci-Blunt sat down beside her, he too raising his eyes toward the hill.

Suddenly a bolt of fire shot from the hill summit toward the starry sky, becoming lost among the astral bodies. Other bolts—of gold and silver, of red, green, white, blue, and yellow—shot up here and there, rising into the black sky strewn with sparkling points of light, descending in the distance like falling stars. And as if the bolts had been heralds of the fury of some Vesuvius, a tremendous explosion of light turned the hillside blood red, and from this unexpected volcano gushed a tall column of flames, similar to the tall column of incandescent rocks and fiery-hot ash that gushed from the mouth of Vesuvius. In the middle of this column of fire spun fiery pinwheels; fiery stars were born, burned, and went out. The entire hill appeared transformed into the cave of the god Vulcan: you could see nearly naked men running before the flames, black against the fire's red blaze, who seemed to be drawing out the flames with long iron poles and beating hammers on a gigantic anvil, on which some sort of giant tortoise writhed, sending up flashes and blue and green sparks.

The scene, in which the master pyrotechnists (whom Count Pecci-Blunt, in his magnificence, had brought in from Naples) outdid themselves, depicted Vulcan and his helpers at work forging the shield of Achilles, as it is sung in Homer's *Iliad*. Once the prerogative of the fireworks shows that the kings of Naples offered to the people on special occasions (births, baptisms, weddings, coronations), this pantomime, fittingly known as *The Shield of Achilles,* was reprised that night on the hill of La Marlia, in front of those two sole spectators, Count and Countess Pecci-Blunt. Seated on the benches of the nymphaeum, they contemplated this marvelous phantasmagoria of flames nearly in each other's arms, embracing each other as if there really were a god stoking a fire and hammering metal on an anvil, there, on the summit of the hill. Slowly, lifted by red iron chains, the tortoise rose into the air. And by the miracle of the Neapolitan pyrotechnists, unsurpassed masters of the art of fireworks, this ancient art that also has some magic about it, one could see, in silhouette on the shield, the battles, Achilles's horses, the work in the fields, the bulls yoked to the plow, the hunt for the Calydonian Boar, all as described by Homer in his divine poem. And suddenly, with a final burst of flames that rose high into the sky and seemed to blot out the twinkling stars, the whole hill caught fire, and the trees, the horizon, the pyrotechnists, the god Vulcan himself disappeared in an immense rose of fire that covered the entire sky and little by little faded into the black folds of the night.

Count Pecci-Blunt rose and held out a hand to his consort, and both walked down from the nymphaeum to the Minotaur's labyrinth. I saw them disappear, and we waited for them, guided by Ariadne's thread, to emerge from the labyrinth. First came Laetitia, almost at a run; stopping at the threshold of the labyrinth, she turned to wait for Count Pecci-Blunt. It seemed to me that her face was lit up by a youthful joy, that a new rosiness reanimated her pale cheeks. The count arrived, laughing, and they embraced at the entrance to the labyrinth, as Theseus and Ariadne did. Gracefully coupled, we saw, they went down toward the dance floor, right beside the lake, where little tables were spread out on the grass, discreetly illuminated by a pale pink light. They sat down at a table next to the edge of the shining marble floor. Shortly after, a sweet music rose from an invisible orchestra, caressing the tree leaves wet with dew, the grass and the naked shoulders of the statues. It was a Chopin waltz, whispered by violins and occasionally accompanied by a raspy saxophone in a cypress grove. Count Pecci-Blunt rose and bowed to Laetitia, who smiled and gave a graceful nod of her head. Rising, she placed her left hand (never has a woman's hand seemed to me so white, so small) on her husband's shoulder, and the two slowly, tenderly, began to dance.

Princess Jane gripped my arm tight, trembling. I saw tears roll down her pallid cheeks.

"Let's go greet them," I said. "They'll be happy to see us."

"No," said Princess Jane. "If they see us, they'll realize they're alone."

And Princess Jane pulled me gently through the trees toward the park gate.

NOTES

TRANSLATOR'S NOTE

1   If it has become conventional wisdom to refer to the "civil war" in Italy
     between September 1943 and April 1945, it is thanks to the late preemi-
     nent historian of the Italian resistance, Claudio Pavone, who, as Stan-
     islao Pugliese explains, "first used the loaded term 'civil war' at a
     conference in Belluno in October 1988. Previously, only the Fascists and
     neo- or post-Fascists had used the phrase. Just as only a Nixon could go
     to China, only an historian with such impeccable anti-Fascist creden-
     tials as Pavone could propose looking at the Resistance in this manner."
     Pugliese, introduction to *A Civil War: A History of the Italian Resis-
     tance*, by Claudio Pavone, ed. Stanislao Pugliese, trans. Peter Levy (New
     York: Verso, 2013), x.

2   Maurizio Serra, *Malaparte: Vies et légendes* (Paris: Grasset, 2011), 429–30.

3   Giordano Bruno Guerri, *L'arcitaliano: Vita di Curzio Malaparte* (Mi-
     lan: Leonardo, 1990), 232–33.

4   Serra, *Malaparte*, 197.

5   Ibid., 105.

6   Ibid., 67–68, 76–78.

7   Ibid., 463–66. The critic was Francis Ambrière (1907–1998), winner of
     the Prix Goncourt for *Les Grandes vacances* (1946), a novel chronicling
     the lives of French prisoners of war in the period 1939–45.

8   Curzio Malaparte, *Diario di uno straniero a Parigi*, ed. Enrico Falqui,
     trans. Giuseppe Argentieri (Florence: Vallecchi, 1966); *Journal d'un
     étranger à Paris*, trans. Gabrielle Cabrini (Paris: Denoël, 1967). In 2014,

the Denoël edition was reissued by La Table Ronde (Paris). The same year also saw the appearance of both Dutch and Spanish translations.

9 Falqui, "Nota bibliografica," in Malaparte, *Diario*, 313. The Denoël edition does not name an editor.

10 Ibid., 315.

11 Needless to say, it would make considerably less sense to refer to differences in *words* if the two languages in question, French and Italian, were not so closely related in terms of grammar and lexicon.

12 For example, "Annie Ducaux" in the French edition versus "Annie Ducos" in the Italian; "Mounet-Sully" (French) versus "Monet Sully" (Italian). A prefatory note to the Denoël edition indicates that the text written in French has been "*relu et corrigé*" (proofread and corrected). By all accounts, Malaparte paid little heed to the spelling of foreign names.

13 On a related note, in terms of the omissions explicitly signaled in the text by means of either ellipses or asterisks (converted in the present edition to two em dashes [——]), I would not be tempted to attribute any of them to censorship. When they do not reflect Malaparte's own sense of tact, they appear to simply indicate information that he intended to fill in at a later date. This would seem to be the case, for instance, with the likes of "Naples, its Riberas; Turin, its ——"; "the extraordinary popularity of the Persian poet ——"; or in Malaparte's citations of Chateaubriand, which occasionally appear as "Book ——, chap. —— of *Memoirs from Beyond the Grave*." To explain such omissions, there is no need to look beyond the book's unfinished state. I have filled in a few of the citations, within square brackets. There are also a few instances of bracketed ellipses, which I have reproduced when they appear in both editions.

14 According to Maurizio Serra, diplomat and author of the definitive biography of Malaparte (written and originally published in French), his subject, while possessed of a flair for languages, lacked the perseverance to become a fully bilingual writer, and would typically begin writing in French only to switch back to Italian after a few pages. How to account, then, for the dozens of consecutive pages of roman type—i.e., material marked as originally composed in French—in the Denöel edition? See Serra, introduction to *Malaparte: Vite e leggende*, trans. Alberto Folin (Venice: Marsilio, 2012), 28.

SKETCH OF A PREFACE

There exists an earlier (very similar) draft of this sketch of a preface—cited in its entirety as part of the bibliographic note of the Vallecchi edition—one of many signs of the importance that Malaparte attributed to the *Diary*.

1947

1   Big Bertha (*Dicke Berthe*) is the name of the superheavy German mortar used to destroy forts in Belgium and northern France at the start of World War I, a name that subsequently came to be applied generically by the Allies to any very large German gun, including the ultra-long-range Paris Gun (*Paris-Geschütz*), several of which were used to bombard Paris from March to August 1918.

2   In Rome. Since 1961 the official residence of the prime minister of the Italian Republic, Palazzo Chigi was at the time the seat of the Italian foreign minister.

3   Louis Aragon, from "Lancelot," in *Les Yeux d'Elsa* (1942).

4   Malaparte fails to note that he also describes a first meeting with Mauriac since 1933 just three days earlier, in the entry for July 8.

5   That is, *evidence to the contrary*.

6   Gilbert Gadoffre (1911–1995) was a historian of French literature and Resistance fighter. In 1947, he helped found, alongside Henry Goüin, the Centre culturel international de Royaumont, an important cultural center housed in the Royaumont Abbey, a former Cistercian monastery approximately thirty kilometers north of Paris.

7   The Vallecchi edition dates this entry September 18.

8   I have been unable to identify a textual source for this quotation.

9   Founded in 1901, the Radical Party was initially classically liberal in political orientation, opposing the monarchists and clerical elements on the one hand, the Socialists on the other. With the emergence of the French Section of the Workers' International in 1905, the Radicals shifted toward the political center and eventually became the most important party of the Third Republic (1870–1940).

10   Action Française was an influential right-wing antirepublican group in France during the first forty years of the twentieth century. *Action Française* was also the name of a daily newspaper (published from March 21, 1908, to August 24, 1944) that expressed the group's ideas. The Action Française movement originated at the close of the nineteenth century to champion the antiparliamentarian, anti-Semitic, and strongly nationalist views inspired by the controversy over the Dreyfus affair.

11   The three preceding, apparently self-contradictory sentences, from "It is a piazza" to "with an extreme result," are absent from the corresponding entry in the French edition.

12   Malaparte misquotes. The second line of Alfieri's epigram (VIII) is "*Tutto sanno, e nulla fanno*," or "They know everything, and do nothing."

13   The Denoël edition places this entry in its undated section, under "September 2," perhaps because its editor deemed it impossible to establish the year.

14   The memoirs of Jean François Paul de Gondi, Cardinal de Retz (1613–1679), contain vivid portraits of its author's contemporaries and are addressed to an unknown woman, possibly Mme de Sevigné. Evidently the "retrospective feeling" of Racine, born in 1639, did not look back very far.

15   Mathilde de Chavigny is the young heroine of de Musset's play.

16   An informal French term for doctor, still in use to this day, *toubib* was nineteenth-century military slang and derives from the North African Arabic بْيِطَ (*tabīb*, "doctor").

17   Malaparte is apparently somewhat imprecise here. Nerval's reference to the "modulated tremor" ("*frisson modulé*") of a voice does appear in *Sylvie*, the most celebrated of the stories in his collection *Les Filles du feu*: "*La mélodie se terminait à chaque stance par ces trilles chevrotants que font valoir si bien les voix jeunes, quand elles imitent par un frisson modulé la voix tremblante des aïeules*" ("The melody ended at each stanza in those wavering trills that show off young voices so well, [especially] when, in a modulated tremor, they imitate the quavering voices of old women"). However, the phrase is used not with specific regard to the character

Sylvie, the narrator's childhood sweetheart, whose love he eventually squanders, but in an observation occasioned by the narrator's impression of the singing of a girl who is in some sense Sylvie's rival, Adrienne, the beautiful fair-haired aristocrat whom he encounters once as a child, as if in a vision or dream, and never forgets. Of course, since this comes in the context of Malaparte's portrait of the actress Véra Korène, and for Nerval's narrator the image of Adrienne was inextricably bound to that of the actress he went to the theater every night to see, it does not seem out of the question that this apparent imprecision may have been a calculated move.

18   Latin, "goes forth masked." The phrase was used by Descartes of his decision, following Galileo's 1633 conviction for heresy, to publish his correspondence with Marin Mersenne anonymously.

19   The text of the actual plaque is somewhat longer and begins as follows: "*Ici est tombé pour la France le 25 août 1944 ...*" That is, inconveniently for Malaparte's chosen theme, it recognizes Bonenfant's death as being not just for the Hôtel Majestic (which it does in fact go on to note), but also for France.

20   A reference to Pascal's *Pensées*: "If Cleopatra's nose had been shorter, the whole face of the earth would have changed" (162).

21   André Le Nôtre (1613–1700), French landscape architect who designed the park of the Palace of Versailles.

22   Malaparte's words here—"*chiare e fresche e dolci acque*"—echo Petrarch's canzone 126, "*Chiare, fresche et dolci acque.*" The poem, written between 1340 and 1341, was likely inspired by the source of the Sorgue river, in Fontaine-de-Vaucluse in southeastern France.

23   The Quai d'Orsay in Paris, location of the French Ministry of Foreign Affairs, is often used as a metonym for the ministry.

24   The Third Republic was the French government in place from 1870 to 1940, from the fall of the Second Empire in the Franco-Prussian War to the fall of France to the Germans in 1940. The Fourth Republic began in 1946, after the postwar provisional president Charles de Gaulle resigned, and went through twenty-one different administrations before collapsing in 1958.

25   Malaparte appears to be mistaken. The quoted phrase can be found in a letter from Mme de Sévigné to the Comte de Bussy dated March 10, 1687, in which she describes the splendid funeral pomp in honor of Louis de Bourbon, Prince of Condé, which took place in Paris eight days earlier: "*Ses pères sont représentés par des médailles jusqu'à saint Louis, toutes ses victoires par des basses-tailles, couvertes comme sous des tentes dont les coins sont ouverts et portés par des squelettes dont les attitudes sont admirables.*" It is perhaps not impossible that Mme de Sévigné is repeating a phrase first used by Bossuet; however, I have found no trace of this. Christina, Queen of Sweden, died in 1654, in Rome.

26   This is the French translation (1947) of Malaparte's own book *Donna come me* (1940).

27   The very long 1897 drama *Jeanne d'Arc*, by Charles Péguy (1873–1914), was performed in a three-hour abridgment by the author's son Marcel Péguy at the Théâtre Hébertot in occupied Paris in 1941. On September 18, 1947, a different three-hour abridgment, also by Marcel Péguy, began a run at the Théâtre Hébertot to mark the postwar reopening of the theater.

28   In the Battle of Berezina of November 26–29, 1812, the French Grande Armée of Napoleon, retreating after his invasion of Russia and crossing the Berezina River in Belarus, suffered very heavy losses but managed to cross the river and avoid being trapped. Since then "Bérézina" has been used in French as a synonym for "disaster."

29   Malaparte refers to the first edition of Junger's Paris diaries, whose first volume was published in 1942 as *Gärten und Straßen* (Gardens and Streets) and in French translation as *Jardins et routes* the same year. As a captain in the Wehrmacht, Jünger served as an administrator in the German occupation of France and became acquainted with many prominent artists and intellectuals there.

30   At this point the French edition of the diary places—incongruously, without transition—the "story of the ties," which in the Italian edition (as well as in the present one) appears as part of the December 4, 1947, entry.

31   This entry can be tentatively so dated based on the fact that the theatrical adaptation in question debuted at the Théâtre Marigny, Paris, on October 10, 1947.

32 The English translation from the French translation of Nemeth's book is mine.

33 This entry can be tentatively so dated based on its concluding "ibid." citation, which refers to André Németh's *Kafka, ou Le mysteère juif.* The English translation from the French translation of Bloch as cited by Nemeth is mine.

34 This entry can be so dated thanks to the reference to Jean-Pierre Aumont's play, which had its debut at the Théâtre des Mathurins, Paris, on October 25, 1947. It may well be that the "lunch at André Lichtwitz's" described in a later entry in this section refers to the same occasion described in the present entry, but this has not been confirmed.

35 Petrarch, canzone 128, *"Italia mia, benché 'l parlar sia indarno,"* line 74. The canzone is the first known work of poetry to imagine Italy united from the Alps to Sicily and free from factional strife.

36 This entry can be so dated thanks to newspaper reports of the demonstration, which took place on October 28, 1947.

37 This entry can be tentatively so dated thanks to Malaparte's reference to a ballet by Italian composer Goffredo Petrassi (1904–2003). The full version of Petrassi's *Ritratto di Don Chisciotte* (*Portrait of Don Quixote*) was first staged by the Ballets des Champs-Élysées on November 21, 1947.

38 According to Giordano Bruno Guerri, citing the Italian painter Orfeo Tamburi, Malaparte was so afraid of the potential consequences of a resounding victory by the Italian Communist Party in the 1948 national elections, held on April 18, that, "not feeling safe even in Paris, he winters in Chamonix, and says to Tamburi, who is with him: 'One must be careful these days. Here I'm just steps away from Switzerland.' One day he considers the possibility of fleeing on skis, if they come to arrest him, and another day, more pessimistic, he foresees the moment in which 'we will hear the bell toll, a man will enter and before we can breathe a word he will slaughter us like goats.'" Guerri, *L'arcitaliano: Vita di Curzio Malaparte* (Milan: Leonardo, 1990), 235.

39 The central Helsinki neighborhood of Kaivopuist, also known by its Swedish name Brunnsparken, is where most of the Finnish capital's foreign embassies, including Spain's, are located.

40 This may be a reference to the Hotel Kämp, on the Pohjoisesplanadi (North Esplanadi) in central Helskini. The historic grand hotel opened in 1887 and is roughly a twenty-minute walk from the Spanish Embassy.

41 Then the largest in Eastern Europe, surpassed only with the construction, in Moscow, of the Central Lenin Stadium (opened 1956), now known as the Luzhniki Stadium.

1948

1 Couttet appears to have won his world championship in 1938. The competition was interrupted by World War II in 1940 and not held again until 1948.

2 The French expression *violon d'Ingres* refers to an activity other than that for which one is well known, or at which one excels, and derives from the story that the famous neoclassical painter preferred to play his violin—at which he was only modestly skilled—for visitors instead of showing them his pictures.

3 The contradiction contained in the final words of this paragraph (we would expect him to reaffirm that the obsession with corpses *does* appear...), a feature of both the French and Italian editions, would appear explicable only by one of two not terribly convincing explanations: either a major transcription error or a mental slip on the author's part.

4 Shortly after the Molotov–Ribbentrop Pact of 1939, Maurice Thorez (1900–1964), secretary-general of the French Communist Party, was drafted. Refusing to fight the Germans, he deserted and fled to the Soviet Union.

5 This would appear to be the line Malaparte recalls: "The white shell-like mass beneath it is a small glacier, which in its beautifully curved outline appears to sympathise with the sweep of the rocks beneath." John Ruskin, *Modern Painters*, vol. 4 (London: George Allen, 1904), 230.

6 "A free man thinks of death least of all things; and his wisdom is a meditation not of death but of life" (*Ethics*, part IV, prop. LXVII).

7 Both quotations are from *Mémoires d'Outre-Tombe*; the first is found in book VIII, chap. 4. Here and later, for the quotations from Chateaubri-

and, I have drawn on and modified the English translation of A. S. Kline, available at poetryintranslation.com/PITBR/Chateaubriand/Chathome.htm. At times Malaparte seems to plagiarize Chateaubriand, but it's also possible he was merely copying down passages he liked in his diary, and previous editions' editors failed to observe the distinction.

8   Charles Brockden Brown (1771–1810) was an American novelist, historian, and editor, whose first major work was the 1798 novel *Wieland; or, The Transformation: An American Tale*.

9   In the original text of *Wieland*: "I brought thee hither to fulfil a divine command. I am appointed thy destroyer, and destroy thee I must."

10 In the original text of *Wieland*: "Surely, surely Wieland, thou dost not mean it. Am I not thy wife? and wouldst thou kill me? Thou wilt not, and yet—I see—thou art Wieland no longer! A fury resistless and horrible possesses thee—Spare me—spare—help—help—"

11 The original French term here, *dessin*, derives from the word used in the Italian version of the diary, *disegno*. Both bring with them the art historical connotations of *disegno*, a major component of Renaissance art theory, referring to both design and drawing, an idea and its execution, an underlying plan and a sketch.

12 Jean Vilar (1912–1971) began his career as a director in 1943, with a season in a small Paris theater. In 1947 he directed the first annual drama festival at Avignon, to some acclaim.

13 A play on words (*"Les sots et les sauvages"*), alas, that cannot readily be reproduced in English—or in Italian (*"Gli imbecilli e i selvaggi"*).

14 For reasons that remain obscure to me, the Denoël edition places this entry, *with this date*, between those of November 23 and December 4, 1948.

15 The Vallecchi edition instead identifies this entry as "December 12." I have elected to follow the Denoël edition's dating in this instance, on the basis of how the November 18, 1948, entry begins.

16 This street's name was changed back to Nevsky Prospect by Stalin in 1944.

17 The text from the annotated break to here does not appear in the De-noël edition. The rest of this entry appears in the Denoël edition as part of the September 1947 entry (see note 30 in the 1947 section).

18 The Denoël edition includes a note here indicating that D'Annunzio lived at the address in question for a matter of months, not years, be-tween December 1914 and May 1915.

19 The reference to the German writer and politically liberal newspaper editor Theodor Wolff (1868–1943) as having "just fled the threat of Hit-ler in Germany" makes Malaparte's dating of this evening to 1931 prob-lematic: Wolff fled Berlin only in 1933, after the Nazi Party came to power; he moved into an apartment in Nice, on the Promenade des An-glais. In 1943, the Italian occupation authorities delivered Wolff to the Nazis. Deported to the Sachsenhausen-Oranienburg concentration camp, he was later moved, gravely ill, to the Jewish Hospital of Berlin, where he died.

20 Born the son of a small landowner in the then province of Catania (Sic-ily) and orphaned at the age of four, Giacomo Barone (1887–1961) would add his mother's surname, Russo, to distinguish himself from many others with the same name. In 1920 he married Camilla, the daughter of Count Raniero Paulucci di Calboli. In 1924 he adopted the surname Paulucci di Calboli and the title of marchese at the request of Raniero, who intended thereby to pass on the family name, otherwise destined to die out.

21 The use of the name Mesopotamia Island (*Isola Mesopotamia*) for Tiber Island (*Isola Tiberina*), the only island in the part of the Tiber River that runs through Rome, can be found in the Acts of the Martyrs and in medieval works, and apparently derives from an error in a Latin transla-tion of a work by the Greek writer Plutarch.

22 Malaparte apparently forgot he had included virtually this same anec-dote in a July 1947 entry.

UNDATED ENTRIES

1 Latin, "An excuse that has not been sought [is] an obvious accusation." In French, *qui s'excuse, s'accuse.*

2   The subject of Holbein's 1536 painting, commonly known as *Portrait of Sir Richard Southwell*, was a privy councilor of Henry VIII of England, but not a duke. Malaparte's confusion may be connected to the fact that the painting was given to Grand Duke Cosimo II de' Medici by Thomas Howard, Duke of Arundel, in 1621.

3   Colette Clément, née Grunbaum (1898–1982), was a medical doctor and the author, under the pseudonym Constance Coline, of novels, plays, and adapted pieces for the theater.

4   These paragraphs echo parts of Malaparte's account of the "Lunch at Taillevent," in an earlier undated entry. Somehow, the lunch in his honor, where he meets for the first time a woman who will become at least an acquaintance later, Claudine Chonez, blends with his meeting up with a woman who's an old friend, Constance Coline.

5   *Sidi*, an honorific prefix in Arabic, became a pejorative French term for North Africans; their connection to the banks of the Seine is unclear. *Bougnat* indicates a person who moved to Paris from the Auvergne region. The Auvergnat population in Paris became known in the nineteenth century for selling coal and running modest café establishments.

6   The Vallecchi edition has "rue Amélie" here rather than "rue Saint-Dominique." Both streets are located on the Rive Gauche, in the 7th arrondissement, and in fact intersect. I have followed the Denoël edition in this detail largely because, of the two streets, Rue Saint-Dominique is bigger and considerably longer.

7   *Ardèle ou la Marguerite*, by the French dramatist Jean Anouilh (1910–1987), was first presented in Paris at the Comédie des Champs-Élysées on November 4, 1948.

8   Unable to locate the cited passages in an edition of Tolstoy's novel, I have translated Malaparte's version.

9   Malaparte here presumably refers to Glaukos's speech in the *Iliad*, when he responds to the question in Diomedes's challenge: "Why ask of my generation? As is the generation of leaves, so is that of humanity. The wind scatters the leaves on the ground, but the live timber burgeons with leaves again in the season of spring returning. So one generation of men will grow while another dies." Richard Lattimore, trans. (Chicago: University of Chicago Press, 1951), 6.145–150.

10   This sentence, presented as Malaparte's own original contemporary thought, paraphrases Chateaubriand writing in 1822 about 1792: "*Si Sanson en avait eu le temps, il aurait joué le rôle de Colin, et mademoiselle Théroigne de Méricourt celui de Babet*" (*Mémoires d'Outre-Tombe*, book IX, chap. 2).

11   Following the first sentence, Malaparte appears to have adapted Chateaubriand's text for his own purposes, referring to three mid-twentieth-century newspaper editors with the same terms Chateaubriand used for members of the National Convention (1792–1795), the third government of the French Revolution, and putting himself in the place of their victims: "*Les Conventionnels se piquaient d'être les plus bénins des hommes: bons pères, bons fils, bons maris, ils menaient promener les petits enfants ils leur servaient de nourrices; ils pleuraient de tendresses à leurs simples jeux; ils prenaient doucement dans leurs bras ces petits agneaux, afin de leur montrer le dada des charrettes qui conduisaient les victimes au supplice. Ils chantaient la nature, la paix, la pitié, la bienfaisance, la candeur, les vertus domestiques; ces béats de philanthropie faisaient couper le cou à leurs voisins avec une extrême sensibilité, pour le plus grand bonheur de l'espèce humaine.*" (Ibid.)

12   That is, François-René de Chateaubriand.

13   The words actually appear in the second paragraph of Book I after the preface.

14   According to Chateaubriand, though Richmond in fact lies southwest of central London.

15   The initialisms refer to several political parties and one trade union confederation: the MRP, or Mouvement républicain populaire (Popular Republican Movement), a Christian democratic party during the Fourth Republic; the RPF, or Rassemblement du peuple français (Rally of the French People), a party led by Charles de Gaulle; PC, or Parti communiste (Communist Party); the SFIO, or Section française de l'Internationale ouvrière (French Section of the Workers' International), a socialist political party founded in 1905 and replaced in 1969 by the current Socialist Party (PS); and the CGT, or Confédération générale du travail (General Confederation of Labour), the first of the five major French confederations of trade unions.

16 Montesquieu, *Persian Letters* (1721), letter 30.

17 According to Imogen in *Cymbeline* (act III, scene 4), "In the world's volume / Our Britain seems as of it, but not in it; / In a great pool a swan's nest."

18 Teresa, Contessa Guiccioli (1800–1873), was the married lover of Lord Byron while he was living in Ravenna, Italy, and writing the first five cantos of *Don Juan*.

19 The preceding two entries appear to be missing from the Denoël edition. The present entry, which may well represent a marginal note rather than an entry proper, appears in the Vallecchi edition immediately after the entry that I have tentatively dated October 11, 1947, which recounts the author's response to a performance of Kafka's *Trial* as adapted for the stage by Jean-Louis Barrault and André Gide.

20 A reference, presumably, to Henri de Montherlant's best-selling and widely translated four-volume novel *Les Jeunes Filles* (1936–39), which sets out a philosophy of life based on the idea that a free man cannot sustain a stable relationship with a woman except at the cost of his freedom and happiness.

21 The Denoël edition ends here, having placed the next entry first in the undated entries rather than last.

22 It seems probable that "Il ballo del Conte Pecci-Blunt" was originally part of an unfinished novel, *Una tragedia italiana*, which Malaparte began to publish in installments, in June 1939, in the magazine *Circoli*. Giordano Bruno Guerri, *L'arcitaliano: Vita di Curzio Malaparte* (Milan: Leonardo, 1990), 199–200.

23 Elisa Bonaparte Baciocchi abandoned the villa in 1814 after the fall of her older brother, and it passed through several owners, eventually falling into disuse and being threatened with demolition, before Count and Countess Pecci-Blunt purchased the villa, in 1923.

24 The American Jane Allen Campbell (1865–1938), who married Carlo Bourbon del Monte, Prince di San Faustino (1867–1917), was the mother of Virginia Bourbon del Monte (1899–1945), who married Edoardo Agnelli, the son of Senator Giovanni Agnelli, a cofounder of Fiat, in 1919. Edoardo died in a plane crash in July 1935. According to Malaparte,

he and Virginia were scheduled to marry in October 1936. The wedding was apparently called off due to the violent opposition of Virginia's father-in-law, who threatened to not only disinherit Virginia but also take custody of her seven children by Edoardo. See Maurizio Serra, *Malaparte: Vite e leggende*, trans. Alberto Folin (Venice: Marsilio, 2012), 241–42.

TITLES IN SERIES

For a complete list of titles, visit www.nyrb.com or write to:
Catalog Requests, NYRB, 435 Hudson Street, New York, NY 10014

J.R. ACKERLEY Hindoo Holiday
J.R. ACKERLEY My Dog Tulip
J.R. ACKERLEY My Father and Myself
J.R. ACKERLEY We Think the World of You
HENRY ADAMS The Jeffersonian Transformation
RENATA ADLER Pitch Dark
RENATA ADLER Speedboat
AESCHYLUS Prometheus Bound; translated by Joel Agee
ROBERT AICKMAN Compulsory Games
LEOPOLDO ALAS His Only Son *with* Doña Berta
CÉLESTE ALBARET Monsieur Proust
DANTE ALIGHIERI The Inferno
KINGSLEY AMIS The Alteration
KINGSLEY AMIS Dear Illusion: Collected Stories
KINGSLEY AMIS Ending Up
KINGSLEY AMIS Girl, 20
KINGSLEY AMIS The Green Man
KINGSLEY AMIS Lucky Jim
KINGSLEY AMIS The Old Devils
KINGSLEY AMIS One Fat Englishman
KINGSLEY AMIS Take a Girl Like You
ROBERTO ARLT The Seven Madmen
U.R. ANANTHAMURTHY Samskara: A Rite for a Dead Man
IVO ANDRIĆ Omer Pasha Latas
WILLIAM ATTAWAY Blood on the Forge
W.H. AUDEN (EDITOR) The Living Thoughts of Kierkegaard
W.H. AUDEN W. H. Auden's Book of Light Verse
ERICH AUERBACH Dante: Poet of the Secular World
EVE BABITZ Eve's Hollywood
EVE BABITZ I Used to Be Charming: The Rest of Eve Babitz
EVE BABITZ Slow Days, Fast Company: The World, the Flesh, and L.A.
DOROTHY BAKER Cassandra at the Wedding
DOROTHY BAKER Young Man with a Horn
J.A. BAKER The Peregrine
S. JOSEPHINE BAKER Fighting for Life
HONORÉ DE BALZAC The Human Comedy: Selected Stories
HONORÉ DE BALZAC The Memoirs of Two Young Wives
HONORÉ DE BALZAC The Unknown Masterpiece *and* Gambara
VICKI BAUM Grand Hotel
SYBILLE BEDFORD A Favorite of the Gods *and* A Compass Error
SYBILLE BEDFORD Jigsaw
SYBILLE BEDFORD A Legacy
SYBILLE BEDFORD A Visit to Don Otavio: A Mexican Journey
MAX BEERBOHM The Prince of Minor Writers: The Selected Essays of Max Beerbohm
MAX BEERBOHM Seven Men
STEPHEN BENATAR Wish Her Safe at Home
FRANS G. BENGTSSON The Long Ships
WALTER BENJAMIN The Storyteller Essays
ALEXANDER BERKMAN Prison Memoirs of an Anarchist
GEORGES BERNANOS Mouchette

FRANÇOISE GILOT Life with Picasso
NATALIA GINZBURG Family Lexicon
JEAN GIONO Hill
JEAN GIONO A King Alone
JEAN GIONO Melville: A Novel
JOHN GLASSCO Memoirs of Montparnasse
P.V. GLOB The Bog People: Iron-Age Man Preserved
ROBERT GLÜCK Margery Kempe
NIKOLAI GOGOL Dead Souls
EDMOND AND JULES DE GONCOURT Pages from the Goncourt Journals
ALICE GOODMAN History Is Our Mother: Three Libretti
PAUL GOODMAN Growing Up Absurd: Problems of Youth in the Organized Society
EDWARD GOREY (EDITOR) The Haunted Looking Glass
JEREMIAS GOTTHELF The Black Spider
A.C. GRAHAM Poems of the Late T'ang
JULIEN GRACQ Balcony in the Forest
HENRY GREEN Back
HENRY GREEN Blindness
HENRY GREEN Caught
HENRY GREEN Doting
HENRY GREEN Living
HENRY GREEN Loving
HENRY GREEN Nothing
HENRY GREEN Party Going
HENRY GREEN Surviving
WILLIAM LINDSAY GRESHAM Nightmare Alley
HANS HERBERT GRIMM Schlump
EMMETT GROGAN Ringolevio: A Life Played for Keeps
VASILY GROSSMAN An Armenian Sketchbook
VASILY GROSSMAN Everything Flows
VASILY GROSSMAN Life and Fate
VASILY GROSSMAN The Road
VASILY GROSSMAN Stalingrad
LOUIS GUILLOUX Blood Dark
OAKLEY HALL Warlock
PATRICK HAMILTON The Slaves of Solitude
PATRICK HAMILTON Twenty Thousand Streets Under the Sky
PETER HANDKE Short Letter, Long Farewell
PETER HANDKE Slow Homecoming
THORKILD HANSEN Arabia Felix: The Danish Expedition of 1761–1767
ELIZABETH HARDWICK The Collected Essays of Elizabeth Hardwick
ELIZABETH HARDWICK The New York Stories of Elizabeth Hardwick
ELIZABETH HARDWICK Seduction and Betrayal
ELIZABETH HARDWICK Sleepless Nights
L.P. HARTLEY Eustace and Hilda: A Trilogy
L.P. HARTLEY The Go-Between
NATHANIEL HAWTHORNE Twenty Days with Julian & Little Bunny by Papa
ALFRED HAYES In Love
ALFRED HAYES My Face for the World to See
PAUL HAZARD The Crisis of the European Mind: 1680–1715
ALICE HERDAN-ZUCKMAYER The Farm in the Green Mountains
WOLFGANG HERRNDORF Sand
GILBERT HIGHET Poets in a Landscape

FREYA AND HELMUTH JAMES VON MOLTKE Last Letters: The Prison Correspondence
MICHEL DE MONTAIGNE Shakespeare's Montaigne; translated by John Florio
HENRY DE MONTHERLANT Chaos and Night
BRIAN MOORE The Lonely Passion of Judith Hearne
BRIAN MOORE The Mangan Inheritance
ALBERTO MORAVIA Agostino
ALBERTO MORAVIA Boredom
ALBERTO MORAVIA Contempt
JAN MORRIS Conundrum
JAN MORRIS Hav
GUIDO MORSELLI The Communist
PENELOPE MORTIMER The Pumpkin Eater
MULTATULI Max Havelaar, or the Coffee Auctions of the Dutch Trading Company
ROBERT MUSIL Agathe; or, The Forgotten Sister
ÁLVARO MUTIS The Adventures and Misadventures of Maqroll
L.H. MYERS The Root and the Flower
NESCIO Amsterdam Stories
DARCY O'BRIEN A Way of Life, Like Any Other
SILVINA OCAMPO Thus Were Their Faces
YURI OLESHA Envy
IONA AND PETER OPIE The Lore and Language of Schoolchildren
IRIS ORIGO A Chill in the Air: An Italian War Diary, 1939–1940
IRIS ORIGO Images and Shadows: Part of a Life
IRIS ORIGO War in Val d'Orcia: An Italian War Diary, 1943–1944
MAXIM OSIPOV Rock, Paper, Scissors and Other Stories
LEV OZEROV Portraits Without Frames
RUSSELL PAGE The Education of a Gardener
ALEXANDROS PAPADIAMANTIS The Murderess
BORIS PASTERNAK, MARINA TSVETAYEVA, AND RAINER MARIA RILKE Letters, Summer 1926
CESARE PAVESE The Moon and the Bonfires
CESARE PAVESE The Selected Works of Cesare Pavese
BORISLAV PEKIĆ Houses
ELEANOR PERÉNYI More Was Lost: A Memoir
LUIGI PIRANDELLO The Late Mattia Pascal
JOSEP PLA The Gray Notebook
DAVID PLANTE Difficult Women: A Memoir of Three
ANDREY PLATONOV The Foundation Pit
ANDREY PLATONOV Happy Moscow
ANDREY PLATONOV Soul and Other Stories
NORMAN PODHORETZ Making It
J.F. POWERS Morte d'Urban
J.F. POWERS The Stories of J.F. Powers
J.F. POWERS Wheat That Springeth Green
CHRISTOPHER PRIEST Inverted World
BOLESŁAW PRUS The Doll
GEORGE PSYCHOUNDAKIS The Cretan Runner: His Story of the German Occupation
ALEXANDER PUSHKIN The Captain's Daughter
QIU MIAOJIN Last Words from Montmartre
QIU MIAOJIN Notes of a Crocodile
RAYMOND QUENEAU We Always Treat Women Too Well
RAYMOND QUENEAU Witch Grass
RAYMOND RADIGUET Count d'Orgel's Ball
PAUL RADIN Primitive Man as Philosopher